Great Britain
Quiz
Book

Great Britain

Quiz

Book

Angela Griffiths

Bounty
Books

First published in 2005 by Bounty Books,
a division of Octopus Publishing Group Ltd
2–4 Heron Quays, London E14 4JP

Copyright © Octopus Publishing Group Ltd 2005

ISBN 0 7537 1092 7
ISBN13 9780753710920

A CIP catalogue record for this book is available from the
British Library

Printed and bound in Great Britain

CONTENTS

AUTHORS &
LITERATURE

1. Which publisher was taken to court on a charge of obscenity over the publishing of 'Lady Chatterley's Lover'?

2. What collective name was given to Wordsworth, Coleridge and Southey?

3. D.H. Lawrence died from which ailment?

4. Name the drinking house where the pilgrims met in Canterbury in Chaucer's tales.

5. Which book by Kit Williams involved millions of readers around the world searching for a golden hare?

6. Whose memoirs are contained in his work 'It's a Long Way from Penny Apples'?

7. Which of Shakespeare's plays ends with the line "One feast, one house, one mutual happiness."?

8. 'Jigs and Reels '(2004) is a collection of 22 short stories from which popular writer?

9. Which war correspondent wrote 'The Kindness of Strangers'?

10. Catherine Morland is the heroine of which Jane Austen novel?

11. Which novel opens with the words 'Last night I dreamt I went to Manderley again.'?

12. What was the subject of Carol Lee's book 'To Die For'?

13. Which poet wrote the comic ballad, 'John Gilpin' (1782)?

14. Which trilogy is set in Middle Earth?

15. 'Tomorrow's People' and 'The Private Life of the Brain' are the works of which high-profile Oxford professor?

16. Sue Miller wrote 'The Story of My Father ' documenting his life coping with which disease?

17. The phrase 'ignorance is bliss' is taken from a work entitled 'Ode on a Distant Prospect of Eton College'. Who wrote this?

18. Which Oscar Wilde play concerns Algernon Moncrieff's courtship of Cecily Cardew?

19. Dorothea Brooke, Edward Casaubon and Will Ladislaw are characters from which classic novel?

20. Which poetic drama by T.S. Eliot focuses on the inner conflict of Thomas à Becket as he contemplates martyrdom?

WHICH PLAYWRIGHTS DO YOU ASSOCIATE WITH THE FOLLOWING PLAYS?

1. The Admirable Crichton

2. Amadeus

3. Chips With Everything

4. John, Paul, George, Ringo ....and Bert

5. Dancing at Lughnasa

6. How The Other Half Loves

7. Bouncers

8. Private Lives

9. The Rivals

10. Inadmissible Evidence

11. Jumpers

12. Boys from the Blackstuff

13. Entertaining Mr Sloane

14. Talking Heads

15. Under Milk Wood

16. Androcles and the Lion

17. The Birthday Party

18. Like a Virgin

19. Lady Windermere's Fan

20. The Alchemist

MULTIPLE CHOICE

1. Who wrote children's books and romances under the pseudonym Mary Westmacott?

   a. Maeve Binchy
   b Enid Bagnold
   c. Fanny Burney
   d. Agatha Christie

2. Anne Elliot was the heroine of which Jane Austen novel?

   a. Persuasion
   b. Northanger Abbey
   c. Pride and Prejudice
   d. Sense and Sensibility

3. Which author and illustrator achieved success with 'Borka, the Adventures of a Goose without Feathers' (1963)?

   a. Douglas Adams
   b. John Burningham
   c. Raymond Briggs
   d. Richard Adams

4. Who was the author of the autobiographical 'Confessions of an Opium-Eater'?

   a. Thomas de Quincey
   b. Geoffrey Chaucer
   c. Arthur Conan Doyle
   d. Oscar Wilde

5. Catherine, Hindley and Hareton were all members of the same family in which classic novel?

   a. Lorna Doone
   b. Wuthering Heights
   c. Tess of the D'Urbervilles
   d. Agnes Grey

6. Who wrote 'Possession,' a Booker Prize-winning novel in 1990?

   a. A.S. Byatt   c. Margaret Drabble
   b. Edna O'Brien   d. Iris Murdoch

7. The schoolmaster Wackford Squeers is a character from which Dickens's novel?

   a. Barnaby Rudge   c. Martin Chuzzlewit
   b. David Copperfield   d. Nicholas Nickleby

8. In which Shakespearean play do the spirits Iris, Ceres and Juno appear?

   a. The Tempest   c. A Midsummer Night's Dream
   b. As You Like It   d. Troilus and Cressida

9. 'The Barchester Chronicles' is the collective title of six novels by which author?

   a. Anthony Trollope   c. John Buchan
   b. Arnold Bennett   d. GK Chesterton

10. Who won the Carnegie Medal for his work 'The Amazing Maurice and his Educated Rodents'?

    a. Tom Wolfe   c. Terry Pratchett
    b. Kingsley Amis   d. Malcolm Bradbury

11. The film, 'Men of Respect' (1990), was based on which of Shakespeare's plays?

    a. Hamlet   c. Macbeth
    b. Othello   d. Julius Caesar

12. What is the setting for Marian Keyes novel 'The Other Side of the Story'?

a. Publishing
b. Modelling
c. Gardening
d. Film Industry

13. What is the name of the bedridden boy in the Children's classic 'The Secret Garden'?

a. Frederick
b. Colin
c. John
d. Alistair

14. Who won the Whitbread Prize in 1996 for the children's Book of the Year with 'The Tulip Touch'?

a. Anne Fine
b. Gillian Cross
c. Judy Allen
d. Diana Hendry

15. Which author's autobiography of 1929 was entitled 'As I Walked Out One Midsummer's Morning'?

a. H.E. Bates
b. Roald Dahl
c. Laurie Lee
d. John Bunyan

16. Which classic tale begins, 'As I walked through the wilderness of this world, I lighted on a certain place where was a Den, and I laid me down in that place to sleep; and, as I slept, I dreamed a dream.'

a. The Way of All Flesh
b. Alice's Adventures in Wonderland
c. The Canterbury Tales
d. The Pilgrim's Progress

17. 'Virginia', 'Madame Bovary' and 'Flesh and Blood' are works by which playwright?

a. Edna O'Brien
b. J.B. Priestley
c. Peter Shaffer
d. Richard Harris

18. Which poet wrote 'Lycidas', 'On His Blindness' and 'Nativity Ode'?

a. Alexander Pope
b. John Dryden
c. John Milton
d. Thomas Gray

19. In 'Jane Eyre' what is the name of Mr Rochester's home?

a. Wildfell Hall
b. Thornfield Hall
c. Wykeham Hall
d. Whitworth Hall

20. The first line of which book is, 'It is a truth universally acknowledged, that a single man in possession of a good fortune, must be in want of a wife.'?

a. Pride and Prejudice
b. Emma
c. Persuasion
d. Mansfield Park

NAME THE BOOK WHERE YOU WOULD FIND THE FOLLOWING CHARACTERS AND THE AUTHOR:

1. Sir Danvers Carew

2. Paul Morel

3. Cedric Errol

4. James Dixon

5. Sergeant Cuff

6. Mrs Proudie

7. Rikki Tikki Tavi

8. Mr Charles Chipping

9. Norah Nesbit

10. Ford Prefect

11. Bathsheba Everdene

12. Captain Charles Ryder

13. Flashman

14. Sam Weller

15. Captain Cat

16. Maxim de Winter

17. Yahoos

18. Fanny Price

19. Basil Hallward

20. Dr Slop

NAME THE POET, NOVELIST OR PLAYWRIGHT YOU ASSOCIATE WITH THE FOLLOWING WORKS:

1. 'The Eve of St Agnes'; 'Ode on a Grecian Urn'; 'La Belle Dame sans Merci'

2. 'Barrack-Room Ballads'; 'The Just So Stories'; 'The Light that Failed'

3. 'Down and Out in Paris and London'; 'The Road to Wigan Pier'; 'Homage to Catalonia'

4. 'Changing Places'; 'The British Museum is Falling Down'; 'How Far Can You Go?'

5. 'Prester John'; 'The Thirty-Nine Steps'; 'Mr Standfast'

6. 'The Man of Property'; 'In Chancery'; 'To Let'

7. 'First Among Equals'; 'The Fourth Estate'; 'Kane and Abel'

8. 'The Entertainer'; 'Inadmissable Evidence'; 'Look Back In Anger'

9. 'Fungus the Bogeyman'; 'When the Wind Blows'; 'The Snowman'

10. 'The Van'; 'The Woman Who Walked into Doors'; 'Paddy Clarke Ha Ha Ha'

11. 'Witness for the Prosecution'; 'The Mysterious Affair at Styles'; 'Hound of Death'

12. 'The Third Man'; 'The Power and the Glory'; 'The Heart of the Matter'

13. 'Jacob's Room'; 'To the Lighthouse'; 'Night and Day'

14. 'Next of Kin'; 'The Choirboy'; 'A Village Affair'

15. 'The First Men in the Moon'; 'The Invisible Man'; 'The Time Machine'

16. 'Dirty Linen'; 'Night and Day'; 'The Real Inspector Hound'

17. 'Aaron's Rod'; 'The Plumed Serpent'; 'The White Peacock'

18. 'Affliction'; 'Down Among the Women'; 'The Life and Loves of a She-Devil'

19. 'Clayhanger'; 'The Old Wives' Tale'; 'Anna of the Five Towns'

20. 'The Lost World'; 'The Sign of Four'; 'The White Company'

IDENTIFY THE SHAKESPEAREAN PLAY FROM THE CHARACTERS:

1. Bertram, Count of Rousillon

2. Prospero

3. Touchstone

4. Banquo

5. Goneril

6. Iago

7. Brutus

8. Katharina

9. Bottom

10. Shylock

11. Friar Lawrence

12. Costard

13. Benedick

14. Laertes

15. Sir Toby Belch

16. Octavia

17. Duke of Buckingham

18. Valentine

19. Balthasar

20. Cadwal

21. Mistress Quickly

22. Priam, King of Troy

23. Isabella

24. Leontes, King of Sicily

25. Menenius Agrippa

THE FOLLOWING ARE THE FIRST LINES OF POEMS FROM WHICH AUTHORS?

1. A little learning is a dangerous thing;
   Drink deep, or taste not the Pierian spring;

2. Blow, blow, thou winter wind,
   Thou art not so unkind
   As Man's ingratitude;

3. Drink to me only with thine eyes,
   And I will pledge with mine;

4. Do not go gentle into that goodnight,
   Old age should burn and rave at close of day;
   Rage, rage against the dying of the light.

5. Come live with me and be my love,
   And we will all the pleasures prove,

6. The King asked
   The Queen, and
   The Queen asked
   The Dairymaid:
   'Could we have some butter for
   The Royal slice of bread?'

7. They went to sea in a Sieve, they did,
   In a Sieve they went to sea:
   In spite of all their friends could say,
   On a winter's morn, on a stormy day,
   In a Sieve they went to sea!

8. The Camel's hump is an ugly lump
    Which well you may see at the Zoo;
    But uglier yet is the hump we get
    From having too little to do

9. 'Will you walk a little faster' said a whiting to a
    snail.
    There's a porpoise close behind us, and he's treading
    on my tail.

10. Hamelin Town's in Brunswick
    By famous Hanover city;
    The river Weser, deep and wide,
    Washes its wall on the southern side

11. The world is so full of a number of things,
    I'm sure we should all be as happy as kings.

12. Jellicle Cats come out tonight
    Jellicle Cats come one and all:
    The Jellicle Moon is shining bright-
    Jellicles come to the Jellicle Ball

13. Little Boy kneels at the foot of the bed,
    Droops on the little hands little golden head.
    Hush! Hush! Whisper who dares!
    Christopher Robin is saying his prayers

14. 'Is there anybody there?' said the Traveller,
    Knocking on the moonlit door;

15. I will arise and go now, and go to Innisfree,
    And a small cabin build there, of clay and wattles
    made:

16. If I should die, think only this of me:
    That there's some corner of a foreign field
    That is for ever England...

17. Tiger! Tiger! Burning bright
    In the forests of the night,

18. Faster than fairies, faster than witches
    Bridges and houses, hedges and ditches;
    And charging along like troops in a battle,
    All through the meadows the horses and cattle

19. There was a naughty boy,
    A naughty boy was he,
    He would not stop at home,
    He could not quiet be

20. Gentle Jesus, meek and mild,
    Look upon a little child;
    Pity my simplicity,
    Suffer me to come to thee.

SHAKESPEARE: NAME THE CHARACTER AND THE PLAY FROM THE FOLLOWING LINES:

1. "Now is the winter of our discontent, made glorious summer by this son of York"

2. "Thus with a kiss I die"

3. "Be not afraid of greatness. Some are born great, some achieve greatness, and some have greatness thrust upon 'em'"

4. "Full fathom five thy father lies. Of his bones are coral made"

5. "Our remedies oft in ourselves do lie which we ascribe to heaven."

6. "We few, we happy few, we band of brothers."

7. "He hath eaten me out of house and home"

8. "Men are April when they woo, December when they wed, maids are May when they are maids, but the sky changes when they are wives."

9. "When sorrows come, they come not single spies, but in battalions."

10. "Cowards die many times before their deaths; the valiant never taste of death but once."

11. "Double, double, toil and trouble, fire burn, and cauldron bubble."

12. "The quality of mercy is not strained. It droppeth as the gentle rain from heaven, upon the place beneath."

13. "They say, best men are moulded out of faults; and for the most, become much more the better, for being a little bad."

14. "You may my glories and my state depose, but not my griefs; still am I king of those"

15. "The course of true love never did run smooth."

16. "Oh, what men dare do! What men dare do! What men daily do, not knowing what they do"

17. "She is a woman, therefore may be wooed; she is a woman, therefore may be won; she is Lavinia, therefore must be loved."

18. "Who is Silvia? What is she, that all our swains commend her?"

19. "A woman moved is like a fountain troubles, muddy, ill seeming, thick, bereft of beauty."

20. "O beware, my lord, of jealousy; it is the green-eyed monster which doth mock the meat it feeds on"

1. Which was the first of Charles Dickens works to bring him fame and fortune, which was published when he was 24 years old?

2. Which author created the animal expert Dr Dolittle?

3. Thomas Hardy in his novels renamed which market town Casterbridge?

4. Which knight wrote 'Kenilworth'.

5. Which cathedral town of Staffordshire is famous for its association with Samuel Johnson?

6. Who was appointed Poet laureate in 1984?

7. 'The Hunting of the Snark' (1876) was a nonsense poem by whom?

8. 'Brave New World' (1928) is the best-known work of which author?

9. Which London thoroughfare gave its name to a Helen Hanff book and is associated with second-hand bookshops?

10. In Roald Dahl's 'Charlie and the Chocolate Factory', what are the pygmies called?

11. Bentley Drummie, Joe Gargery and Abel Magwitch are characters from which Dickens novel?

12. What was the pen name of the spy novel writer David Cornwell?

13. Name the three volumes of 'Lord of the Rings'.

14. Who wrote the lines 'Fair daffodils, we weep to see / You haste away so soon.'?

15. What were the Christian names of the writer and poet A.A. Milne?

16. Who, during World War II told the nation to take heart with the words from Kipling 'If you can dream and not make dreams your master; If you can think and not make thoughts your aim, If you can meet with Triumph and Disaster and treat those two impostors just the same.'?

17. Who wrote, 'The Dong with the Luminous Nose'?

18. Who wrote the narrative poem 'Evangeline'?

19. 'Strangers and Brothers' (1940-70) were a sequence of books by which author?

20. Who came out in defence of modern grammar in her top-selling work 'Eats, Shoots and Leaves'?

1. Name the author of the blockbuster first novel of Emma Harte who went from poverty to the head of a business empire.

2. In the game of croquet in 'Alice's Adventures in Wonderland,' which animals were used as mallets?

3. Who became the first Children's Laureate in 1999?

4. Which playwright do you associate with 'Forty Years On' and 'Kafka's Dick'?

5. Name the dog in 'Peter Pan'.

6. Who was the central character in John Osborne's 'Look Back in Anger'?

7. Which classic children's book is set in Vendale?

8. In Dickens 'A Tale of Two Cities', which were the two cities?

9. P.D. James is one of Britain's leading crime writers. What do the initials P.D. represent?

10. Dogberry is a character from which Shakespearean play?

11. Who was Soames Forsyte's wife who left him for the architect Bosinney?

12. Which Joanna Trollope novel documents the search of two thirtysomethings looking for their birth mothers?

13. Who reached the best-seller list in 2004 with 'The Bad Mother's Handbook'?

14. In 'Tess of the D'Urbervilles', whom does Tess marry?

15. Name 'The Railway Children'.

16. What was Winston Smith's greatest fear in Orwel's 'Nineteen Eighty-Four'?

17. Dorothea Brooke was the heroine in which George Eliot novel?

18. In 2004, who was listed as the world's richest author, worth $1 billion, aged 38?

19. Who owned 'Animal Farm' in the book of the same name?

20. Which classic novel do Mr Lockwood and Nelly Deane narrate?

1. Name the two boys from the 'Famous Five' books by Enid Blyton.

2. Devotees of which 18th-century writer are known as Janeites?

3. Who created the characters Bertie Wooster and his manservant Jeeves?

4. Sherlock Holmes lived at which fictional address?

5. Alfie is the central character of which prolific children's author and illustrator?

6. Bob Cratchit was the underpaid clerk in which Dickens novel?

7. Chief Inspector Wexford is the fictional detective of which author?

8. Name the parsonage where the Brontë sisters lived in Yorkshire.

9. To which writer is 'Jane Eyre' dedicated?

10. Name the close-fitting cloth hat that is forever associated with Sherlock Holmes.

11. 'Moll Flanders' and 'Robinson Crusoe' were among the works of which prolific author?

12. Who described his own boarding-school experience in 'Stalky and Co'?

13. Who adopts 'Oliver Twist' at the end of the story?

14. Which book is subtitled 'Travels into Several Remote Nations of the World'?

15. Eliza Dolittle's father described himself as "one of the undeserving poor". What was his occupation?

16. Sir Anthony Absolute is a character from which of Sheridan's plays?

17. Complete Coleridge's line, 'In Xanadu did Kubla Khan...'

18. In which Hardy novel does Henchard sell his wife and daughters for five guineas?

19. Who created the Mr Men series of books?

20. In which novel do you meet cows named Aimless, Feckless, Graceless and Pointless?

1. Name Shakespeare's four great tragedies.

2. Who wrote the narrative poem 'The Lady of the Lake' (1810)?

3. Kenneth Grahame is known for his children's classic, 'The Wind in the Willows'. What was his profession?

4. Who told of the ups and downs of his own life in the poem 'Maud '(1855)?

5. Which Yorkshire Dales school inspector's fourth book of memories is entitled 'Up and Down in the Dales'?

6. Who is the criminal investigator in Ian Rankin's 'A Question of Blood'?

7. What handicap did the novelist and playwright Somerset Maugham suffer from?

8. In which novel did Mr Bumble, the beadle, declare 'the law is an ass - a idiot'?

9. Which actor tells of his turbulent life in his autobiography 'Ricky'?

10. In which novel by Conan Doyle did Sherlock Holmes first appear?

11. What was 'The Moonstone', in the book of the same title?

12. Monsignor John O'Connor, a Roman Catholic priest was the model for which G.K. Chesterton character?

13. 'All animals are created equal but some animals are more equal than others' is a line from which book?

14. Name Shakespeare's shortest play.

15. Who established his reputation as a leading Romantic poet with such works as 'Childe Harold's Pilgrimage' (1812) and 'Don Juan' (1819-24)?

16. Which poet of World War I do you associate with the 'Anthem for Doomed Youth'?

17. Name the four fairies in Shakespeare's 'A Midsummer Night's Dream'.

18. Which of Tennyson's works tells of a mysterious lady who never raises her eyes from her loom until Lancelot passes by on his way to Camelot?

19. Which disease is chronicled in Julie Gregory's work 'Sickened'?

20. Which poet's dying words were, 'I've had 18 straight whiskies, I think that's a record...after 39 years this is all I've done.'

TWENTY QUESTIONS ON SHAKESPEARE:

1. Name the fat knight in 'Henry IV'

2. How does 'Othello', the Moor of Venice meet his death?

3. Which country do you associate with 'Hamlet'?

4. Name Hamlet's mother

5. Complete the line of the sonnet 'Shall I compare thee to a summer's day?'

6. Name the airy spirit in 'The Tempest'.

7. By what other name was Portia known in 'The Merchant of Venice?'

8. In what year was Shakespeare born?

9. Bertram, Reynaldo and Lord Dumaine are characters from which play?

10. Which character says "All the world's a stage and all the men and women merely players..."?

11. Name Katherine's sister in 'The Merchant of Venice'.

12. Which play do you associate with the line 'A horse, a horse, my kingdom for a horse'?

13. Who was King Lear's youngest daughter?

14. Bassanio, Gobbo and Stefano are characters from which play?

15. Which play tells of Sir John Falstaff's unsuccessful attempts to seduce Mistress Ford and Mistress Page?

16. What is the setting for 'Much Ado About Nothing'?

17. Name Iago's wife in 'Othello'.

18. Peter Quince, the carpenter, Snug the joiner and Robin Starveling, the tailor are characters from which play?

19. Whose final words are 'O happy dagger, this is thy sheath! There rust, and let me die.'?

20. Which play ends with the line 'Ere bloody hands were washed, with such a peace.'?

1. In which Oscar Wilde play do Lady Gertrude Chiltern and Mrs Laura Cheveley appear?

2. Which animal, according to Charles Lutwidge Dodgson 'vanished quite slowly...ending with the grin.'?

3. Which adventure story, published in 1886, tells of the exploits of a young Scottish boy named David Balfour?

4. Who wrote the poem, 'Ode to the West Wind'. (1820) which was inspired by a walk in Florence on an October day?

5. Who were the fictional pair of old men who answered readers' letters in the Daily Mirror between 1936-90?

6. Name the book of poems by T.S. Eliot, made popular by the musical 'Cats'?

7. What was the Artful Dodger's true name?

8. Whose novels featured the agent Harry Palmer?

9. 'Memoirs of a Midge', a poetic fantasy, is one of the best-known books by which author?

10. Who created the despairing singleton Bridget Jones?

11. Who won the Booker Prize in 1995 with 'The Ghost Road'?

12. Which two books are castaways given on BBC radio's 'Desert Island Discs'?

13. Name the street on which professor Henry Higgins lived in 'Pygmalion'.

14. In 'The Radiant Way' (1987), three middle-aged women look back on their younger selves. Who wrote this novel?

15. In which fictional diary do you meet the suburban anti-hero, Charles Pooter?

16. 'The Black Prince', 'The Sea, The Sea' and 'The Time of the Angels' are works by which acclaimed author?

17. Which book closes with the line 'And they were both ever sensible of the warmest gratitude towards the persons, who, by bringing her into Derbyshire, had been the means of uniting them.'?

18. Who illustrated the 'Winnie the Pooh' stories?

19. Who was the central character of Thackeray's 'Vanity Fair'?

20. Which television personality named her autobiography 'Memoirs of an Unfit Mother'?

**NAME THE CHILDREN'S BOOK AND AUTHOR
WHERE YOU WOULD FIND THE FOLLOWING
CHARACTERS:**

1. Bagheera

2. Great-Uncle-Matthew 'Gum'

3. Mrs Bedonebyasyoudid

4. Cruella deVille

5. Caractacus Potts

6. Mr Tumnus

7. Hunca Munca

8. Gollum

9. Fiver

10. Violet Elizabeth Bott

11. Albus Dumbledore

12. Tinkerbell

13. Flashman

14. Ben Gunn

15. Push-me-pull-you

16. Dumbiedikes

17. Toad

18. The Bastable Family

19. Charlie Bucket

20. 'Arrietty

1. Whose verse-autobiography is entitled 'Summoned by Bells'?

2. Penelope Keeling is the main character in which Rosamunde Pilcher novel?

3. Calypso, Walter and Polly arrive by the London train at Penzance at the start of their summer visit, in which Mary Wesley novel?

4. 'The Loving Spirit', 'The Birds' and 'My Cousin Rachel' are works by which author?

5. Who made her name with 'The Murder of Peter Ackroyd' in 1926?

6. 'Sanditon' was the unfinished novel of which author?

7. R.D. Blackmore is famous for his romance 'Lorna Doone'. What did his initials represent?

8. Who wrote the trilogy 'A Horseman Riding By'?

9. Which Charles Kingsley swashbuckling Elizabethan story was based on 'the little white town of Bideford'?

10. Which playwright and satarist was the author of 'The Beggar's Opera'?

11. Little Nell was the tear-jerking heroine of which Dickens novel?

12. Who wrote 'Room at the Top'?

13. Whose fourth novel 'Hotel du Lac' (1984) won the Booker Prize?

14. Name the secret agent John Buchan introduced in 'The Thirty-Nine Steps'.

15. Carl Peterson, an international criminal, was the chief adversary of which character in the books by Sapper?

16. Who wrote 'The Ballad of Peckham Rye' and 'The Comforters'?

17. Which book opens with the line, 'All children, except one, grow up.'?

18. Which dancer's autobiography was entitled Precious Little Sleep'?

19. Name the elephants in the Winnie the Pooh stories.

20. In which novel do Gudrun Brangwen and Gerald Crich appear?

1. 'Decline and Fall' (1928) charted the rise and fall of Oxford student Paul Pennyfeather. Who wrote this novel?

2. Whose 'story of a simple soul' told of an inarticulate draper's assistant named Arthur Kipps?

3. Which underground magazine was founded in London in the sixties by the Australian Richard Neville?

4. Who was the linguistics expert in George Bernard Shaw's 'Pygmalion'?

5. 'Theirs not to reason why,
   Theirs but to do or die;'
   gives a bleak picture of a soldier's duty in which poem?

6. What was Adam Bede's occupation in George Eliot's book of the same name?

7. Who wrote 'The Rime of the Ancient Mariner'?

8. In George Orwell's 'Animal Farm', what type of animal was Boxer?

9. Who initially published her novel 'The Bell Jar' under the pseudonym Victoria Lucas?

10. Name the five daughters of Mr and Mrs Bennett in Jane Austen's 'Pride and Prejudice'.

11. Which novel by Evelyn Waugh does Charles Ryder narrate?

12. In E.F. Benson's satirical stories, who are the consecutive owners of the house known as Mallards?

13. Name the poets known collectively as The Liverpool Poets.

14. Which book is set during 18 hours on 16 June 1904 in Dublin?

15. Where did John Fowles set 'The French Lieutenant's Woman'?

16. Who wrote 'South Riding', the story of left-wing headmistress Sarah Burton, at odds with the community and her husband?

17. Which Merseyside-born writer wrote 'Thursday's Child', 'Liverpool Daisy' and 'Three Women of Liverpool'?

18. Who made Farringford house, near Freshwater his home for nearly 40 years?

19. Who wrote about 'Carrie's War'?

20. Which Graham Greene novel begins' Hale knew, before he had been three hours in Brighton, that they meant to murder him'?

IDENTIFY THE SHAKESPEAREAN PLAY FROM THE FOLLOWING OPENING LINES AND WHICH CHARACTER SAYS THEM:

1. If you shall chance, Camillo, to visit Bohemia

2. When shall we three meet again? In thunder, lightning, or in rain?

3. In sooth, I know not why I am so sad

4. As I remember, Adam, it was upon this fashion

5. Cease to persuade, my loving Proteus

6. I learn in this letter that Don Pedro of Aragon comes this night to Messina

7. Two households, both alike in dignity in fair Verona

8. If music be the food of love, play on

9. Now, fair Hippolyta, our nuptial hour draws on apace

10. I thought the King had more affected the Duke of Albany than Cornwall

11. Proceed, Solinus, to procure my fall

12. In delivering my son from me I bury a second husband

13. Hence, home, you idle creatures, get you home

14. Boatswain!

15. In Troy there lies the scene. From isles of Greece

16. You do not meet a man but frowns

17. Nay, but this dotage of our General's overflows the measure

18. Who's there?

19. Let fame, that all hunt after in their lives

20. Sir Hugh, persuade me not. I will make a Star Chamber matter of it

WHICH AUTHORS CREATED THE FOLLOWING CHARACTERS?

1. Doctor Faustus

2. Rumpole

3. Moll Flanders

4. Dracula

5. I Claudius

6. Bilbo Baggins

7. Agnes Grey

8. Dr Finlay

9. Sir Benjamin Backbite

10. Ivanhoe

11. Barnaby Rudge

12. Joseph Andrews

13. Major Barbara

14. Adrian Mole

15. Fanny Price

16. Lord Jim

17. Humphrey Chimpden-Earwicker

18. Daniel Deronda

19. Beatie Bryant

20. Ethan Frome

NAME THE AUTHORS YOU ASSOCIATE WITH THE FOLLOWING LINES:

1. Death will be an awfully big adventure.

2. An alcoholic is someone you don't like who drinks as much as you do.

3. Pylons, those pillars
bare like nude giant girls that have no secret.

4. He is the Napoleon of crime.

5. I like the English. They have the most rigid code of immorality in the world.

6. Live now, pay later (book title).

7. Only connect.

8. A drama critic is a man who leaves no turn unstoned.

9. We are all born mad. Some of us remain so.

10. Other people have a nationality. The Irish and the Jews have a psychosis.

11. I was much too far out all my life. And not waving but drowning.

12. Always fornicate between clean sheets and spit on a well-scrubbed floor.

13. There is nothing - absolutely nothing - half so much worth doing as simply messing about in boats.

14. 'My esteemed chums', murmured Hurree Jamset Ram Singh. 'This is not an occasion for looking the gift horse in the mouthfulness'.

15. Something nasty in the woodshed.

16. As I grow older and older
    And totter towards the tomb
    I find that I care less and less
    Who goes to bed with whom

17. Better drowned than duffers if not duffers won't drown.

18. That whiskey priest. I wish we had never had him in the house.

19. It is said that the effect of eating too much lettuce is 'soporific'.

20. There's no money in poetry, but then there's no poetry in money either.

NAME THE AUTHORS WHO WON THE BOOKER PRIZE WITH THE FOLLOWING NOVELS;

1. G (1972)

2. Saville (1976)

3. The Sea, The Sea (1978)

4. Rites of Passage (1980)

5. Schindler's Ark (1982)

6. Hotel du Lac (1984)

7. The Old Devils (1986)

8. Moon Tiger (1987)

9. Oscar & Lucinda (1988)

10. Possession (1990)

11. Sacred Hunger (1992) joint winner

12. Paddy Clarke Ha Ha Ha (1993)

13. The Ghost Road (1995)

14. Last Orders (1996)

15. Amsterdam (1998)

1. Which contemporary writer created Dr. Temperance Brennan?

2. Who told of the rivalry between Queen Mary and Elizabeth in 'The Queen's Fool?

3. Which media queen's autobiography is entitled 'Baggage: My Childhood' (2004)?

4. Name the four children in C.S. Lewis' stories of Narnia.

5. Which controversial author and academic wrote 'The Boy', challenging the way we look at the boy in art?

6. Name the boat in which Percy Bysshe Shelley was drowned in 1822.

7. Complete the sentence:
   'The clever men at Oxford
   Know all that there is to be knowed
   But none of them know one half as much
   As intelligent ....'

8. Which novelist, with religious themes, speaking in 1980 said "I didn't invent the world I write about - it's all true!?

9. Miss Matty is a character from which of Elizabeth Gaskell's books?

10. In 1902, whose first book of poems was entitled 'Songs of Childhood'?

11. Who won the Nobel Prize for Literature in 1932?

12. What article did Sherlock Holmes use as a tobacco pouch?

13. Born in 1903, this writer changed his name and adopted a Suffolk River's name for his surname. Who was he?

14. Who wrote 'Under the Tuscan Sun', which was filmed in 2003?

15. Which writer said, "An archaeologist is the best husband any woman can have - the older she gets the more interested he is in her"?

16. Who wrote the shopaholic series of books?

17. Who did Noel Coward write 'Private Lives' for?

18. What was Dickens' first published novel?

19. Name the association that awards the Gold Dagger for fiction.

20. Who was the author of 'Girl with a Pearl Earring'?

WHICH WRITERS DO YOU ASSOCIATE WITH THE FOLLOWING LINES:

1. The child is the father of the man

2. East is East and West is West and never the twain shall meet

3. Kind hearts are more than coronets

4. We are American at puberty. We die French

5. O what a tangled web we weave when first we practise to deceive

6. Go and catch a falling star

7. Experience is the name everyone gives to his mistakes

8. Into each life some rain must fall

9. For fools rush in where angels fear to tread

10. Knowledge is power

11. Some books are undeservedly forgotten, none are undeservedly remembered

12. Comedy is tragedy interrupted

13. Every man over forty is a scoundrel

14. I am a camera with its shutters open, quite passive, recording, not thinking

15. Four legs good, two legs bad

16. God's in his heaven - all's right with the world

17. The past is a foreign country: they do things differently there

18. Love is a fan club with only two fans

19. Anno-domini - that's the most fatal complaint of all

20. Literature is mostly about sex and not much about having children and life is the other way round

WHICH CONTEMPORARY AUTHORS WROTE THE FOLLOWING POPULAR STORIES:

1. Beggars Banquet

2. Equal Rites

3. The House of Flowers

4. Atlantic Shift

5. The Other Side of the Story

6. The Rules of Engagement

7. Olivia Joules and the Overactive Imagination

8. The Mermaid and the Drunks

9. The Boy Who Taught the Beekeeper to Read

10. The Other Woman's Shoes

11. Two for Joy

12. Paradise House

13. Where Did It All Go Right?

14. Waiting for the Day

15. The Kid

16. The Family Way

17. The Making of Henry

18. The Distance Between Us

19. Crossing the Lines

20. Buddha Da

ENTERTAINMENT

1. What are the nicknames of the following 'London's Burning' characters?

   a) Mike Wilson
   b) Rob Sharpe
   c) Bert Quigley
   d) Roland Cartwright
   e) Stuart Mackenzie

2. In 'Upstairs Downstairs' which actors played the following servants:

   a) Rose
   b) Daisy
   c) Thomas
   d) Edward
   e) Sarah

3. Name the seven children played by these actors in 'The Waltons'

   a) Mary Elizabeth McDonoogh
   b) Judy Norton Taylor
   c) David W. Harper
   d) Kami Cotler
   e) Richard Thomas
   f) Eric Scott
   g) Jon Walmsley

4. In which TV shows did the following doctors appear:

   a) Dr. Claire Maitland played by Helen Baxendale
   b) Dr. Beth Glover played by Amanda Burton
   c) Dr. Geoffrey Brent played by Ian Hendry
   d) Prof. Geoffrey Hoyt played by Tom Baker
   e) Dr. Judith Vincent played by Brigit Forsyth
   f) Dr. Toby Latimer played by Tony Britton

5. Name the shows you associate with the following fictional locations:

    a) St. Angela's Hospital, Battersea
    b) Grace Brothers
    c) Holby City Hospital
    d) Le Château Anglais
    e) Tarrant
    f) Hartley in Lancashire

6. Who created the following series:

    a) Just Good Friends
    b) Peak Practice
    c) Up the Workers
    d) The House of Elliott
    e) London's Burning
    f) When the Boat Comes In

7. In what year did the following long-running series first come to our screens:

    a) Coronation Street
    b) Changing Rooms
    c) General Hospital
    d) The Bill
    e) Minder
    f) Brookside

8. Name the following vehicles in the children's series 'Bob the Builder':

    a) The yellow digger
    b) The orange cement mixer
    c) The red dumper truck
    d) The blue nervous crane
    e) The green steamroller

9. Name the characters played by David Jason in the following series:

    a) The Darling Buds of May
    b) A Touch of Frost
    c) Only Fools and Horses
    d) The Wind in the Willows (voice)
    e) Open all Hours

10. Which TV series were set at the addresses below:

    a) 'Dalentrace', Bryan Close, Essex
    b) Huskinson Street, Liverpool
    c) 'Mallards', Tilling-on-Sea, Sussex
    d) 1313 Mockingbird Lane, Mockingbird Heights
    e) 3 Duchess Mews, London

ENTERTAINMENT 2

1. Which entertainer said, "What you said hurt me very much. I cried all the way to the bank"?

2. Which classic actor played Lord Marchmain in TV's 'Brideshead Revisited'?

3. Name the four actors who were TV's 'The Monkees'.

4. What character did Una Stubbs play in 'Worzel Gummidge'?

5. Barrie Gill, Quentin Willson, Chris Goffey and Tiff Needell have all been presenters on which programme?

6. In which comedy series did Wendy Craig play Sally Harrison/Redway?

7. Desmond Morris, Chris Kelly and Harry Watt all presented which TV programme?

8. Name the first man to win a million on 'Who Want's to be a Millionaire'?

9. 'Trumpton' was a spin-off from which children's series?

10. In the TV series 'Alias Smith & Jones', by what other names were they known?

11. Who starred as Guy and Harriet Pringle in 'Fortunes of War'?

12. Who created 'Teletubbies'?

13. What did the initials B.A. stand for in Sgt. Bosco 'B.A.' Baracus' name in 'The A-Team'?

14. Johnny Morris and the appropriately named Terry Nutkins presented which TV programme?

15. Who played Alf's long-suffering wife in 'Till Death Us Do Part'?

16. David Nixon, Barbara Kelly, Isobel Barnett and Gilbert Harding were the original panel of which TV game show?

17. Who played TV's 'Banacek'?

18. Who narrated 'The Magic Roundabout'?

19. Name the TV sketch show, which featured Kenny Everett, Germaine Greer and Jonathan Routh.

20. Which TV drama was loosely based on the life of Rosa Lewis, a kitchen maid who became manageress of the Cavendish Hotel?

WHICH TV SERIES DO YOU ASSOCIATE WITH THE FOLLOWING CHARACTERS?

1. Eddie Hitler

2. Bubble

3. Nurse Hathaway

4. Sir Greville

5. Windy Miller

6. Dawn Tynsley

7. Guy Buchanan

8. Yosser Hughes

9. Rangi Ram

10. Herr Flick

11. Seymour Utterthwaite

12. Queenie

13. 'Boss' Hogg

14. William Bodie

15. Ling Woo

16. Eric Catchpole

17. Maddie Hayes

18. Blakey

19. Granny Sushila

20. C.J. Parker

21. Zoe Angell/Callender

22. Mike Gambit

23. Harry Farthing

24. Joe Friday

25. Assumpta Fitzgerald

NAME THE ACTORS WHO HAVE THE FOLLOWING TV SHOWS TO THEIR CREDIT:

1. Murphy's Law; Cold Feet

2. William and Mary; Men Behaving Badly; Dr. Who

3. Coronation Street; Heartbeat; Keeping Up Appearances

4. The Good Life; To the Manor Born; No Job for a Lady

5. All Creatures Great & Small; At Home with the Braithwaites; Second Thoughts

6. Angels; Shine On Harvey Moon; Down To Earth

7. Beiderbecke Affair; Only When I Laugh; Executive Stress

8. Robin's Nest; Don't Wait Up, Don't Tell Father

9. A Very Peculiar Practice; Holding the Fort; Sink or Swim

10. Hollyoaks; Casualty; Two Pints of Lager and a Packet of Crisps

11. Ain't Misbehavin'; Faith in the Future; Jonathan Creek

12. Last of the Summer Wine; 'Allo, 'Allo; Born & Bred

13. Our Friends in the North; Goggle Eyes; Inspector Morse

14. Z Cars; Love in a Cold Climate; As Time Goes By

15. EastEnders; On The Buses; The Newcomers

16. Auf Wiedersehen Pet; The Boys From The Bush; Common As Muck

17. Rumpole of the Bailey; Lytton's Diary; Only When I Laugh

18. The Liver Birds; Bergerac; Midsomer Murders

19. Goodnight Sweetheart; Only Fools & Horses; The Two of Us

20. Rings on Their Fingers; The Forsyte Saga; The Pallisers

1. Which Dimbleby do you associate with Radio 4's 'Any Questions'?

2. Who presents radio's mix of music, comedy and conversation 'Loose Ends'?

3. Which poet is known for the ending of a poem with the words "not waving but drowning"?

4. Who chairs Radio 4's 'Gardeners' Question Time'?

5. Who created Dr Finlay?

6. Which Mike Stott radio comedy was set in possibly the worst estate agent's north of Watford?

7. Which smash hit musical was based on the songs of Abba?

8. 'A Cat in the Hat' (2004) brings happy chaos to the lives of a bored brother and sister. The film is adapted from whose book?

9. With which opera do you associate the character 'Yum Yum'?

10. Which musical is based on the extraordinary lives of Zelda and F. Scott Fitzgerald?

11. Name the character Russell Crowe played in 'Master and Commander: The Far Side of the World'.

12. Which Yorkshire Dales school inspector wrote 'Up and Down in the Dales'?

13. Which best-selling author wrote a collection of short stories entitled 'Jigs and Reels'?

14. Name Roddy Doyle's memoir of his parents' lives.

15. Teddy Lloyd was the art teacher in which book that was made into a very successful film starring Maggie Smith?

16. Who composed and sung the theme tune for TV's 'One Foot in the Grave'?

17. In which city would you find Chetham's School of Music?

18. What is the setting for TV's 'Casualty'?

19. Who played the character 'Worzel Gummidge' in the TV series of the same name?

20. Who created TV's 'Brookside'?

ENTERTAINMENT 6

1. Sarah Frances & Eleanor Prescott were characters from which radio and TV series?

2. Who owns a hamster known as SPG?

3. Name the three horror characters resurrected in Stephen Sommers film of 2004 'Van Helsing.

4. Name the character Dervla Kirwan played in 'Ballykissangel'.

5. Which actor plays Bill in 'Kill Bill Vol 2'?

6. Which funny man married Jennifer Saunders in 1985?

7. 'Tenko', 'Bad Girls' and 'Dynasty' were all dramas starring which actress?

8. Maureen Lipman played Jane Lucas in the TV series 'Agony'. Which agony aunt co-wrote it with Len Richmond?

9. Which actress played Queen Elizabeth I in TV's 'Blackadder'?

10. Who wrote 'The Singing Detective'?

11. Which brutal film of 2004 was based on John King's novel about Chelsea Headhunters?

12. Which footballer-turned-chef is known for his four-letter expletives on TV?

13. Name the twins in 'The Woodentops'.

14. Name the joiner in TV's 'Changing Rooms'.

15. What do Rachel de Thame, Diarmuid Gavin and Matt James have in common?

16. Who was the presenter of TV's 'Hell's Kitchen'?

17. Who was found in the Ten Acre Field on Scatterbrook Farm by John and Sue Peters?

18. Frank Pickle, Owen Newitt & Jim Trott are characters from which TV comedy series?

19. 'Go Let it Out', and 'Some Might Say' were No.1 hits for which band?

20. The play 'Jumpers' is the work of which playwright?

NAME THESE TV AND RADIO PROGRAMMES FROM THEIR THEME TUNES:

1. '5-4-3-2-1' by Manfred Mann

2. 'Minute Waltz' by Chopin

3. 'This Wheel's on Fire' by Julie Driscoll

4. 'Approaching Menace' by Neil Richardson

5. 'A Musical Joke' by Mozart

6. 'Barwick Green' suite by Arthur Wood

7. 'Who Do You Think You're Kidding, Mr. Hitler?' sung by Bud Flanagan

8. 'Barnacle Bill the Sailor' adapted by Mike Oldfield

9. 'By the Sleepy Lagoon' by Eric Coates

10. 'Nunc Dimittis' arranged by Geoffrey Burgon

11. 'Handbags & Gladrags' by Mike D'abo

12. 'Liberty Bell' by John Paul Souza

13. 'That's Living Alright' sung by Joe Fagin

14. 'Soul Limbo' by Booker T. and The M.G.'s

15. 'Variations on a Theme of Paganini' by Julian Lloyd Webber

16. 'Hit and Miss' by John Barry

17. 'Eine Kleine Nachtmusik' by Mozart

18. 'William Tell' overture by Rossini

19. 'I Could Be So Good For You' by Pat Waterman & Gerard Kenny

20. 'Walking in the Air' sung by Aled Jones

1. 'Paradise Found' (2002) was a biopic of which artist?

2. The controversial BBC film 'Tumbledown' was broadcast in May 1988. What was its subject matter?

3. Jim Bowen is known as a comedian and game-show presenter. What was his previous profession?

4. Which character said 'gis a job' in Boys from the Blackstuff?

5. Who played Bluebottle in the Goon Show?

6. Name the eight celebrities in the first I'm, a Celebrity Get Me Out of Here'.

7. Whose autobiography is entitled 'Banjaxed'?

8. Who said, "Television is an invention that permits you to be entertained in your living room by people you wouldn't have in your home".

9. Which nineties play written and directed by Tom Stoppard is based on Shakespeare's 'Hamlet'?

10. In which series did Michelle Collins play single mum Abby Wallace?

11. Who played the arrogant Trojan prince Paris in Wolfgang Petersen's film 'Troy'?

12. The TV & Radio presenter Sue Lawley first made her name on which programme (1972-83)?

13. Name the original four performers in the unpredictable comedy radio show 'The Goon Show'.

14. Which bandleader formed the BBC Dance Orchestra in 1932 and became a household name with his weekly 'Guest Night'?

15. Which actress starred opposite Pierce Brosnan in the romantic comedy 'Laws of Attraction' (2004)?

16. Who said on collecting an Oscar for 'Chariots of Fire', "The British are coming"?

17. 'Mastermind' came to our screens in which year?

18. Who played the old professor in the title role of 'Emile' (2004)?

19. Which debut single launched Oasis?

20. Name the third Harry Potter film.

NAME THE ACTORS WHO PORTRAYED THE FOLLOWING TV COPS:

1. Det Sgt Jane Tennison

2. Det Inspector Jack Frost

3. Det Sgt Lewis

4. Sgt Shelagh Murphy

5. Inspector Barlow

6. Det Sgt Johnny Ho

7. Det Supt Andrew Dalziel

8. Det Sgt George Carter

9. Inspector Jean Darblay

10. Sgt Oscar Blaketon

11. Sgt Suzanne 'Pepper' Anderson

12. Det Chief Insp Alan Craven

13. Det Sgt Albert 'Charlie' Chisholm

14. Det James 'Sonny' Crockett

15. Inspector Charlie Eden

16. Det Chief Supt Charlie Barlow

17. Det Chief Inspector Tom Haggerty

18. Chief Inspector Barney Crozier

19. Det Chief Inspector Jim Taggart

20. Undercover cop Liam Ketman

NAME THE FOLLOWING PERSONALITIES:

1. He grew up in Port Talbot, the son of a baker and struggled with dyslexia at school. He first tried acting at his local YMCA and he later won a place at RADA and joined the National Theatre in 1965. He became an American citizen in 2000. He won a best actor Oscar in 1992 for his performance playing opposite Jodie Foster, which launched him into Hollywood's big league. Name him.

2. He was born on August 29 1958 in Dudley, West Midlands, one of seven children. He went to Bluecoats School where his natural comic ability was recognised. At the age of 16, he won TV's 'New Faces'. He made his debut in the sitcom 'The Fosters' in 1976. He also appeared in 'Tiswas', 'Three of a Kind' and 'Chef!'. Name him.

3. This actress was formerly a teenage model and at the age of 4 was the star of a Fairy Liquid advert. She played computer whiz kid Fred Smith in 'C.A.T.S. Eyes'. She has also danced with the Black & White Minstrels, co-presented 'The Tube' and regularly appears in a TV commercial. Name her.

4. Born on 17 January 1957, this cynical but witty funnyman grew up in South London. He went to a Catholic Comprehensive school, gained 2 'A' levels but decided against University. He worked in Tooting Employment Office while gaining experience at the London Comedy Store. His first wife was actress Caroline Quentin. Name him.

5. Born in Wales in 1958, this TV presenter began her TV and radio career in Hong Kong. She got her big break on an adventurous game show on Channel 4. TV am's 'Good Morning Britain', 'Wish You Were Here...' and 'Holiday', are also among her credits. Name her.

6. Born in 1941, this actor began working on the stage aged 10 and was in films as a child. He played Lennie in Britain's first TV soap opera 'The Grove Family'. His other TV work has included 'Upstairs, Downstairs', 'The Rag Trade' and 'In Loving Memory'. Name him.

7. Born in Colerain, Northern Ireland, this actor is best known as Adam Williams in a popular TV show. 'Touching Evil', 'Playing the Field' and 'Waking Ned', are among his other credits. Who is he?

8. Born in 1968, this baby-faced English actress and singer has been in commercials, programmes and films as a child. Her films include 'The Great Gatsby' (1974), 'Absolute Beginners' (1986) and 'Kleptomania' (1993). In 'The One and Only' (2002) she struggled to maintain a 'Geordie' accent. Name her.

9. This British leading actress was born in Casablanca in 1947 and is now based in the United States. She trained at RADA and was married to the actor John McEnery. Her TV work includes 'Connie', 'The Colbys' and 'Napoleon & Josephine'. Who is she?

10. This character comedienne described herself thus - "I was very tall and very plain - I wasn't going to get very far on looks - so I thought I'd better be the funny girl." Her TV work includes 'Moving', 'Executive Stress', 'Law and Disorder' and 'No Job for a Lady'. Name her.

11. Born in 1935 in Rothwell, Northamptonshire as James Smith. He trained as a dancer, began as a comedian in the early fifties and first came to the public's attention on TV rock shows as a performer and host, with several hit records in the late fifties. He turned to acting in the sixties and achieved great success on the stage, particularly in the title role of 'Barnum'. Name him.

12. This English actor, seen mainly on stage and television was born in Leicestershire in 1926. He worked in various jobs, including an apprentice butcher before training at RADA. His TV work includes 'Bouquet of Barbed Wire', '84 Charing Cross Road' and 'Common As Muck'. Can you name him?

13. In 1960, he appeared in the title role of 'Billy Liar' and starred in 'Saturday Night, Sunday morning'. He later played Hercule Poirot in 'Murder on the Orient Express'. Name him.

14. He made his TV debut in an episode of 'Blackadder' in 1983 and later became a household name thanks to the sitcom 'One Foot in the Grave'. He later fronted the comedy current affairs quiz 'Have I Got News For You'. Who is he?

15. Born in Beeston, Nottinghamshire in 1931. This light actor studied at the Central School of Speech and Drama. He married the singer and actress Judith Shergold. His TV work included the series 'Skyport' and 'The Troubleshooters' but he is popularly known as the Dutch detective 'Van der Valk'. Name him.

1. Emma Thompson won an Oscar for Best Actress for her role in which nineties film?

2. Name the failed British spy in John Le Carré's, 'The Spy Who Came in from the Cold' (1963).

3. Which radio programme did Melvyn Bragg take over as host from Richard Baker in 1988?

4. In which George Bernard Shaw play is the hero John Tanner pursued by the heroine Ann Whitefield?

5. In which pantomime does a boy steal a hen that lays golden eggs?

6. Name the fictional prison setting for TV's 'Bad Girls'.

7. What is Shane's occupation in the sitcom of the same name?

8. Wich TV comedy series stars Frank Thornton, Peter Sallis and Robert Fyfe?

9. Which comedy chat show is hosted by Sanjeev Bhaskar?

10. Name the block of flats where Del Boy lives in 'Only Fools & Horses'.

11. Who wrote the sitcom. 'Up the Garden Path'?

12. Which police drama series starred Dennis Waterman, Amanda Redman, Alun Armstrong and James Bolam?

13. In which erotic murder mystery did Ewan McGregor play Joe, a barge worker?

14. Which comedian played Professor Johnston in the travel adventure film 'Timeline' (2003)?

15. Which British actress played opposite Jim Carrey in 'Eternal Sunshine of the Spotless Mind'?

16. Which former 'Watchdog' and 'Points of View' presenter's autobiography is entitled 'Memoirs of an Unfit Mother'?

17. Who is the Chairman of Radio 4's 'Just a Minute'?

18. Who was the first Director General of the BBC?

19. Name the police station where 'The Bill' is set.

20. Name Ozzy Osbourne's two children who took part in the Reality TV show 'The Osbournes'.

ADVERTISEMENT SLOGANS;

1. Full of Eastern Promise

2. Nice one, Cyril

3. Spreads straight from the fridge

4. Made to make your mouth water

5. Things go better with .....

6. Don't you just love being in control

7. Fortifies the over forties

8. Because life's complicated enough

9. Put a tiger in your tank

10. Good to the last drop

11. To our members, we're the fourth Emergency Service

12. You press the button, we do the rest

13. Cleans and polishes in one go

14. Prevents that sinking feeling

15. Wot a lot I got

16. Graded grains make finer flour

17. Nothing works faster than

18. You'll look a little lovelier each day

19. Simply years ahead

20. I never knew it had so much in it

1. Which Collins Wilkie spine-chilling novel did Andrew Lloyd-Webber bring to the stage?

2. Which TV series of the late sixties, was a spin-off from the ever-popular Z cars?

3. Who did Elizabeth Taylor marry in 1991?

4. Which character did Anthony Hopkins portray in his Oscar-winning performance of 1991?

5. 'Power to the People' was the catchphrase of the leader of the Tooting Popular Front in which TV series?

6. Who won the Lawrence Olivier Award for Best Theatre Actor with 'Stanley' in 1997?

7. What is Edina's surname in 'Absolutely Fabulous'?

8. Name the captains of TV's 'Have I Got News for You'.

9. Which TV show was presented by James Cameron, Brian Inglis & Bernard Braden?

10. What was Batman's alias?

11. In 'When Harry Met Sally' (1989) who played the title characters?

ENTERTAINMENT 13

12. Who played René Artois in "Allo 'Allo'?

13. Who hosted 'I'd Do Anything', the TV game show in which people face up to their greatest fears?

14. How many questions do contestants have to answer correctly to take the top prize in 'Who Wants to be a Millionaire'?

15. Which TV series was set in St. Angela's Hospital, Battersea?

16. Which actress played Cathy Gale in TV's 'The Avengers'?

17. Which presenter played Cupid in the TV series 'Love on a Saturday Night'?

18. Which Nick Hornby novel told of an idle playboy who learns about commitment when he is forced to befriend an unhappy child?

19. Which actor had Top Ten hits with 'Ain't No Doubt' and 'Love Don't Live Here Anymore'?

20. Name the character played by James Bolam in 'When the Boat Comes In'.

WHICH ACTORS DO YOU ASSOCIATE WITH THE FOLLOWING AUTOBIOGRAPHIES?

1. Beginning

2. Blessings in Disguise

3. Bring on the Empty Horses

4. Diet for Life

5. 80 Not Out

6. Farce about Face

7. In Darkness & Light

8. Just Resting

9. The Long Banana Skin

10. Moab is my Washpot

11. The Moon's a Balloon

12. The Other Side of the Street

13. Stamp Album

14. Stare Back & Smile

15. Travelling Player

16. What's It All About

17. Just Williams

18. All I Ever Wrote

19. Reminder

20. The Dynamite Kid

1. Which politician said in 1969, "Broadcasting is much too important to be left to the broadcasters"?

2. 'TTFN' was a catchphrase in which forties show?

3. Name the author, art historian and public official who remarked in 1977, "Television is a form of soliloquy".

4. Name the comedian who starred in 'Up the Elephant and Round the Castle'.

5. Name the public house which is frequented by the inhabitants of Ambridge in radio's 'The Archers'.

6. Which classic cop series began 'Ladies and Gentlemen, the story you are about to hear is true. Only the names have been changed to protect the innocent'?

7. Name the dramatist who wrote 'Alphabetical Order' (1975) and 'Donkey's Years' (1976).

8. Who was 'Faster than a speeding bullet! More powerful than a locomotive!'?

9. Name the comedy series centred on the Porter family of 142 Chepstow Road, Chiswick.

10. Which comedian was quoted in 'The Times' (1969) saying, "Comedy, like sodomy, is an unnatural act"?

11. Who did Glenda Jackson portray in the title role 'Stevie' in 1978?

12. Name the British science writer who worked with Stanley Kubrick on the script for '2001 : A Space Odyssey'.

13. In the sixties, Judy Carne's catchphrase was 'Sock it to me!'. Name the TV show.

14. Name the radio comedy series starring a Lancashire comedian, which ran from 1958 to the death of its star in 1972.

15. In which television cop show did you hear the line 'Kookie, lend me your comb'.

16. Which British film director said, "I have a perfect cure for a sore throat - cut it"?

17. Who played Tom Chance in TV's 'Chance in a Million'?

18. Which children's entertainment took place in the garden of Sir Basil and Lady Rosemary?

19. Name the Cardiff-born comedian and actor who hosted the literary review 'Bookworm'.

20. What is the slang term for a cue card displaying lines or instructions held near a camera to help forgetful presenters?

1. Name the children's series, which featured Fleegle, Bingo, Drooper & Snorky.

2. Who wrote 'Till Death Us Do Part'?

3. Which Scottish actor married Eve Mavrakis in 1994?

4. Who played the title role in the comedy series 'Rhoda'?

5. Who was the second Dr Who?

6. Which soap is remembered for its bikini-clad star, Kate O'Mara?

7. Who were TV's 'Two Fat Ladies'?

8. In which classic TV comedy series did Vienna the cat appear?

9. Who was the writer and narrator of TV's 'Bagpuss'?

10. Name the character Jason Connery played in 'Robin of Sherwood'.

11. Who played Maggie Moon in TV's 'Shine on Harvey Moon'?

12. Which cartoon series is set in Springfield?

13. Which character did Donna Douglas play in 'The Beverly Hillbillies'?

14. Which comedian toured in 2004 with his show 'Park Troll'?

15. Who won the Lawrence Olivier Award for Best Theatre Actor in 1992 for 'The Madness of GeorgeIII'?

16. Who in 'The Avengers' lived at 3 Duchess Mews, London?

17. Which character did Adrian Edmondson play in 'The Young Ones'?

18. What was Phoebe's surname in 'Friends'?

19. Who play husband and wife Ben and Susan in 'My Family'?

20. Which car is advertised on TV as 'the ultimate driving machine'?

1. Which Shakespearean play was the film 'West Side Story' (1961) based on?

2. Which character did Brad Pitt play in the film 'Troy' (2004)?

3. What was the stage-name of the slapstick comedian Arthur Jefferson?

4. Name the weekly radio talk that, until its closure in 2004, was the longest-running solo performance in the history of broadcasting.

5. Name the four actors who played the two couples in TV's 'The Good Life'.

6. Which comedian do you associate with 23 Railway Cuttings, East Cheam?

7. Name the debut single of 'Frankie Goes to Hollywood' which was banned by Radio 1.

8. Which director won Oscars for 'Bridge on the River Kwai' and 'Lawrence of Arabia'?

9. Name the musical by Queen and Ben Elton.

10. Who was the youngest of Britain's chat-show hosts in the early nineties?

11. Name the four actors who were the regulars in the 'alternative' comedy TV show 'The Young Ones'.

12. Which actress won the Laurence Olivier Award for Best Theatre Actress for 'The Rise & Fall of Little Voice'?

13. Who played 'Bubble' in 'Absolutely Fabulous'?

14. The Hamden Veterinary Hospital in Aylesbury was one of the the locations of which TV programme?

15. In what year did 'Big Brother' come to our TV screens?

16. 'Handbags & Gladrags' by Mike D'Abo is the theme tune for which comedy series?

17. Name Morticia's husband in TV's 'The Addams Family'.

18. Which TV programme has been presented by Anne Robinson, Nick Ross and Alice Beer?

19. 'Respectable' was a No. 1 hit for which duo?

20. What was Captain Pugwash's first name?

TV & FILM QUICKIES

1. Name the sequel to 'Get Shorty' starring John Travolta

2. Trinity, Morpheus & Nev are characters from which film

3. Name Bill Nighy's wife

4. What is the ITV TV equivalent of the Oscars?

5. Buzz Lightyear is a character from which animated film?

6. Spielberg's film about the Holocaust.

7. Oscar-winning song from 'The Lord of the Rings'

8. Actor who produced 'My Big Fat Greek Wedding'

9. Impersonates Posh Spice, Carol Smillie, Jerry Hall on Alistair McGowan's 'Big Impression'

10. Samuel L. Jackson wore a kilt in Liverpool in which 2001 film?

11. Former soap star who hosted TV's 'Sixty Minute Makeover'

12. She made over £3million for her role in 'Titanic'

13. Catherine Zeta-Jones has a £1million a year deal with which Cosmetics company?

14. Name David Bowie's model wife

15. Which TV chef do you associate with the Sainsbury's commerical?

16. In which film did we see John Travolta as an angel?

17. Bolton-born comedian associated with 'Phoenix Nights'

18. Actor who plays schoolboy wizard Harry Potter

19. He played a bumbling British secret service agent in the spoof spy film 'Johnny English'

20. The setting for TV's 'Byker Grove'

1. Who created the secret agent, James Bond?

2. Which actor, best known for his film work, is famous for his performance in Keith Waterhouse's 'Jeffrey Bernard is Unwell'?

3. Who played Harry Palmer in the film 'The Ipcress File' (1962) and 'Funeral in Berlin' (1964)?

4. Who made her name playing Kat Moon in BBC1's 'Eastenders'?

5. Name the first Asian comedy sketch shown on British television starring and co-written by Meera Syal.

6. The top television dramas 'Fat Friends' and 'Between The Sheets' are works by which writer?

7. Which film producer had his greatest success with 'Chariots of Fire' (1981)?

8. Parminder Nagra played the Asian girl who made it against the odds in which hit film of 2002?

9. Which TV presenter do you associate with 'Panorama', the '10 o'clock News' and BBC's 'Crimewatch'?

10. Name the eighties TV comedy which starred Judi Dench and her husband Michael Williams

11. Who devised and was the first presenter of radio's 'Desert Island Discs'?

12. Which radio play broadcast in 1938 caused panic?

13. Which comedienne was Mrs Merton?

14. Who wrote the play 'Dancing at Lughnasa'?

15. Who played Dave in 'Drop the Dead Donkey'?

16. Bob Louis, Dave Briggs and Supt Frank Cottam were characters in which TV spoof?

17. Name the pet dinosaur in 'The Flintstones'

18. What have Larry Grayson, Bruce Forsyth and Jim Davidson in common?

19. According to the TV adverts, what product 'Cuts cleaning time in half'?

20. In which TV cartoon series did Officer Dibble appear?

WHICH ENTERTAINERS DO YOU ASSOCIATE WITH THE FOLLOWING QUOTATIONS:

1. "All done in the best possible taste"

2. "Alright at the back"

3. "I mean that most sincerely, friends"

4. "How's about that then, guys and gals"

5. "Don't touch me"

6. "Didn't he do well"

7. "Nah ... Luton airport"

8. "It's the way I tell 'em"

9. "I wanna tell you a story"

10. "Respec"

11. "Short, fat, hairy legs"

12. "Stone me"

13. "Rock on Tommy"

14. "Not a lot"

15. "Bernie, the bolt"

16. "It's goodnight from me ... and it's goodnight from him"

17. "It's turned out nice again"

18. "Rodney, you plonker"

19. "Shut that door"

20. "Not 'arf"

21. "Swinging"

22. "Without hesitation, deviation or repetition"

23. "Hello, good evening and welcome"

24. "Orft we jolly well go"

25. "You lucky people"

1. Name Rumpole's wife in 'Rumpole of the Bailey'

2. What are the three options open to contestants if they get stuck on 'Who Wants To Be A Millionaire'?

3. Name the local pub in the TV comedy series 'Shane'

4. What was the registration of Lady Penelope's Rolls Royce?

5. Which Scottish actor, born 1971, was inspired to take to the profession by his Uncle Denis Lawson?

6. Who presents TV's 'Bargain Hunt'?

7. Name the actor who plays Dr Carter in E.R.

8. Name 'The Simpsons' pet dog

9. Name the Harold Brighouse classic Lancashire comedy concerning a cantankerous Salford-based boot-maker who spends most of his time drinking while his three daughters run his shop and home.

10. Which actress played Tara King in TV's 'The Avengers'?

11. Sarah Jessica Parker kept many riveted to the screen in 'Sex and the City'. Name the character she played.

12. Which actor played 'The Six Million Dollar Man'?

13. In which Stephen Daldry film of 2000 did Jamie Bell and Julie Walters win Baftas?

14. Name Frank & Betty's daughter in 'Some Mothers Do 'Ave 'Em'

15. Which TV comedy starring Nichola McAuliffe and Duncan Preston, took place in the fictional Gillies hospital?

16. Name the two presenters of TV's 'Crimewatch'.

17. What was Rigsby's first name in 'Rising Damp'?

18. How did Rolling Stone, Brian Jones' die, aged 27?

19. Who was DJ Peter Powell's first wife?

20. Which singer's real name is Graham McPherson?

WHAT WERE THE FIRST NAMES OF THE FOLLOWING TV CHARACTERS:

1. Corporal Jones, 'Dad's Army'

2. Glover, 'Only When I Laugh'

3. Mrs. Merton

4. Captain Peacock, 'Are You Being Served?'

5. Scottie, 'Star Trek'

6. Morse

7. Banacek

8. Colonel Hannibal Smith

9. Petrocelli

10. Shelley

11. Miss Jones, 'Rising Damp'

12. Hoss Cartwright, 'Bonanza'

13. Callan

14. Hinge & Bracket

15. Bootsie, 'The Army Game'

16. Jeeves

17. Professor Quatermass

18. Crane

19. Mrs. Slocombe, 'Are You Being Served'

20. Bodie & Doyle, 'The Professionals'

1. Which British actor put in a guest appearance in 'Cheers' in 1987 and won an Emmy for his performance?

2. Which Geordie duo are often seen as the successors to Morecambe & Wise?

3. Who created the glove puppet Sooty?

4. Who hosts TV's 'The South Bank Show'?

5. Which actress received great acclaim for her role in the film 'Truly, Madly, Deeply' (1991)?

6. In 'Casualty', who was the admin. assistant who was so devastated by the end of her relationship with the senior house officer Simon, that she attempted suicide with an overdose?

7. Name the character Stephanie Beacham played in 'Bad Girls'.

8. Which entertainer wrote and starred in the sitcom 'Shane' (2004)?

9. Which actor sang the theme tune to the police drama series 'New Tricks'.

10. With which satirical news quiz do you associate the names Paul Merton and Ian Hislop?

11. Which comedian/actor plays an archaeologist trapped in 14th-century France in the film 'Timeline' (2003)?

12. Which actress is out to 'Kill Bill' in the 2003 film of the same name?

13. Who played the hyperactive priest Father Noel Furlong in Father Ted?

14. Who hosts the daytime chat show 'Now You're Talking!'?

15. Evelyn Waugh's novel 'Vile Bodies' was adapted into which film of 2003 starring and directed by Stephen Fry?

16. Which television dramatist do you associate with 'Touching Evil', 'Reckless' and 'Clocking off'?

17. What was Pop Larkin's favourite word of approval?

18. 'Dead Belgians Don't Count' was the original working title for which popular TV comedy?

19. Little Weed and Slowcoach the Tortoise, are characters in which children's programme?

20. Who played Det Insp Maggie Forbes in TV's 'The Gentle Touch'?

1. Who presented radio's 'Desert Island Discs' briefly from 1986-88?

2. Who won an Oscar in 1986 for 'Hannah and her Sisters'?

3. The gentleman burglar Simon Templar was commonly known as what?

4. Who gave an Oscar-winning performance as Scarlett O'Hara in 'Gone With The Wind' (1939)?

5. Which skiffle artist had a hit with 'My Old Man's a Dustman' (1960)?

6. Which character did Alec Guinness play in TV's 'Tinker, Tailor, Soldier, Spy'?

7. 'The Singing Detective' was a drama series in the eighties. Who wrote it?

8. Who played Jim Hacker in the TV Comedy 'Yes, Minster'?

9. Which radio special agent, with the help of Jock & Snowy, foiled a wide range of criminal activities?

10. What was Roger Moore's first Bond movie?

11. Who brought the character Alf Garnett to life in 'Till Death Us Do Part'?

12. Which comedian created a character whose catch phrase was 'Loadsamoney'?

13. What was the rag doll called in the Andy Pandy BBC programme?

14. What was the family name of the children in P.L. Travers 'Mary Poppins'?

15. Which Scottish author created 'Peter Pan'?

16. Which Irishman won the Nobel Prize for Literature in 1995?

17. Who succeeded John Masefield as Poet Laureate in 1968?

18. Who played TV's 'Cracker'?

19. Who wrote the plays, 'The Dock Brief' and 'A Voyage Around My Father'?

20. Which TV series features the character Pop Larkin, a man who loves the excesses of food, alcohol and sex?

1. Whom did Michael Aspel succeed as anchorman on 'Antiques Roadshow'?

2. Name the three children in 'At Home with the Braithwaites'

3. 'Laverne & Shirley' and 'Mork & Mindy', were spin-offs of which TV series?

4. Which entertainer said, "The trouble with Freud is that he never played the Glasgow Empire Saturday night"?

5. Who created the comedy series 'Bread'?

6. Captain Snort, Sgt. Major Growt and P.C. McGarry, are characters from which children's series?

7. 'The Good Old Days' variety show always ended with the same song. Name it.

8. Name the actors who played 'The Lovers' Geoffrey & Beryl in the popular comedy series.

9. Which model hit Russell Harty about the head as she thought he was ignoring her on his chat show?

10. Name the two journalists who took it in turns to learn new skills in TV's 'In At the Deep End'.

11. Who sang the theme song for the comedy series 'Me and My Girl'?

12. The words, 'This tape will self-destruct in five seconds' were regularly heard on which TV series?

13. Who portrayed Peter Mayle in the TV series 'A Year in Provence'?

14. Who narrated TV's 'World at War'?

15. The theme tune of which police series was based on the folk song 'Johnny Todd'?

16. Which actress plays dizzy Alice Tinker in 'The Vicar of Dibley'?

17. Who sang the title song 'You Rang, M'Lord' in the TV comedy?

18. Name Dick Dastardly's dog

19. What was the meaning of the abbreviation C.A.T.S. in the series 'C.A.T.S. Eyes'?

20. Kingsley Martin, Brian Inglis and Stuart Hall have all presented which programme?

WHICH ACTORS PLAYED THE TITLE ROLES IN THE FOLLOWING SERIES:

1. Boon

2. Dempsey & Makepeace

3. Frasier

4. Inspector Morse

5. Campion

6. Lord Peter Wimsey

7. Petrocelli

8. Callan

9. Kojak

10. Dr Kildare

11. Jonathan Creek

12. Budgie

13. Lou Grant

14. Sharpe

15. Cagney & Lacey

16. Wycliffe

17. Tripper's Day

18. Mr Pastry

19. Steptoe & Son

20. The Peter Principle

21. Marcus Welby MD

22. The Virginian

23. Perry Mason

24. Sexton Blake

25. McCloud

1. Which actresses star in Radio 4's comic series 'Ladies of Letters'?

2. Name the host of 'Film 2004'.

3. Which comedy actor played Mr. Chipping in 'Goodbye Mr. Chips'?

4. Who plays Arthur Dent in the film version of 'The Hitchhiker's Guide to the Galaxy'?

5. Who won a Bafta for best supporting actor in 2004 for 'Love Actually'?

6. Which TV presenter and mother of three, wrote a handbook for working mums?

7. Born in 1938, this conjuror made his first TV appearance on 'Opportunity Knocks' in 1970. Name him.

8. What character will Rowan Atkinson play in 'Harry Potter and the Goblet of Fire' (2005)?

9. Who is known as 'Pop Idol's' Mr. Nasty?

10. By what name is Sacha Baron Cohen better known?

11. In what year was Channel 4 launched?

12. Who received a BAFTA for Best Actress in 2002 for 'My Beautiful Son'?

13. Who did Frank Muir call 'Thinking Man's Crumpet'?

14. John Eric Bartholomew is more familiarly known as whom?

15. Radio 4's 'Desert Island Discs' has had 3 presenters. Name them.

16. Which political commentator and interviewer, knighted in 1981 was one of the pioneers of the aggressive political interview?

17. Which TV series has been hosted by Matthew Kelly, Henry Kelly, Sarah Kennedy, Jeremy Beadle and Rustie Lee?

18. 'The Hornblower' was the theme music to which children's programme?

19. Who played Ria's husband, Ben Parkinson in the TV comedy 'Butterflies'?

20. Who created TV's 'Cracker' series?

REVEAL THE TV SHOW FROM THE NAME OF THE ASSOCIATED BUSINESS:

1. Eyecatchers Advertising Agency

2. Luxtons Bus Company

3. Sunshine Cabs

4. Bentinck Hotel

5. Blue Moon Detective Agency

6. Sunshine Desserts

7. Globelink News

8. Mole Valley Valves

9. New York School of Arts

10. Mackintosh Textiles

11. Henshaw-Ferraday Hairdressing

12. Ginsberg Publishing

13. Coleman and Sons

14. Central Perk

15. The Silver Diner, East End, London

QUICKIES

1. The central family in 'Bonanza'

2. The DIY expert on 'Changing Rooms'

3. What is Frasier's Surname?

4. First presenter of 'You've been Framed'

5. Played the title role in 'Winston Churchill - The Wilderness Years'

6. Comedy series featuring a lorry named 'Thunderbird Three'

7. Classic actress who played Queen Mary in 'Edward and Mrs Simpson'

8. He played the title role of the absent-minded teacher 'A.J. Wentworth'

9. The family featured in 'Bread'

10. The voice of 'Bob the Builder'

11. This family lived at Cemetery Ridge

12. 'Doctor in the House' was based on his books

13. He coined the phrase 'Television is chewing gum for the eyes'

14. 'She knows, y'know' was her catchphrase

15. Comedian who spent seven years in the Horse Guards before becoming known for his bungled tricks

16. He created TV's 'Fraggle Rock'

17. Played spycatcher George Smiley

18. Quiz game which took its name from Superman's home planet

19. 'Hello playmates' was his catchphrase

20. The voice of 'Thomas the Tank Engine'

NICE WORK IF YOU CAN GET IT

WHAT ARE THE OCCUPATIONS OF THE FOLLOWING TV CHARACTERS:

1. Ben Harper in 'My Family'

2. William Shawcross in 'William & Mary'

3. Martin Platt in 'Coronation Street'

4. Henry Crabbe in 'Pie in the Sky'

5. Paddy Kirk in 'Emmerdale'

6. A.J. Wentworth B.A. in the series of the same name

7. Sam Ryan in 'Silent Witness'

8. Desmond Ambrose in 'Desmonds'

9. Nicki Matthews in 'Sunburn'

10. Norm from 'Cheers'

11. Sam Tyler in 'Three Up, Two Down'

12. Godfrey Egan in 'No Job For a Lady'

13. Assumpta Fitzgerald in 'Ballykissangel'

14. Carol Johnson in 'Band of Gold'

15. Tom in 'Take Me Home'

16. Miles Stewart in 'This Life'

17. Gary Sparrow in 'Goodnight Sweetheart'

18. David Marsden in 'Cold Feet'

19. Danny Kavanagh in 'The Lakes'

20. Lorraine Watts in 'The Other 'Arf'

1. Which British actress won the Best Actress award in 'A Touch of Class' (1973)?

    a) Maggie Smith   c) Emma Thompson
    b) Glenda Jackson   d) Geraldine James

2. Who won the Dennis Potter Award 2004?

    a) Paul Abbott   c) Jimmy McGovern
    b) Russell Davies   d) Andrew Davies

3. Which playwright wrote 'Benefactors' and 'Noises Off'?

    a) Noel Coward   c) Christopher Fry
    b) Michael Frayn   d) Alan Bennett

4. Which of the following presented TV's 'Candid Camera'?

    a) Bob Monkhouse   c) Matthew Kelly
    b) Jeremy Beadle   d) Danny Baker

5. Who composed and sang the theme tune for TV's 'Supergran'?

    a) Ringo Starr   c) Dennis Waterman
    b) Jon Pertwee   d) Billy Connolly

6. Who won her 6th Best Actress BAFTA in 2004 for 'The Wife of Bath'?

    a) Victoria Wood   c) Julie Walters
    b) Penelope Keith   d) Jennifer Saunders

7. Who won the Lawrence Olivier Award for Best Theatre actress for 'Absolute Hell' in 1996?

a) Juliet Stevenson c) Fiona Shaw
b) Judi Dench d) Alison Steadman

8. In which year did Edinburgh launch the International Festival of Music and Drama?

a) 1947 c) 1967
b) 1957 d) 1977

9. What was Michael Caine's previous occupation before becoming an actor?

a) Coffin polisher c) Electrician
b) Milkman d) Billingsgate fish porter

10. Which comedian's autobiography is called 'The Full Monty'?

a) Frank Skinner c) Jim Davidson
b) Les Dawson d) Ben Elton

11. Who said "Women should be obscene and not heard"?

a) Johnny Rotten c) Mel B
b) John Lennon d) Mick Jagger

12. Dr. Frank'n'Furter is a character from which musical?

a) Phantom of the Opera c) Blood Brothers
b) Rocky Horror Show d) Starlight Express

13. In the TV sit-com 'After Henry', which actress played Sarah France?

    a) Joan Sanderson   c) Prunella Scales
    b) Elizabeth Estensen   d) Brenda Blethyn

14. Beatrice Arthur gained international recognition late in her career with which character in 'The Golden Girls'?

    a) Blanche   c) Dorothy
    b) Rose   d) Sophia

15. Which car do you associate with 'Knight Rider'?

    a) Kitt   c) Karr
    b) Fast   d) Witt

16. Which TV drama concerned the life of sociologist Charity Walton?

    a) The Bretts   c) Blue Heaven
    b) A Very Peculiar Practice   d) The Men's Room

17. 'That's Living Alright' by Joe Fagin, was a top 10 hit in 1984. It was the closing theme song of which TV series?

    a) The Likely Lads   c) Harry
    b) Byker Grove   d) Auf Wiedersehen Pet

18. Who played Nicky Hutchinson in the drama 'Our Friends in the North'?

    a) Christopher Eccleston   c) James Bolam
    b) Kevin Whately   d) Stephen Tompkinson

19. The Catholic priest Father Peter Clifford, took up his new posting at which church in 'Ballykissangel'?

    a) St. Mary's   c) St. Joseph's
    b) St. Assumpta's   d) St. David's

20. Who wrote and sang the closing theme song for 'On The Up'?

    a) Dennis Waterman   c) Jimmy Nail
    b) Dora Bryan   d) Wendy Richards

QUICKIES

1. Catchphrase of Billy Cotton

2. His advice to his peers was "Just know your lines and don't bump into the furniture"

3. The psychotic 'Oddjob' featured in this Bond movie

4. Setting of the classic sixties series 'The Prisoner'

5. Character Thelma Barlow played for 26 years

6. Rangi Ram in 'It Ain't Half Hot Mum'

7. She replaced Eve Matheson in 'May to September'

8. Sport featured in 'Fallen Hero'

9. Bobby Ewing in 'Dallas'

10. He wrote the whodunnit 'An Inspector Calls'

11. He joined Julie Driscoll on the theme song for 'Absolutely Fabulous'

12. U.S. series described as 'Hill Street Blues' in a courtroom

13. First presenter of 'The Crystal Maze'

14. The voice of 'Dangermouse'

15. Controversial DJ who compered the 1967 'Miss World'

16. The housekeeper in 'Father Ted'

17. Family who live at 368 Nelson Mandela House

18. 'Benson's' surname

19. 'Mim' Dervish in 'Outside Edge'

20. 'Can you hear me, mother?' was his catchphrase

NAME THE HOSTS OF THE FOLLOWING TV QUIZ/GAMESHOWS:

1. Countdown

2. Didn't They Do Well

3. Fifteen to One

4. Who Wants to be a Millionnaire?

5. Today's the Day

6. QI

7. Criss Cross Quiz

8. Come and have a go ... if you think you're smart enough

9. Sale of the Century

10. University Challenge

11. Top of the World

12. Every Second Counts

13. 1000 to One

14. Whose Line is it Anyway?

15. The People Versus

16. The Vault

17. Play your Cards Right

18. Headjam

19. The Cram

20. The National IQ Test 2004

1. Name the public houses in the following TV programmes:

   a) Heartbeat
   b) Coronation Street
   c) Harbour Lights
   d) Only Fools and Horses
   e) Love Thy Neighbour

2. Name the characters played by James Bolam in the following series:

   a) Only When I Laugh
   b) When the Boat Comes in
   c) Beiderbecke Affair
   d) Second Thoughts
   e) The Likely Lads

3. In which cities are the following series set?

   a) The Fresh Prince of Bel-Air
   b) Cutting it
   c) Band of gold
   d) Ellen
   e) Badger

4. Who created the following series?

   a) E.R.
   b) Widows
   c) The Lakes
   d) Grange Hill
   e) Lovejoy

5. Who wrote the book on which the following TV series were based?

   a) Colditz
   b) The Darling Buds of May
   c) Logan's Run
   d) Wycliffe
   e) Lord Peter Wimsey

6. Give the full names of the characters in 'Friends' played by the actors below:

   a) Lisa Kudrow
   b) Courteney Cox Arquette
   c) Matt Le Blanc
   d) Jennifer Aniston
   e) David Schwimmer
   f) Matthew Perry

7. Name the comedy actresses who played the four wacky girls in 'Girls on Top'

   a) Candice Valentine
   b) Shelley Dupont
   c) Jennifer Marsh
   d) Amanda Ripley

8. Who wrote the following series?

   a) The Beiderbecke Affair
   b) Grandad
   c) Luv
   d) One Foot in the Grave

9. Who narrated the following:

    a) The Wombles
    b) Roobarb
    c) Walking with Dinosaurs
    d) Willo The Wisp
    e) Bananaman

10. Name the programmes in which John Thaw played the following roles:

    a) Peter Mayle
    b) Tom Oakley
    c) Jack Regan
    d) Henry Willows
    e) Sgt. John Mann

11. Name the TV series from their theme tunes:

    a) Eye Level by Simon Park
    b) Suicide is Painless
    c) On the Inside sung by Lynne Hamilton
    d) Hornblower played by Tommy Edwards
    e) I'll Be There For You by 'The Rembrandts'

12. Name the presenters of the following TV series:

    a) The Good Sex Guide
    b) Dream Holiday Homes
    c) Big Brother
    d) The Golden Oldie Picture Show
    e) Location, Location, Location

13. Cars - Cars - Cars

   a) He drove a Morris Minor named Miriam
   b) A 1969 Dodge Charger featured in this series
   c) Emma Peel drove this car
   d) Registration of Lady Penelope's Rolls Royce
   e) Series which featured a vehicle known as Jupiter, registration J999

14. Identify the programme from its fictional setting:

   a) Skelthwaite
   b) Hatley Station
   c) Aldbridge C & P Bank
   d) Scott Furlong Aircraft Factory
   e) Gallowshield

15. Identify the drama series from the named character:

   a) Frank Carver
   b) Maddie Hayes
   c) Dr. Robyn Penrose
   d) Mary Soulsby/Cox
   e) Dolly Rawlins

WHAT ARE THE STAGE-NAMES OF THE FOLLOWING ENTERTAINERS?

1. Robert Davies (Comedian)

2. Minnie Higginbottom (Actress)

3. George Logan (TV Transvestite)

4. Margaret Lake (TV Personality)

5. Bruce Johnson (Entertainer)

6. Jim Moir (Comedian)

7. Thomas Woodward (Vocalist)

8. Stanley Kirk Burrell (Rapper)

9. Barbara Deeks (Actress)

10. Anthony Robert McMillan (Actor/Comedian)

11. Paul O'Grady (Female Impersonator)

12. Chris Collins (Comedian)

13. Michael Dumble-Smith (Actor/Singer)

14. Michael Pennington (Comedian)

15. Leslie Hornby (Model/Actress)

FOOD
& DRINK

1. Which town's name is associated with liquorice cake?

2. Talisker is a single malt whisky originating from where?

3. Who had their first hit with 'Food for Thought' (1980)?

4. Which cookery writer, born 1913, had a major and beneficial influence on British culinary standards from the fifties?

5. If you were given a firkin of beer, what quantity would you possess?

6. Who devised and presented BBC Radio 4's 'The Food Programme' from 1979?

7. Name the chef/restaurateur who became known through his popular TV series 'Taste Of the Sea' (1995).

8. Who wrote the best-selling 'River Cottage' series of cookbooks?

9. He has hosted 'Masterchef' and is known for his trademark spiky haircut. Who is he?

10. Whose definition of oats was "A grain, which in England is generally given to horses but in Scotland supports the people"?

FOOD & DRINK 1

11. Which food chain does Jamie Oliver promote on TV commercials?

12. Name the two women who opened the successful River Café in Hammersmith, London.

13. Which fast food is promoted as 'Fingerlickin' Good'?

14. Which TV presenter is known for her Detox series of cookbooks?

15. Which best-selling novelist created the slogan 'Go to work on an egg' when she worked at the advertising agency of Mather & Crowther in 1957?

16. Who were the resident drinks' experts on TV's 'Food & Drink'?

17. By what name was bully beef more commonly known in Britain?

18. What spirit is added to coffee to make an Irish or Gaelic coffee?

19. Which milk is referred to as gold top?

20. Name the cookery writer who wrote 'al dente', subtitled 'The adventures of a gastronome in Italy'?

1. A light savoury dish baked from a batter of flour, eggs and milk and traditionally served with roast beef.

2. Which cheese do you associate with 'Wallace & Gromet'?

3. What is laver bread?

4. What is known as the 'Great Chieftain o' the Puddin-race'?

5. In Britain, kedgeree is traditionally served for which meal?

6. The cowboy, Desperate Dan, relied on a supply of which particular dish to keep up his great strength?

7. What type of fish is a kipper?

8. Which food was launched in Britain in 1984 as the result of a joint research programme by Rank Hovis McDougall and Imperial Chemical Industries?

9. VSOP may appear on a bottle of sherry. What is the meaning of these letters?

10. The television cook Phyllis Primrose-Pechey was more familiarly known by what name?

11. Name the chef who has a restaurant at the Calabash Hotel on Grenada

12. Lancashire hotpot is traditional made with which meat?

13. A noisy-sounding dish of leftover meat, potatoes and cabbage.

14. What do the initials UHT denote?

15. By what name are Lima beans more commonly known?

16. Which purple/black berries are the basic ingredient of gin?

17. Which drink was advertised with the slogan 'Any time, any place, anywhere'?

18. What name is given to English or Irish beef cooked in pastry?

19. 'Model White', 'Veitch's Red Globe' and 'Green Globe' are all varieties of which vegetable?

20. Which British writer and caricaturist commented "Port: the milk of donhood"?

QUICKIES

1. A sausage made of pig's blood and fat

2. Scottish leek and chicken soup

3. Mixture of white wine and cream - dates back to Elizabethan times

4. Cheese on toast - sometimes with mustard or beer added

5. Food associated with Melton Mowbray

6. A Cumberland sweet called a cake

7. Famous Tearooms in Harrogate and York

8. Scottish soup of Finnan haddock and potatoes

9. English dish of sausages in batter

10. Another name for a split smoked herring

11. Cross between a raspberry and blackberry

12. Irish, potato and cabbage dish

13. Sweet associated with Pontefract

14. Meaning of MSG

15. Scottish sheep's stomach filled with offal, oatmeal and seasonings

16. Bun named after a legendary lady from Bath

17. A smooth, creamy white cheese, named after an Ayrshire town

18. Northern spicy currant pastries

19. An alewife is a kind of what?

20. What is a 'Singin' inny'?

1. Which Scottish whisky liqueur claims romantic origins in the '45 Rebellion?

2. Mint sauce or jelly is the traditional British accompaniment with which meat?

3. Which biscuit, consisting of think layers of currants, has been referred to as squashed flies?

4. What is the popular name of a suet pudding with currants or raisins?

5. What is TVP?

6. Which cook said, "When you get to fifty-two, food becomes more important than sex"?

7. What was the weekly ration of tea during WWII?

8. What name is given to a dish of puréed stewed fruit, mixed with cream or custard?

9. Who were the original hosts of TV's 'Food & Drink'?

10. 'Eat your Greens' (1993), 'Travels à la Carte' (1994) and 'Taste of the Times' (1997) are all works by which English cookery writer and broadcaster.

11. According to the advertising campaign of 1929-41, what drink '... is good for you'?

12. Which food company had the image of '57 Varieties'?

13. Which British Prime Minister, known for his bluntness, said "If I had the choice between smoked salmon and tinned salmon, I'd have it tinned. With vinegar" (1962)?

14. Who wrote the best seller 'How to be a Domestic Goddess' (2000)?

15. Which chef created ATV's 'Hell's Kitchen'?

16. What is the traditional drink taken before hunting?

17. Which British writer penned the line 'The cook was good cook, as cooks go and as cooks go, she went"?

18. Name the pudding, that usually accompanies roast beef?

19. "Meat is a status dish in which the sizzle counts for more than the intrinsic nutritional worth' said which leading nutritionist in 1978?

20. The calorie-controlled 'Count On Us' range of goods is found in which store?

1. The Stout 'Murphy's' has its birthplace in which town?

2. Name the two ingredients of 'Angels on Horseback'?

3. Who said, "The House of Lords is like a glass of champagne that has stood for 5 days"?

4. Which food writer told of his early life in his book 'Toast'?

5. What is Yarg?

6. Which shop in Piccadilly has a reputation for lavish and exotic food?

7. Who succeeded Michael Barry as resident chef on BBC TV's 'Food & Drink'?

8. Name the Scottish dish of oatmeal, soda and salt, usually served with butter, honey or jam

9. Which English cookery writer wrote for Sainsbury's from 1978 and was cookery editor for the 'Sunday Telegraph' from 1982?

10. What was the slogan designed in 1958 to extol the virtues of milk and its British Marketing Board?

11. Who in 'How to Survive Children' (1975) write 'A food is not necessarily essential just because your child hates it'?

12. Name the ex Liberal MP, gastronome and cookery writer who has also advertised dog food.

13. Which British cookery writer declared in 1981 "Everything tastes better outdoors"?

14. Which supermarket launched the 'Taste the Difference' range?

15. 'How to cheat at cooking' (1973), was the first of many books by which cookery writer and broadcaster?

16. Born in Leeds in 1961, this chef and restaurateur learned from Albert Roux, Nico Ladenis and Raymond Blanc. Name him.

17. What was advertised with the slogan 'Stop me and buy one'?

18. Which English chef's restaurants have included 'Ménage à Trois', '190 Queensgate', 'Dell'ugo' and 'Notting Grill'?

19. Which British humorist wrote, 'It was my Uncle George who discovered that alcohol was a food well in advance of modern medical thought' (1923)?

20. What is added to Irish Whiskey to make 'Irish Mist'?

HISTORY

HISTORY 1

1. Who founded the 'Daily Express' in 1900?

2. Which King, who reigned from 1272-1307, was also known as 'Longshanks' and 'Hammer of the Scots'?

3. Which politician famously said, "One man's wage rise is another man's price rise"?

4. Which special homes for the disabled and incurably ill were set up by a retired RAF Officer when he founded this charity in 1948?

5. Who became the 100th Archbishop of Canterbury in 1961?

6. What date is known as D-Day?

7. Which King was crowned on the battlefield?

8. Who did Winston Churchill call 'a sheep in sheep's clothing'?

9. The first car numberplate was issued to Lord Russell in 1903. What was the registration?

10. Name the first British feature film of August 1912.

11. Which King's dying words were said to be "Bugger Bognor"?

12. Who was the first woman doctor in the U.K?

13. Which King was born in Pembroke Castle?

14. Name the club in London, founded in 1831, by Conservative Members of Parliament and their supporters.

15. Who was the mother of Elizabeth I?

16. Which British Prime Minister was known as 'Old Wait and See'?

HISTORY 2

1. The Rye House Plot of 1683 was a conspiracy to murder which King?

2. In what year was the Labour Party established, being originally named the Labour Representation Committee?

3. Name Charles Darwin's ship, which surveyed the South American islands.

4. Commander-in-Chief of British troops fighting on the western front in WWI and the first president of the British Legion. Who was he?

5. Name the au pair who faced life in prison after Matthew Eappen, the baby in her care died.

6. Who was Prime Minister 1976-79?

7. Which politician in an attack on Harold Macmillan in 1962 said, "Greater love hath no man than this, that he lay down his friends for his life"?

8. The only legitimate daughter of Henry I was Matilda. What was her nickname?

9. Which King was known as the Lionheart?

10. In the seventies what was the collective name for Gerard Conion, Carole Richardson, Paul Hill and Patrick Armstrong?

11. Who was King of Scotland from 1306?

12. In what year did Victoria become Queen of the UK?

13. Who wrote the historical novel 'I Claudius' (1934)?

14. How many Britons died in the terrorist attack on the World Trade Centre?

15. 'Who breaks a butterfly on a wheel' was 'The Times' leader of 1 July 1967. To what did it refer?

16. What name was given to the document published by the Labour government in 1969 setting out its policy for controlling industrial relations?

17. Name the political agitators of the 1640's who were led by John Lilbume.

18. By what name is a judge known in Scotland?

19. Emily Davison brought attention to which pressure group when she died after throwing herself among galloping horses during the Derby of 1913?

20. In what year did the Great Train Robbery take place?

HISTORY 3

CAN YOU IDENTIFY THE YEAR BY THE FOLLOWING EVENTS?

1. Richard Eyre was named to succeed Sir Peter Hall as Director of the National Theatre; flamboyant pianist, Liberace died; The Herald of Free Enterprise ferry capsized off Zeebrugge.

2. Spurs beat QPR 1-0 in the FA Cup Final replay; Laker Airways collapsed leaving 6000 passengers stranded; Mercury receives a licence to operate telephones in competition with B.T.

3. The Aircraft carrier HMS Ark Royal was launched; Mr Lloyd Thomas's Royal Mail won the centenary Grant National; Oxford won the Boat Race after 13 successive Cambridge victories

4. The Hawker Hunter jet made its maiden flight; The Austin A40 went up in price to £685; British trade unionist and statesman Ernest Bevin died.

5. Comedian Tommy Cooper died after collapsing on stage; The Thames Barrier was officially opened; Government abolished dog licences.

6. This year saw the deaths of comedian Larry Grayson; writer, zoo pioneer and Conservationist Gerald Durrell; tennis player Fred Perry; author and vet, James Herriot; and four-time general election winner Harold Wilson

7. A British Midlands jet crashed on a motorway; Mrs Thatcher became a grandmother; 95 people died in the Hillsborough disaster.

8. Comedian Max Miller died; the first British-made oral contraceptive became available on prescription; Christine Keeler was jailed for 9 months for perjury and conspiracy to pervert the course of justice.

9. Welsh miners agreed to work on a Sunday for the first time; A photo finish camera was used for the first time at Epsom; UK's first atomic reactor started up at Harwell.

10. The Open University awarded its first degrees to 867 students; Women were allowed on the Stock Exchange Floor for the first time; British playwright, Sir Noel Coward died.

11. 80,000 people celebrated Nelson Mandela's birthday at Wembley Stadium; Broadcaster Russell Harty died; Paddy Ashdown was elected leader of the Social and Liberal Democrats.

12. James Joyce and Virginia Woolf died; The BBC promoted the V for Victory campaign; The Atlantic Charter was agreed after a meeting of Mr. Churchill and President Roosevelt.

13. Cecil Day-Lewis became Poet Laureate and Trevor Nunn took over as head of the Royal Shakespeare Company; Enoch Powell triggered fierce controversy over race relations with his 'rivers of blood' speech; Jaguar unveiled their new XJ-6 luxury saloon.

14. The 800th episode of BBC radio's 'The Archers' was broadcast; The Queen and the Duke of Edinburgh visited Sydney for the first visit to Australia by a reigning monarch; Royal Tan won the Grand National, after a race in which four horses died.

15. Thousands queued all night to file past Churchill's coffin as he lay in State in Westminster Hall; Roger Moore and Patrick McGoohan were Britain's top-earning actors, on £2,000 a week; David Steel, aged 26, became Britain's youngest M.P.

16. An extremist group, The Angry Brigade, bombed the home of Robert Carr, the Secretary of State for Employment; The new divorce law, making 'irretrievable breakdown of marriage'; the sole grounds for divorce, came into force; Henry Cooper retired after losing his British, European and Commonwealth titles to Joe Bugner.

17. The Prince of Wales opened Britain's longest road bridge, the Royal Tweed Bridge; The women's rights campaigner Emmeline Pankhurst died; Captain de Havilland set a world record by flying his place 'Gipsy Moth' at 21,5000 feet.

18. Red Rum became the first horse to pull off the Grand National hat trick; Britons celebrated the Queen's Silver Jubilee; 'Mull of Kintyre' and 'Don't Cry For Me, Argentina' were in the pop charts.

19. The Queen Mother celebrated her 90th birthday on 4 August; Dr. David Owen announced that the Social Democratic Party had come to an end with just 6,200 members; John Gummer was photographed feeding his daughter a beef burger in an attempt to calm fears over BSE.

20. The first test-tube baby was born by Caesarian section to Mrs Lesley Brown; David Gower scored his first Test century on the first day of the second Test against New Zealand; The BBC began permanent radio broadcasting from the House of Commons

WHO WERE ELECTED TO THE FOLLOWING CONSTITUENCIES IN THE JUNE 2001 ELECTIONS?

1. Derby South (Labour)

2. Richmond, Yorkshire (Conservative)

3. Tunbridge Wells (Conservative)

4. Hull East (Labour)

5. Maidstone & The Weald (Conservative)

6. Livingston (Labour)

7. Folkestone & Hythe (Conservative)

8. Sedgefield (Labour)

9. Rushcliffe (Conservative)

10. Pontypridd (Labour)

11. Hampstead & Highgate (Labour)

12. Ross, Skye & Inverness West (Liberal Democrat)

13. Hackney North & Stoke Newington (Labour)

HISTORY 4

14. Dumfermline East (Labour)

15. Chingford & Woodford Green (Conservative)

16. Wokingham (Conservative)

17. Linlithgow (Labour)

18. Kensington & Chelsea (Conservative)

19. Camberwell and Peckham (Labour)

20. Bath (Liberal Democrat)

1. Who was the only English-born son of King William I?

2. What name was given to the supporters of the parliamentary cause in the English Civil War?

3. Which King was nicknamed Blackbird, and The Merry Monarch?

4. Which report, published in 1942, laid down the framework for the development of the Welfare State?

5. Who was known as the 'Third Man' after the defections of Donald Maclean and Guy Burgess in 1951?

6. Who became King of Scotland from 1371, founding the royal house of Stuart?

7. Which sixties group sang 'I'm Henery the Eighth I am'?

8. Who was the father of Edward, the Black Prince?

9. Name the daughter of Ferdinand II of Spain and Isabella of Castile who married Henry VIII?

10. Who were the first two leaders of the Labour Party?

11. What was the date of 'Big Bang'; the day on which the deregulation of the stock Exchange came into effect?

12. Name the main rifle shooting contest and headquarters of the National Rifle Association in Surrey.

13. Who was the engineer who gave his name to a simple form of hut made of curving strips of corrugated iron?

14. Who famously declared he had "nothing to declare except my genius"?

15. What is the Mildenhall Treasure?

16. Which royals do you associate with the Ridolfi Plot and the Babington Plot?

17. Name the Conservative MP who was Secretary of State for Defence (1981-3), during the Falklands War.

18. Which house in London SW1 is known as No. 1 London?

19. Who is considered to have been the first Prime Minister, in 1721?

20. Which M.P., philanthropist, reformer and evangelical Christian, is known for his work on the Factory Acts 1847?

HISTORY 6

1. Which King, who reigned from 1399-1413 was also known as Bolingbroke?

2. Which Lord founded the Sunday Express?

3. What was Enoch Powell's first name?

4. Which King asked, "Will no one rid me of this turbulent priest"?

5. Which newspaper was originally part of the Mirror Group and was founded by three 'Daily Telegraph' journalists in 1986?

6. Which King was crowned twice?

7. Which religious group were founded in Dublin by the reverend John Nelson Darby in 1827 and named after a Devon town?

8. In 1946, the TV licence came into being. How much did this first licence cost?

9. Which politician has been known by numerous nicknames - 'Tarzan', 'Veronica Lake', 'Goldilocks' and 'Action Man'?

10. Which Welsh philosopher, author and mathematician wrote 'Theory and Practice of Bolshevism'?

11. Which peer was moved from Wayland Jail in Norfolk to North Sea Camp Prison in Lincolnshire in October 2001?

12. In England, what name was given to the financial panic caused in London on the news that Charles Edward Stuart had marched into Derby (December 6th 1745)?

13. Which Prime Minister, speaking on 5 November 1923 said, "It is fitting that we should have buried the Unknown Prime Minister by the side of the Unknown Soldier"?

14. What is the popular name of the maxim 'Anything that can go wrong will go wrong'?

15. Name the organisation Mrs Pankhurst founded in 1903.

16. Who did Dennis Healey put down in his comment "like being savaged by a dead sheep"(1978)?

17. Which journalist commenting on the permissive society of the sixties said "The orgasm has replaced the cross as the focus of longing and the image of fulfillment"?

18. Which King so overwhelmed by demonstrations of loyalty at his jubilee said, "I can't understand it. I'm really quite an ordinary sort of chap"?

19. Who were referred to as 'The Lost Generation'?

20. Which politician in 1976 branded Moscow with the Nazi image, saying "The Russians are bent on world dominance ... (they) put guns before butter"?

WHICH POLITICIANS SAID THE FOLLOWING:

1. The lady's not for turning.

2. I have always thought that every woman should marry, and no man.

3. Unpleasant and unacceptable face of Capitalism.

4. A week is a long time in politics.

5. Democracy means government by discussion but it is only effective if you can stop people talking.

6. There are three groups that no British Prime Minister should provoke: the Vatican, The Treasury and the miners.

7. The House of Lords is the British Outer Mongolia for retired politicians.

8. Bunnies can (and will) go to France.

9. Nagging is the repetition of unpalatable truths.

10. The wind of change is blowing through the continent.

11. I have nothing to offer but blood, toil, tears and sweat.

12. Nothing matters very much and very few things matter at all.

13. A lie can be halfway round the world before the truth has got its boots on.

14. My father did not riot. He got on his bike and looked for work. And he kept on looking until he found it.

15. She is so clearly the best man among them.

16. I read the newspapers avidly. It is my one form of continuous fiction.

17. What one generation sees as a luxury, the next sees as necessity.

18. If the British public falls for this, I say it will be stark staring bonkers.

19. I never knew the lower classes had such white skins.

20. There are two problems in my life. The political ones are insoluble and the economic ones incomprehensible.

1. What was Winston Churchill referring to when he commented "a riddle wrapped in a mystery inside an enigma"?

2. Who founded the 'Today' newspaper in 1986?

3. Which King reigned 1066-1087?

4. Parking meters were first seen in the UK and London saw its first traffic wardens in this year?

5. Name the only British person to become Pope.

6. Who was the first female Speaker of the House of Commons?

7. Which statesman and author referred to the hansom cab as 'The gondola of London'?

8. Who was known as the 'Widow of Windsor'?

9. How many women did Peter Sutcliffe murder between 1975 and 1980?

10. Which American-born British MP said to Winston Churchill: "Winston, if I were married to you, I'd put poison in your coffee"?

11. Name the British historian who in his ten-volume work 'A Study of History' posits his theory of the way in which civilisations move in cycles.

12. When was the slogan 'Women of Britain say GO:' used?

13. Which British politician speaking in 1945 said, "No attempt at ethical or social seduction can eradicate from my heart a deep and burning hatred of the Tory Party ...So far as I am concerned, they are lower than vermin"?

14. Which British Prime Minister's last words were "This is not the end of me"?

15. Which Labour Chancellor of the Exchequer in 1924 and 1929-31 based his policies squarely on the traditional values of thrift, hard work, self-denial and economic prudence?

16. Which contemporary historian with extensive media exposure said "There is nothing more agreeable in life than to make peace with the Establishment - and nothing more corrupting"?

17. Which politician, speaking on 20 January 1936, said, "When I was a little boy in Worcestershire reading history books, I never thought I should have to interfere between a King and his mistress"?

18. Name the well-known political cartoonist of the 'Evening Standard' who produced a cartoon of Harold Macmillan as a comic hero superman with the title 'Introducing Supermac'?

19. 'Religion and the Rise of Capitalism' was the major work of which British economist?

20. What historic event happened at 11.59 p.m. on Monday 15 April 1912?

HISTORY 9

QUICKIES - WHAT YEAR?

1. The £1 coin came into circulation

2. The age of majority was reduced from 21 to 18

3. Nancy Astor, first woman to take seat in Parliament

4. The General Strike is called in Britain

5. The Heysel Stadium Disaster

6. Julius Caesar's first invasion of Britain

7. Margaret Thatcher came to power in Britain

8. The Youth Hostels Association was founded

9. The Iranian Embassy Siege

10. The Archbishop of Westminster, Cardinal Basil Home died

11. Terry Waite was taken hostage in Lebanon while seeking to free others

12. The Titanic sank on its maiden voyage

169

13. The Profumo Affair developed into crisis

14. Television broadcasting started in Britain

15. Attlee replaced Churchill after a Labour landslide at the General Election

16. Eden resigned as Prime Minster after the Suez fiasco

17. A coal strike in Britain forced the Government to declare a 3-day working week

18. A terrorist bomb brought down Pan-Am 747 over Lockerbie

19. Edward VII died and was succeeded by his son George V

20. John Major was elected to replace Margaret Thatcher

WHICH POLITICIANS SAID THE FOLLOWING:

1. The members of our Secret Service have apparently spent so much time under the bed looking for Communists, that they haven't had the time to look in the bed.

2. If you resolve to give up smoking, drinking and loving, you don't actually live longer, it just seems that way.

3. History is littered with wars which everybody knew would never happen.

4. The lamps are going out all over Europe; we shall not see them lit again in our lifetime.

5. They are going to be squeezed as a lemon is squeezed - until the pips squeak.

6. We are not at war with Egypt. We are in an armed conflict.

7. There are some of us, Mr. Chairman, who will fight and fight and fight again to save the party we love.

8. A great party is not to be brought down because of a squalid affair between a woman of easy virtue and a proven liar.

9. I am not a product of privilege, I am a product of opportunity.

10. I feel I am getting a down on George V just now. He is all right as a gay young midshipman. He may be all right as a wise old king. But the intervening period when he was just shooting at Sandringham is hard to manage or to swallow. For seventeen years he did nothing at all but kill animals and stick in stamps.

QUICKIES

1. Millionaire newspaper tycoon drowns in the Atlantic Ocean, 5 November 1991.

2. On 22 November 1995, Britain's worst serial killer was sentenced to ten life sentences.

3. The Irish hostage released by terrorists after more than 4 years in Lebanon on 23 August 1990.

4. Group freed on 14 March 1991 after being jailed for a terrorist pub bombing in 1974.

5. She became the first female President of Ireland on 9 November 1990.

6. BBC's 'Panorama' programme of 21 November 1995 drew a massive audience for this sensationally frank interview.

7. A British colony since 1842, it passed back to China on 1 July 1997.

8. Nicknames of the five who introduced 'girlpower' in 1997.

9. The British au pair freed on 10 May 1997 after the baby in her care died from brain injuries.

10. The MP who resigned in 1988 after a TV interview, which suggested that Britain's egg production, was infected by salmonella.

11. He owned and captained the yacht 'Morning Cloud'.

12. This serial killer took his own life in Winson Green Prison in 1995.

13. This year saw the Piper Alpha oil-rig disaster.

14. The Thames pleasure steamer which was rammed and sunk by a dredger in August 1989 with the loss of 51 lives.

15. British destroyer hit by an Exocet missile on 4 May 1982, with the loss of 20 lives.

16. Northern Ireland Secretary who resigned from the Cabinet on 24 January 2001.

17. Shadow Rural Affairs Minister sacked over a racist joke told at a rugby club dinner in 2002.

18. He made a record-breaking crossing of the English Channel in the Gibbs Aquada car in 2004.

19. This former government minister 'disappeared' on 20th November, 1974.

20. He was the architect of Britain's abortion laws when he introduced the 1967 Abortion Act.

MUSIC

MUSIC 1

IDENTIFY THE ARTIST FROM THE FOLLOWING LP'S:

1. Slowhand; From the Cradle; 461 Ocean Boulevard

2. Sacred Love; Nothing Like The Sun; The Soul Cages

3. Abacab; Invisible Touch; Duke

4. The Joshua Tree; Achtung Baby; Rattle and Hum

5. Cloud Nine; All Things Must Pass; Living In The Material World

6. The Division Bell; The Final Cut; Atom Heart Mother

7. Never For Ever; Hounds of Love; The Whole Story

8. La Passione; Tennis; Auberge

9. Beggars Banquet; Let It Bleed; Goat's Head Soup

10. Hunky Dory; Diamond Dogs; Black Tie White Noise

11. Life; A New Flame; Stars

12. Atlantic Crossing; Every Picture Tells A Story; Blondes Have More Fun

13. Stranded; Avalon; Flesh and Blood

14. Face Value; No Jacket Required; Both Sides

15. Love Over Gold; Makin' Movies; Communique

16. Innuendo; A Day At The Races; The Game

17. Caribou; Captain Fantastic and the Brown Dirt Cowboy;

18. The Innocents; Chorus; The Circus

19. High on the Happy Side; Popped in Souled Out; Picture This

20. Revenge; We Two Are One; Touch

MUSIC 2

1. Which singer/songwriter condensed the novel 'Wuthering Heights' to a three-minute song?

2. Whose debut album of 2004 was 'Call Off the Search'?

3. Who was thrust into the limelight with the number one single 'Mad World'?

4. Born 1944, this conductor has been musical director of Glyndebourne since 1988. He is particularly known for his interpretation of operas by Strauss. Name him.

5. Whose recording of Vivaldi's 'Four Seasons 'reached No 3 in the pop album charts in 1989?

6. A sequence from Mike Oldfield's 'Tubular Bells' was used as theme music for which film?

7. Who was the vocalist of the heavy-metal group Deep Purple?

8. Which composition for violin and orchestra by Vaughan Williams was inspired by a poem by Meredith?

9. Which pop group, formed 1977 were named in recognition of its early financial situation?

10. Which pop group was formed in Sheffield by two computer operators, Martin Ware and Ian Craig in 1977?

11. Who played drums in the rock group Led Zeppelin?

12. Who, having left The Smiths to go solo, went to the top of the album charts with 'Viva Hate'in 1988?

13. Her debut album, 'Come Away With Me' won her eight Grammys. Name her

14. Who had a top ten best-selling album in 1996 with 'Jagged Little Pill'?

15. Who composed the charity song 'Do They Know It's Christmas'?

16. Who came last in the 2003 Eurovision Song Contest with 'Cry Baby'?

17. The three Choirs Festival rotates among which three cathedral choirs?

18. Which orchestra did Sir Thomas Beecham found in 1932?

19. Who was the frontman/vocalist of The Animals?

20. Who was the original drummer with The Beatles?

IDENTIFY THE GROUP FROM ITS MEMBERS;

1. Natalie Appleton, Nicole Appleton, Melanie Blatt, Shaznay Lewis

2. Graeme Clark, Tom Cunningham, Marti Pellow, Neil Mitchell

3. Marcella Detroit, Siobhan Fahey

4. Mark King, Phil Gould, Boon Gould, Mark Lindup

5. Chris Lowe, Neil Tennant

6. Mikkey Dee, Phil Campbell, Ian Kilmister

7. Marc Almond, Dave Ball

8. Anne Dudley, JJ Jeczalik

9. Matt Black, Jonathon Moore

10. Andy Cox, Roland Gift, David Steele

11. Andy Bell, Vince Clarke

12. Martin Ware, Ian Craig Marsh, Glenn Gregory, Carol Kenyon

13. Mike Cole, Ray Dorsey, Colin Earl, Paul King

14. Hugh Cornwell, Dave Greenfield, Jean-Jacques Burnel, Jet Black

15. Ronnie Bond, Peter Staples, Chris Britton, Reg Presley

16. Roland Orzabal, Curt Smith, Ian Stanley, Oleta Adams

17. George Michael, Andrew Ridgeley

18. Chick Churchill, Leo Lyons, Ric Lee, Alvin Lee

19. Mike Joyce, Andy Rourke, Johnny marr, Stephen Morrissey

20. Con Cluskey, Declan Cluskey, John Stokes

1. Which ageing rocker was commissioned by Lord Lloyd-Webber to do a series of paintings for the Theatre Royal in Drury Lane?

2. 'We Will Rock You' is a musical celebrating which band?

3. 'I Don't Mean to be Rude, But...' is the autobiography of which musical commentator?

4. Name Jamiroquai's lead singer and songwriter.

5. He has achieved No 1 hits in each of five decades, selling about 250 million records. He is vice-president of the Tear Fund development agency. Name him.

6. Will Champion is the drummer with which band?

7. Mel C and Mel B were Spice Girls. What are their surnames?

8. Who was runner-up to Will Young in TV's first Pop Idol in 2002?

9. Name Posh Spice's 2 oldest children.

10. 'The Man Who' is a top-selling album for which band?

11. Which sixties group thought that they were the best and named themselves accordingly?

MUSIC 4

12. Who replaced Shane MacGowan in The Pogues?

13. Name the trio who was Scaffold.

14. Which Spice Girl was known as Sporty?

15. Which band's first seven records all reached No 1?

16. Who formed the following groups, King Bees, Hype, Lower Third, Kon-Rads and Feathers?

17. Name the duo that was Yazoo.

18. Who had No1 hits with 'Oh Julie' and 'Green Door'?

19. 'How the West Was Won' is a three CD set compiled from which group's 1972 tour of America?

20. Who composed 'Rocket Man'?

GIRLS, GIRLS, GIRLS - WHO SANG ABOUT THE FOLLOWING GIRLS?

1. Angie Baby (1975)

2. Cecilia (1996)

3. Claire (1972)

4. Diane (1964)

5. Eloise (1986)

6. Emma (1974)

7. Jennifer Eccles (1968)

8. Jennifer Juniper (1968)

9. Judy Teen (1974)

10. Julie Ann (1975)

11. Lady Eleanor (1972)

12. Lady Madonna (1968)

13. Lola (1970)

14. Maggie May (1971)

15. Maria (1999)

16. Nikita (1985)

17. Rosie (1968)

18. Shirley (1982)

19. Sylvia (1973)

20. Virginia Plain (1972)

MUSIC 6

WHO RECORDED THE FOLLOWING SINGLES?

1. Blue Jean; Drive-in Saturday; Modern Love

2. Always Yours; Oh Yes! You're Beautiful; Remember Me This Way

3. Why; Walking on Broken Glass; No More I Love You's

4. Love Letters; That Ole Devil Called Love; Is This Love?

5. Moonlight Shadow; Portsmouth; Sentinel

6. Dog Eat Dog; Prince Charming; Young Parisians

7. Easy Lover; In The Air Tonight; Separate Lives

8. Friday I'm In Love; High; Lullaby

9. Julia Says; Somewhere Somehow; Wishing I was Lucky

10. Breakfast In Bed; Homely Girl; I Got You Babe

11. Always On My Mind; Heart; Suburbia

12. Angel Eyes; Over You; Street Life

13. Holidays In The Sun; Pretty Vacant; Silly Thing

14. So Lonely; Wrapped Around Your Finger; Invisible Sun

15. Start Me Up; Tumbling Dice; Emotional Rescue

16. Angel; For your Babies; Stars

17. Elevation; Beautiful Day; All I Want Is You

18. Condemnation; I Feel You; People are People

19. Girl Crazy; Love is Life; Brother Louie

20. Mirror Man; Open Your Heart; Tell Me When

1. What was the stage-name of the sixties singer Mary O'Brien?

2. Born Michael Barratt in 1948, he played Presley on the West End Stage in 'Elvis' (1977-8). He had a No 1 hit single in 1982 with 'Oh Julie'. Name him.

3. 'Cinnamon Girl' is the title track of whose 2004 album 'Musicology'?

4. Which celebrated trumpeter is known affectionately as Humph?

5. 'Oh What a Circus' is a song from which musical?

6. Who made her debut with the EP 'Come Over' in 2004?

7. Whose album 'Patience', topped the charts in 2004?

8. Which pop chameleon is nicknamed the Thin White Duke?

9. Which eighties group took their name from a French fashion magazine, meaning 'Fast Fashion'?

10. What were 'Walking on Sunshine' in 1981?

11. Name Cleo Laine's musical husband.

12. Their No 1 hit 'Don't You Want Me' (1981) gained further exposure on a television commercial. Who recorded this hit?

13. John Lennon and Yoko Ono recorded which protest song during a 'bed-in' they staged in a Montreal hotel in 1969?

14. Which singing partnership also appeared together in the television series 'Soldier, Soldier'?

15. Who composed the classic song 'First Cut Is The Deepest'?

16. Who had a Top Ten hit with 'Absolutely Fabulous' in 1994?

17. What was the stage-name of the music-hall entertainer, George Galvin, known for his rambling personal anecdotes?

18. Who was 'Walkin' Back To Happiness' (1961)?

19. Which popular seventies group took their name from a cinema chain?

20. 'All Stood Still'; 'Vienna'; and 'Dancing With Tears In My Eyes' were hit singles for which band?

MUSIC 8

POT LUCK

1. Which musicians' daughter won the Miss World Title in 2004?

2. Where was Benjamin Britten's 'War Requiem' first performed?

3. Who was 'Running Up That Hill' in 1985?

4. Which two names do you associate with the songs from the 'Lion King' musical?

5. 'Berlington Bertie' was one of the best-known songs of which music-hall artist's repertoire?

6. What is the meaning of the group named Clannad?

7. Name the female vocalist in Thompson Twins.

8. In Praise of Lemmings and Sex Gang Children were two of the early names of which band?

9. In what year did the singles charts begin?

10. Whose signature tune was 'Leaning On A Lamppost'?

11. Which composer do you associate with the opera 'Billy Budd'?

MUSIC 8

12. Which group won four Brit. Awards in February 1995?

13. Which singer died in a car crash in 1977 aged 30?

14. This pop star launched his own red wine, from grapes off his estate in Portugal in 2002. Name him.

15. Who became the first black female artist to win the prestigious Mercury Music Prize, for her debut album, 'A Little Deeper'?

16. Who replaced Jay Aston in Bucks Fizz in 1985?

17. Which group was also known by the names, The Catch and The Tourists?

18. Who had a Top Ten hit with 'Freeek!' in 2002?

19. Who was 'Walking Wounded' in 1996?

20. Which sixties group named themselves after jazzman Charlie Parker?

MUSIC 9

QUICKIES - NAME THE FOLLOWING:

1. The singer/songwriter forever associated with 'Lady In Red'

2. Lead vocalist in Hot Chocolate

3. Played guitar in the Plastic Ono Band

4. Stage-name of Gordon Sumner

5. Drummer of Queen

6. Manager of The Sex Pistols

7. Victoria Beckham's maiden name

8. The band Robbie Williams left in 1995

9. Her signature tune was 'Sally'

10. The Beatle who wrote the book 'A Spaniard in the Works'

11. The song about marital break-up which was Billy Connolly's first hit in 1975

12. They were 'Dedicated Followers of Fashion' in 1966

13. Duo with a Top Ten hit with 'F.L.M.' (1987)

14. This countdown song was the first hit for Manfred Mann in 1964

15. He had a No 1 hit with 'Goody Two Shoes' in 1982

16. 'Do Ya Do Ya (Wanna Please Me')' was a hit for this Page 3 girl in 1986

17. 'A Hard Rain's Gonna Fall' was his first solo hit of 1973

18. 'I Lost My Heart To A Starship Trooper' was performed by which combination

19. Ex-Spice girl had a No 1 with 'I Turn To You' (2000)

20. Merseyside group who took their name from a caption in a Marvel science fiction novel

MUSIC 10

WHO HAD NO 1 HITS WITH THE FOLLOWING:

1. Ain't No Doubt (1992)

2. Freak Like Me (2002)

3. West End Girls (1985)

4. A Little Time (1990)

5. Dancing In The Street (1985)

6. What Took You So Long (2001)

7. Living On My Own (1993)

8. Skweeze Me Pleeze Me (1973)

9. Long Live Love (1965)

10. Desire (1988)

11. Bootie Call (1998)

12. Just a Little (2002)

13. Never Had a Dream Come True (2000)

14. My Camera Never Lies (1982)

15. A Different Beat (1996)

16. Say You'll be Mine (1996)

17. The Final Countdown (1986)

18. Love Won't Wait (1997)

19. Some Might Say (1995)

20. Country House (1995)

21. I'm Your Man (1985)

22. Breathless (2000)

23. Love Is All Around (1994)

24. What Do You Want (1959)

25. All Or Nothing (1966)

1. Which Somerset town hosts a three-day Festival of Rock Music?

2. 'Lola '(1970) is perhaps the best-known hit of which sixties pop group?

3. 'The Game'(1980); 'The Miracle' (1989) and 'Innuendo' (1991) were albums from which rock group?

4. Which former Atomic Kitten won 'I'm A Celebrity, Get me Out Of Here'?

5. Who had a No 1 hit in 2002 with 'Anyone of us (Stupid Mistake)'?

6. 'Down, Down' (1974) was the only No 1 hit single of which rock group?

7. Who wrote the musical 'Blood Brothers'?

8. What was the title of Gerri Halliwell's No 1 hit of 1999?

9. Which veteran performer followed his hit album 'Re-Load' with a 'Greatest Hits' CD that went to platinum?

10. Name George Harrison's only son.

11. Who in 2004 was named Most Influential Artist of All Time by 'New Musical Express'?

12. Which sixties group were named after a famous agriculturist?

13. The musical 'Forbidden Planet' is based on which of Shakespeare's plays?

14. Name Led Zeppelin's drummer, who died in 1980.

15. Who was the first person to win the Eurovision Song Contest in the UK in 1967?

16. Which former Boyzone member had a number one hit with his debut album?

17. Which Pink Floyd veteran gave the £4 million proceeds of his London house sale to the charity Crisis in 2002?

18. 'Let's Talk About It' and Capped Teeth and Caesar Salad' are songs from which musical?

19. Who composed the tune for the hymn 'Onward Christian Soldiers'?

20. Which comedian's signature tune was 'Love Is Like A Violin'?

MUSIC 12

WHO HAD CHRISTMAS NO 1 HITS WITH THE FOLLOWING:

1. I Love You (1960)

2. I Feel Fine (1964)

3. Green Green Grass Of Home (1966)

4. Merry Xmas Everybody (1973)

5. Lonely This Christmas (1974)

6. When a Child is Born (1976)

7. Mull of Kintyre/Girl's School (1977)

8. Mary's Boy Child (1978)

9. Another Brick In The Wall (1979)

10. There's No One Quite Like Grandma (1980)

11. Only You (1983)

12. Merry Christmas Everybody (1985)

13. Always On My Mind (1987)

14. Do They Know Its Christmas (1984)

15. Bohemian Rhapsody/These are the Days of our Lives

16. Mr Blobby (1993)

17. Too Much (1997)

18. I Have a Dream/Seasons in the Sun (1999)

19. Can We Fix It (2000)

20. Sound of the Underground (2002)

1. Which rock icon fronted Nirvana before violently ending his life in 1994?

2. Which sixties pop group was formed by two brothers named Ray and Dave, with Peter Quaife and Mick Avery?

3. Which Scottish music-hall entertainer wrote 'Keep Right On To The End Of The Road'?

4. Which of the Bach family was known as 'the English Bach'?

5. Which Gilbert and Sullivan opera is also known as 'The King of Barataria'?

6. Who was relatively unknown until Eminem used one of her songs in his hit track 'Stan' in 2000?

7. Who was the principal conductor of the Halle Orchestra from 1943 until his death in 1970?

8. On 21 October 1997 which single was declared the biggest selling single ever, with 31.8 million sales?

9. Who said "Number one, I'm not gonna die. I'm gonna make the tour. I'm not dead. I'm ready to rock man", on coming out of a coma after crashing his quad bike?

10. What do Cliff Richards, Elton John, Paul McCartney and Mick Jagger have in common?

11. 'All That Jazz' is a song from which musical?

12. Which band, created by the talent show 'Popstars', split up in 2002 following a decline in public support?

13. Which eighties group chose their name from a Steely Dan record?

14. Which singer/actress performed her best-selling album 'Best of Friends '(1978) with guitarist John Williams?

15. How often is the Leeds International Piano Competition held?

16. Which librettist died in 1911 of a heart attack after saving a young woman from drowning in a lake at his home?

17. 'O may the long language endure' is the final line of which national anthem.

18. Name The Hollies only No 1 hit of 1965.

19. Which groups' original name was Hollycaust?

20. Who had a Top 10 album in 2002 with 'Escapology'?

1. Which seventies group, originally from Sheffield, took their name from a science fiction computer game?

2. Name Bucks Fizz first No 1 hit of 1981.

3. Who sings lead vocals with Texas?

4. 'The Edge' from U" is also known by what other name?

5. Name the group formed when George Harrison teamed up with Bob Dylan, Roy Orbison, Jeff Lynne and Tom Petty.

6. Which pop singer in 2002 signed a contract worth £70 million with EMI, the largest ever in British music history?

7. 'As Long As He Needs Me' is a song from which musical?

8. Who had a Christmas No 1 with 'Somethin' Stupid' in 2001?

9. Which female vocalist is known as 'Alf'?

10. Name the trio who were Cream.

11. By what name is pop singer Naiomi McLean-Daley more popularly known?

12. In what year did John Lennon marry Yoko Ono?

13. Who played keyboards with Roxy Music?

14. '(What's the Story) Morning Glory' was a Top 10 best-selling album for which band in 1995?

15. The lead singer of Clannad released the haunting single 'Tara' in 2004. Name her.

16. In the TV adaptation of 'The Secret Diary of Adrian Mole, Aged 13 3/4', which pop singer played Pauline Mole?

17. Who was lead vocalist with Take That?

18. Who had No1 hits with 'Black Coffee', 'Never Ever' and 'Pure Shores'?

19. Which sixties group had a No1 hit with 'Blackberry Way'?

20. Name the three presenters of Juke Box Jury

MUSIC 15

1. Which band made its 'Forty Licks' tour in 2003?

2. Jim Kerr topped the charts in the mid-eighties with which band?

3. Bryan McFadden shocked his fans when he announced in 2004 that he was leaving which band?

4. By what names are Paul Hewson and Dave Evans more popularly known?

5. Dave Vanian was the lead singer of which seventies band?

6. Who left The Human League in 1980 to form Heaven 17?

7. Who sang lead vocals with Spandau Ballet?

8. Katrina and the Waves won the Eurovision Song Contest for the UK in 1997. Name the song.

9. Who sang lead vocals with Frankie Goes to Hollywood?

10. In which year did girlpower sweep the land with the advent of The Spice Girls?

11. 'Stars'was a Top 10 best selling album in 1991 for which group?

12. With which group do you associate Captain Sensible?

13. Who in 2004 teamed up with Ronan Keating for the single 'Last Thing On My Mind'?

14. Which member of Bros joined Gordon Ramsay in 'Hell's Kitchen'?

15. Which group played the music in TV's 'Robin of Sherwood 'series?

16. Which member of Westlife married the Irish Prime Minister's daughter in 2003?

17. Which group named themselves after a character from the Tintin cartoons?

18. 'I Got You Babe' and 'Love Can Build A Bridge' topped the charts for which female artist?

19. Who composed the song 'Photograph', which was a top 10, hit in 1973?

20. What was Robbie Williams first hit of 1996, which reached No 2 in the charts?

MUSIC 16

WHO HAD NO 1 HITS WITH THE FOLLOWING:

1. Independent Woman Part 1 (2000)

2. Let's Dance (2001)

3. The Masses Against the Classes (2000)

4. It's Raining Men (2001)

5. Never Be The Same Again (2000)

6. Pure and Simple (2001)

7. Queen Of My Heart (2001)

8. Sorry Seems To Be The Hardest Word (2002)

9. It Feels So Good (remix) 2000

10. Rise (2000)

11. Life Is A Rollercoaster (2000)

12. Sound of the Underground (2002)

13. The Tide is High (Get The Feeling)

14. Survivor (2001)

15. Pure Shores (2000)

16. Light My Fire (2002)

17. Stomp (2000)

18. You See The Trouble With Me (2000)

19. Take On Me (2000)

20. The Long and Winding Road/Suspicious Minds (2002)

QUICKIES

1. Singer who hosted TV's 'Moment of Truth'.

2. He composed the opera 'Gloriana'.

3. Janice Nicholls said "I'll give it foive" on this programme.

4. He played Vendice Partners in the film 'Absolute Beginners' (1986).

5. Rock guitarist who performed in the films 'Tommy' (1975) and 'The Last Waltz' (1978).

6. Hank Marvin, Eric Burdon were born in this city.

7. Setting for the annual Monsters of Rock festival.

8. He sang 'The Ballad of Strangeways' in the sixties.

9. The finale of Elgar's 'Coronation Ode' - with words by A.C. Benson.

10. Town where you would find the grave of Rolling Stones founder Brian Jones.

11. They thanked us very much for the Aintree Iron.

12. As M.P. for Huyton, he presided over the re-opening of the Cavern Club in July 1966.

13. Composer and writer who said, "One should try everything once, except incest and folk dancing".

14. Rock musician's anthem 'I hope to die before I get old' (1965).

15. Nicknamed 'The Moptops'.

16. "Strange how potent cheap music is" taken from which Noel Coward play?

17. North-eastern town, the birthplace of Bryan Ferry.

18. Leading actor who is also an accomplished pianist who composed the score for his directorial debut, 'August' (1996).

19. Rock star who commented "Rock and Roll is instant coffee".

20. He said "I want to manage those four boys. It wouldn't take me more than two half days a week".

1. Who had a Top 10 hit with the album 'Fly or Die'?

    a) Usher
    b) Nerd
    c) Guns N'Roses
    d) Eminem

2. The raucous piece of music entitled 'The Whale' brought which composer to wide public attention?

    a) Richard Rodney Bennett
    b) Steven Martland
    c) John Tavener
    d) Thomas AdËs

3. On which TV show did Adam Faith make his debut?

    a) Ready Steady Go!
    b) Six-five special
    c) Top of the Pops
    d) Old Grey Whistle Test

4. In 1969 The Hollies had a Top 10 hit with this song, and on re-release in 1988 it reached No. 1. What was it?

    a) The Air that I Breath
    b) Stop Stop Stop
    c) Here I Go Again
    d) He Ain't Heavy, He's my Brother

5. Which duo took 'I know Him So Well' to the No. 1 spot in 1985

    a) Marti Webb & Kiki Dee
    b) Elton John & Kiki Dee
    c) Elaine Paige & Barbara Dickson
    d) Barbara Dickson & Marti Webb

6. Who had his first solo hit in 1982 with 'No Regrets'?

    a) Robbie Williams
    b) Midge Ure
    c) George Michael
    d) Sting

7. Which Benjamin Britten opera is based on a chilling tale by Henry James

a) Billy Budd   c) Death in Venice
b) The Turn of the Screw   d) Paul Bunyan

8. Who found fame and fortune with his song 'Keep the Home Fires Burning'?

a) Noel Coward   c) Michael Tippett
b) Vaughan Williams   d) Ivor Novello

9. Who hosted Channel 5's karaoke programme 'Night Fever'?

a) Boy George   c) Toyah
b) Suggs   d) Morrissey

10. In which Shakespearean play is the Old English tune 'Greensleeves' mentioned?

a) A Midsummer Night's Dream   c) Henry IV
b) All's Well That Ends Well   d) The Merry Wives of Windsor

11. What was Dusty Springfield's first hit in 1963?

a) I Only Want to be With You   c) All I See is You
b) Some Of Your Lovin'   d) Going Back

12. Who teamed up with Paul Miles-Kingston on the 1985 hit 'Pie Jesu'?

a) Aled Jones   c) Nick Berry
b) Sarah Brightman   d) George Michael

MUSIC 18

13. Which composer's best-known work is Venus & Adonis (1682)?

   a) John Bull
   b) John Blow
   c) Henry Purcell
   d) John Dowland

14. Who won an Oscar for the original score for 'Jaws' (1975)?

   a) Johnny Dankworth
   b) Leo Sayer
   c) John Williams
   d) Mike Oldfield

15. Who sang the theme song, 'Everything I Do, I Do it for You' in the 1991 film 'Robin Hood: Prince of Thieves'?

   a) Phil Collins
   b) Tracy Chapman
   c) U2
   d) Bryan Adams

MUSIC 19

WHICH PEOPLE WITH MUSICAL CONNECTIONS DO YOU ASSOCIATE WITH THE FOLLOWING AUTOBIOGRAPHIES?

1. Acts of Faith

2. Always Playing

3. Arias and Raspberries

4. Good Vibrations

5. Now & Then

6. Take It Like a Man

7. Those twentieth Century Blues

8. Learning to Fly

9. Broken Music Memoirs

10. Oh! What A Circus

QUICKIES

1. He's known as 'Saint Bob'.

2. 'The Weekend begins here' declared which TV show

3. The Beatles' first film

4. Singer who played Anita Braithwaite in TV's 'Band of Gold'

5. Mick Jagger wrote 'Stupid Girl' about this ex.

6. Andy Cox, Roland Gift and David Steele were collectively known by what name?

7. Former All Saints member whose debut album 'Never Felt Like This Before' was released in 2004

8. Boy George's Musical about the glamorous and decadent London club scene of the New Romantic era

9. Her 2004 tour was named 'Back On Track'

10. The year of the first Glastonbury Festival

11. Name the first dancers on Top of the Pops

12. Nickname of DJ, David Jensen

13. Vocalist born Elaine Bookbinder

14. 'Element Four' had a Top 10 hit in 2000 with the theme tune for this TV show

15. Page 3 girl in the charts with 'Touch Me (I Want Your Body)' (1986)

16. The All Saints sisters

17. 'Come Away with Me' was a Top 10 album 2002 for this artiste

18. 'Baby's Got a Temper' was a Top 10 hit for this group in 2002

19. More commonly known as Freddie Mercury

20. The year 'Top of the Pops' was launched

PEOPLE
& PLACES

1. Which castle was named as King Arthur's birthplace by ancient chroniclers?

2. Dylan Thomas spent his honeymoon in this Cornish village, which he proclaimed to be "really the loveliest village in England". Name it?

3. St Mary Mead was the deceptively quiet home village of which sleuth?

4. The Royal Crescent is a fine 18th-century landmark in which city?

5. The paintings, 'The last of England' and 'Work' are two of the best known works of which Victorian artist?

6. Who was the Lancashire-born inventor of the flying shuttle of 1733?

7. Name the moorland location, known for its three giant golf ball shapes which is an Early Warning Station of the Ministry of Defence.

8. Name the world's first custom-built motor racing circuit, which opened near Weybridge in Surrey in 1907.

9. Which peninsula was the UK's first Area of Outstanding Natural Beauty?

10. What name was given to the aircrews of 617 Squadron, who flew the mission on 16 May 1943?

11. Which Cathedral became a place of pilgrimage after the murder of Thomas à Becket?

12. In what year was capital punishment abolished in Britain?

13. With what do you associate the name of Christie's in London?

14. Which poet used the pseudonym Nicholas Blake for his novels?

15. Which Victorian engineer do you associate with the three ships, 'The Great Western', 'The Great Britain 'and the 'The Great Eastern'?

16. Name the 18th-century home of the Duke of Bedford.

17. What is the popular name adopted by the British Expeditionary Force in World War 1?

18. Which Irish lawyer and politician, elected to parliament in 1828, was known as 'the Liberator'?

19. Name the television and radio presenter who became the host of 'Desert Island Discs' in 1988.

20. Which city did Matthew Arnold refer to as 'that sweet city with her dreaming spires.'

WHO'S WHO?

1. Born 1967, this English footballer was offered a record £7.9 million by the Italian club Lazio, but this was reduced to £5.5 million when he injured his knee playing for Spurs in the 1991 Cup Final. Name him.

2. He was a leading British composer of the mid-twentieth century. He achieved international fame for the production of 'Peter Grimes' in 1945. In 1947 he settled in Aldeburgh where he created the annual music festival. Name him.

3. Born in 1909, this painter was known for the nightmarish imagery of his work. His first major work 'Three Studies for Figures at the Base of a Crucifixion' 1944 is in The Tate Gallery. Name him.

4. After serving as a nurse in World War II, she trained as a doctor and set up St Christopher's, London's first hospice. She is credited as the founder of modern palliative care. Name her.

5. Born in Yorkshire 1862, the son of German immigrants, his music is said to capture the spirit of the English countryside. 'On Hearing the First Cuckoo in Spring' (1912) is one of his many loved works. Name him.

6. She was the first British ballerina to dance the great classical roles and was particularly admired for her 'Giselle'. In 1935 she formed the first of several companies with Anton Dolin. She retired in 1962 and was awarded the DBE in 1963. Name her.

7.   Born in the north-east of England, this monk and Bishop of Lindisfarne had his bones finally buried in Durham Cathedral after being moved due to Viking raids. His feast day is March 20th. Name him.

8.   This poet and historian is known as one of the Lake Poets. He was appointed Poet Laureate in 1813. His wife was the sister of Coleridges' wife and they were great friends. He died in 1843.

9.   She was born in Torquay in 1890 and it was her home until after her first, famously failed marriage of 1914. She made a mysterious disappearance to Harrogate in 1926 allegedly due to loss of memory and a nervous breakdown. She was the author of 80 novels, 19 plays and several children's books. Name her.

10. Born in 1716, this landscape gardener transformed the parks of some 140 houses - Blenheim was the greatest of these. Others include Badminton and Burghley. He also worked as an architect, sometimes in partnership with his son-in-law Henry Holland. Who was he?

11. Born in 1834 in Walthamstow, East London. After his death he was described as a poet, artist, manufacturer, socialist, designer, decorator, dyer, weaver, painter, printer, translator, novelist, journalist, collector, and connoisseur... He was a prolific designer of every kind of decorative object from furniture to stained glass. Kelmscott Manor was his country home from 1871 until his death in 1896. Who was he?

12. This author was born in Wales in 1916, the son of Norwegian parents. He wrote both mystery stories that were televised and books for children. The latter have consistently been the most borrowed from children's libraries. He died in 1990. Name him.

13. Born in 1927, this saxophonist, bandleader and composer became Pop Music Director of the London Symphony Orchestra in 1985. He also has had a successful career composing film scores, which include 'Saturday Night and Sunday Morning'. Who is he?

14. Born in 1778, this dandy was known for his sharp wit, private fortune and friendship with the Prince of Wales. By 1816 he had run up great gambling debts and fled to France, before dying in an asylum in 1840. Name him.

15. This engineer was born in Wylam, Northumberland in 1781. He was entirely self-taught in technology and did not learn to read until the age of eighteen. He designed his first locomotive in 1814 and he also produced a safety lamp for miners. Name him.

16. Born in 1573, this architect was the founder of Classical English architecture. In 1616 he designed the Queen's House at Greenwich. Other work included the rebuilding of the Banqueting House at Whitehall and Marlborough Chapel. He also laid out Covent Garden and Lincoln's Inn Fields. Name him

17. This satirist and comedian who described his diet as "two large screwdrivers and smoking a packet of cigarettes for breakfast", died in 1995, aged 57. He came to fame in 1959 in 'Beyond the Fringe'. Name him.

18. He entered the Royal Navy in 1913 and in World War II became Supreme Allied Commander in south-east Asia. He presided over the transfer of power to India and Pakistan. He was a cousin of the Queen and in his later years was a mentor to Prince Charles. Who was he?

19. She grew up in Barnet, Hertfordshire, the daughter of an estate-agent father and milliner mother. She studied at the Aida Foster stage school before joining the original cast of the musical 'Hair'. She released her album 'Centre Stage' in 2004. Name her.

20. Born at 4, The Terrace, Penzance, Cornwall in 1778, this English chemist was knighted by George1V when Prince Regent (1812) and created a Baronet in 1816. He helped to found the Athenaeum Club and London Zoo. His name is particularly remembered for one of his inventions. Name him.

QUICKIES:
LONDON - NAME THE FOLLOWING:

1. The main wholesale, fruit and vegetable market.

2. Another name for The Millennium Wheel

3. Location of The Tate Gallery

4. The large bell housed in St Stephen's Tower

5. Name of the levy on motorists from 17th February 2003

6. Location of the Unknown Warrior's Tomb

7. Horace Walpole's Twickenham residence, built in 1748

8. East London's long-established Sunday market on Middlesex Street

9. Palace where Henry VIII died.

10. Centuries old fish market in Lower Thames Street, which closed 16 January 1982.

11. Official residence of the Bishop of London until 1973.

12. Location of the maze, constructed for William and Mary in 1690.

13. Museum occupying part of the Old Bethlehem Royal Hospital

14. Site of the royal Naval Hospital

15. Palace sited in Muswell Hill

16. Its official title is No 1 Canada Square and is Britain's tallest structure

17. Location of Tin Pan Alley

18. London's largest meat market

19. Where Dick Whittington supposedly 'turned'

20. Location of the British Library

ON WHICH RIVERS DO THE FOLLOWING TOWNS AND CITIES STAND?

1. Jarrow

2. Manchester

3. Aviemore

4. Canterbury

5. Newbury

6. Ipswich

7. Worcester

8. Edinburgh

9. King's Lynn

10. Balmoral

11. Middlesborough

12. Dumfries

13. Lincoln

14. Swansea

15. Derby

16. Perth

17. Exeter

18. Hereford

19. Doncaster

20. Durham

1. In which year was Dartmoor designated a National Park?

2. What do Diana Dors, Sir John Betjeman and Eric Morecambe have in common?

3. Who was awarded the first theatrical knighthood in 1895?

4. Dame Allan's public school is in which city?

5. Roger Bannister is known for his four-minute mile, but what was his profession?

6. Who shot John Lennon, outside his New York apartment in 1980?

7. Which stores slogan is 'never knowingly undersold'?

8. Myra Hindley died; Angus Deayton was sacked from 'Have I Got News For You' and former Take That star Mark Owen won Celebrity 'Big Brother'. What year was this?

9. Name the river on which the city of Cardiff stands.

10. Describe the Scottish flag.

11. What do William Blake, Oscar Wilde, Ben Jonson and John Bunyan have in common?

12. What is the nickname given to in-service teacher training days?

13. Name the highest waterfall in England

14. Who instigated the Citizen's Charter in 1991, with the intention of improving public service standards?

15. Who is the patron saint of Edinburgh

16. Name Shakespeare's three children

17. Who was known as the 'Lady of the Lamp'?

18. By what name is glamour Jordan also known?

19. Who pioneered cheap air travel, particularly with his Skytrain service to the USA in 1977?

20. In which year did the Isle of Man celebrate the 1,000th anniversary of its Parliament?

1. Which Birmingham-born comedian took a drug overdose in a Sydney hotel room in 1968?

2. In 2002, the world's largest maze was opened in Christchurch, Dorset. Which animal is it in the shape of?

3. Name the first National Park in Great Britain.

4. Which criminal was known by the nickname 'The Colonel'?

5. Why was Sarah Jane Hutt in the news in 1983?

6. The city of Leeds stands on which river?

7. What is the more commonly used name for the Royal Courts of Justice?

8. Hamley's is Britain's best-known toyshop. What was its original name?

9. What is the name given to the Scottish equivalent to a coroner in England?

10. Name Britain's leading hospital for heart and lung transplants situated outside of London.

11. Which often-controversial woman journalist earned herself the title of the 'First Lady of Fleet Street'?

12. How did Laura Ashley die in 1985?

13. Which group launched themselves with 'Anarchy in the UK'?

14. Which playwright, who is often referred to as a national treasure, wrote 'The History Boys'?

15. What name is given to the road along the south side of Hyde Park reserved for horse riders?

16. Who was secretary of state for employment (1985-7) and for trade and industry (1987-9)?

17. Whose name do you associate with the Bloody Assizes of 1685?

18. Which prolific novelist, known for his romantic thriller 'The Prisoner of Zenda', gave the fictional country of Ruritania to the English language?

19. Where are the annual Promenade Concerts held?

20. What colour coat has an Irish Setter?

ALL SAINTS - THE ANSWERS TO ALL OF THE FOLLOWING QUESTIONS INCLUDE THE WORD 'SAINT':

1. School for girls created by the artist and cartoonist Ronald Searle

2. City in Hertfordshire, opposite the Roman site Verulamium.

3. Castle-like house on top of the rock on an island off Cornwall

4. Gothic church in Edinburgh's Parliament Square with famous open-work structure on its square tower.

5. One of the five Classic horse races and the last of the season.

6. Tiniest of cathedral towns on a promontory in Dyfed.

7. Scotland's first university was founded here in 1412.

8. A station, church and district of London.

9. Redbrick Tudor palace built by Henry VIII in London SW1

10. London church by Wren associated with the 'Oranges and Lemons' rhyme.

11. The church regarded as the parish church of the House of Commons.

12. Charitable organisation providing volunteers trained in first aid to attend public events.

13. Group of four islands and the first place in Scotland designated an UNESCO world heritage site (1987).

14. The Whispering Gallery is found here.

15. Nurses trained at this London hospital are known as 'Nightingales'.

16. Resort on the north coast of Cornwall, which houses an extension of The Tate Gallery.

17. Charity for blind ex-service men and women founded by Arthur Pearson in 1915

18. Large hospital, known as Jimmy's, popularised through TV exposure.

19. Play by Bernard Shaw, inspired by this young heroine.

20. The nearest open space to the royal palaces in central London.

1. In what year did the Great Famine occur in Ireland, when the potato crop failed?

2. Name Nelson's daughter.

3. What do the Adelphi, Garrick and Mermaid have in common?

4. Which inventor and entrepreneur introduced the C5 and the Zike?

5. Which astronomer became the eccentric presenter of TV's 'The Sky at Night'?

6. Which former BBC cameraman was the author of the Paddington Bear stories?

7. Name the famous monument, built in AD 122 to mark the rough northern limit of the Roman Empire and is now a World Heritage Site.

8. 'Joseph Andrews', 'Amelia' and 'Tom Jones' were all works by which author?

9. Which building in Maidstone would you visit to see the celebrated White Garden?

10. Whose business used the phrase 'Don't ask the price - it's a penny'?

11. Who was Prime Minister of Great Britain 1955 - 1957?

12. In what year did a gunman murder 16 children and one of their teachers, in a horrific and unexplained attack on a primary school in the Scottish town of Dunblane?

13. Who was the 28th and final Governor of Hong Kong?

14. Name the two pop stars who started Band Aid in 1985.

15. In what year was Margaret Thatcher elected for a third term as British Prime Minister?

16. On the 22nd December 1988, Britain experienced its worst air disaster. Name it.

17. How old was Tony Blair when he became Prime Minister?

18. Who took over from Kate Moss as the face of Calvin Klein?

19. Where in Britain could you walk the Royal Mile?

20. He was the first man to sail non-stop and single-handed around the world in 10 months from June 1968 to April 1969. Name him.

1. Which Elizabethan mansion has, since 1961 been the setting for the major autumn three-day horse trials event?

2. Who became a national heroine after rescuing survivors from the steamship 'Forfarshire' in 1838?

3. Which London art gallery, opened in 1897, contains a unique collection of British paintings from the 16th century until the present day, with Turner and Blake particularly well represented?

4. In what year did Margaret Thatcher become leader of the Conservative Party?

5. By what name is the crossroads in London between Trafalgar Square and Whitehall known?

6. Name Darcey Bussell's occupation.

7. Which author and explorer translated 'The Arabian Nights'?

8. Which top security prison was strongly criticised and recommended for closure, unless improvements were made, by the chief inspector of prisons, Judge Stephen Tumim in 1992?

9. Name the small street in central London, famous in the sixties for its fashion shops.

10. 'If' is one of the most popular poems in the English language. Who wrote it?

11. Which company made its fortune with the phenomenally successful 'Tubular Bells' by Mike Oldfield?

12. Which knight starred in 'Sleuth '(1972), 'Marathon Man' (1976) and 'The Boys from Brazil' (1978)?

13. Name the two resourceful Irishmen whose response to the shortage of bodies for dissection by medical students in the nineteenth century led to the passing of the Anatomy Act, which regulated the supply of corpses.

14. In what year did Lord Baden-Powell establish the Scout Movement?

15. What is the collective historic title of the five coastal towns in Southeast England that formerly had special privileges as ports?

16. Which building has been the headquarters of BBC radio's World Service since 1940?

17. Who was the financial dealer whose disastrous trading led to the collapse of Barings Bank in 1995?

18. Name the ancient forest of oak and beech between the Severn and the Wye.

19. Where was the Laura Ashley company originally based?

20. Name the building near Buckingham Palace where the sovereign's coaches are kept.

1. Who became the first ever-female editor of The Sun newspaper, aged 33?

2. In which comic would you read about Dennis the Menace?

3. Which lake runs from Borrowdale to Keswick and is dotted with several small islands?

4. 393 Old Commercial Road, Portsmouth and 48 Doughty Street, London are both museums dedicated to which author who resided there?

5. 'Not a lot of people know that' was a catchphrase associated with which actor?

6. Where is the home of the Saddler's Wells Royal Ballet?

7. Name the housekeeper from 'Dr Finlay's Casebook'.

8. Which top model stripped off on stage in 'The Graduate', at the age of forty-four?

9. Who joined MI5 as a clerk typist and worked her way up to become the organisation's first female Director General?

10. Which lawyer and Master of the Rolls gave his name to the report on the Profumo affair?

11. Who painted the 'Light of the World', the figure of Jesus, bearing a lantern on a moonlit night and knocking on a door?

12. Who became the UK's first female rabbi in the seventies?

13. What name was given to the disaster of August 1987 when Michael Ryan shot and killed 13 people and wounded several others in Berkshire?

14. Name the inlet of the Irish Sea, which separates North west England from South west Scotland.

15. In which Edinburgh square would you find the official residence of the Secretary of State for Scotland?

16. What is the term used to describe civil servants that leak politically embarrassing documents?

17. Who said, 'What is our task? To make Britain a fit country for heroes to live in' (November, 1918)

18. Name the triumphal arch at the east end of The Mall, built as a memorial to Queen Victoria.

19. Which underground station was the scene of a disaster in 1987 when fire started beneath an escalator, resulting in 31 deaths?

20. Name the most important flower show in Britain, held in the grounds of a London Hospital.

LOCATION, LOCATION, LOCATION - IDENTIFY THE FOLLOWING LOCATIONS FROM THE INFORMATION GIVEN:

1. Armley Mills and Kirkstall Abbey are here.

2. The Queen Mary, Queen Elizabeth and QE2 were built in this city.

3. Lady Godiva rode naked through this town.

4. The largest castle in England is found here.

5. Name for the Roman Road from Lincoln to Exeter.

6. London underground station, previously known as Great Central.

7. It is nicknamed The Granite City.

8. The Eureka! Museum is found in this town.

9. Thomas Hardy is associated with this county.

10. The ancient market place, known as Grassmarket is in this city.

11. Cary Grant was born in this city.

12. This is Britain's most northerly town.

13. This London street is associated with the medical profession

14. Location of the Bridge of Sighs.

15. Visit the Holst Birthplace Museum here.

16. Britain's leading hospital for the treatment of spinal injuries.

17. Location of the RAF's Officer Training school.

18. The bookshop in Piccadilly, founded in 1797.

19. This well-preserved city was known to the Romans as 'Deva'

20. Scottish borders town known for the red sandstone ruins of its abbey.

1. Which writer's husband Robert named her 'My Little Portuguese'?

2. Who was the first President of the Royal Academy of Arts, founded in 1768?

3. Who resigned as Director General of the BBC in January 1987?

4. Who or what are ASH?

5. Which two comedians died within a day of each other in 1992?

6. 'Orlando Laborando (by Praying and by Working)' is the motto of which public school?

7. Name the British Ambassador who was killed in 1976 when his car was blown up by an IRA landmine.

8. Who coined the phrase the 'unacceptable face of capitalism' in 1973 when replying to a question in the House of Commons?

9. Which English novelist drowned herself in the River Ouse, near her home at Rodmell in Sussex in 1941?

10. Who was the first woman to become a cabinet minister in the UK, as Minister of Labour?

11. How many women did Jack the Ripper murder?

12. With which profession do you associate the name of Beverly Cobella?

13. Name the range of chalk hills, stretching forty miles northeast of the Thames, near Reading.

14. Name the first of Shakespeare's plays.

15. Known as Jersey Lily, she caused a sensation when she became the first society woman to go on the stage in 1881. Who was she?

16. London was the first city in the UK to install an underground railway. Name the second.

17. Name the main inland waterway in the south of England.

18. Which politician's wife was severely injured in the Brighton bombing of 1984?

19. Name the first women's prison in Britain to have a mother and baby unit.

20. What phrase is used between MPs when addressing each other in the House of Commons?

20 QUICK QUESTIONS:

1. The two letters which signify the local or family doctor.

2. His best known work is 'The Planets'.

3. Conservative MP who made the tabloid front pages with his affair with Antonia de Sancha.

4. Name the only one of the Bronte sisters who married.

5. Statesman and novelist created 1st Earl of Beaconsfield in 1880.

6. City where you would find The Burrell Gallery

7. The person responsible for smallpox vaccination.

8. The nickname of the parachute regiment.

9. Actress Renate Blauel was married to this pop star.

10. Actor who playes Harry Potter on film.

11. York Minster caught fire shortly after which modernist was enthroned as Bishop of Durham.

12. What was the nickname of the Scottish outlaw Robert MacGregor?

13. Who brought 'The Rocky Horror Show' to life in 1973?

14. Which show-business charity has events organised by members known as Barkers?

15. Which distinguished garden designer had a long and successful partnership with the architect Edwin Lutyens?

16. Name the public school for girls founded by the Lawrence sisters near Brighton.

17. Which composer do you associate with the 'Fantasia on a Theme by Thomas Tallis'?

18. Who designed both the Forth and the Severn bridges?

19. Which comedian wrote 'Monty, His Part in my Victory '(1976)?

20. Where was the television series 'The Prisoner' filmed?

PEOPLE & PLACES 14

1. Name the largest lake in Britain.

2. What name is given to a public track or path along which a horse may be ridden?

3. Name the range of rounded hills, mainly in Northumberland, which for about 35 miles forms the border between England and Scotland.

4. OFSTED is a government department, established in 1992. What do the letters represent?

5. Where would you locate the headquarters of The Open University?

6. What name was given to women drafted for agricultural work in each of the two World Wars?

7. Who was the UK's first black female Cabinet member when she became Labour's International Development Secretary in 2003?

8. Name the most westerly point of mainland Britain.

9. Who earned millions with her internet site lastminute.com?

10. Who contributed to newspapers under the pseudonym 'Boz'?

11. In which Cathedral were both Nelson and Wellington buried?

12. What name is given to the bugle call at the end of the day in British Army establishments?

13. Where would you view the annual Military Tattoo?

14. According to the rhyme, how many wives had the man from St Ives?

15. Who were married by a turkey before eating mince and slices of quince with a runcible spoon?

16. Who wrote 'Angela's Ashes', which was later turned into a successful film?

17. 'On the Piste', 'Lucky Sods ' and 'Up'N' Under' are all works of which playwright?

18. Which politician said "Give us the tools and we will finish the job"?

19. Which organisation did the Reverend Chad Varah found in 1953?

20. 'Flash Bang Wallop' is a song from which show?

1. What was the stage name of the actor Richard Jenkins, born 1925?

2. Who launched The Body Shop in the seventies?

3. In 'Dixon of Dock Green', whose catchphrase was 'Evening All'?

4. Name the mountain range, which lies between Aviemore in the Northwest and Braemar in the Southeast.

5. Name the home of Wordsworth and his sister from 1799 until 1808.

6. Which city issues all British driving licences?

7. Matthew Webb achieved fame in August 1875 with which feat?

8. Name the first sea captain to sail around the world.

9. Who were collectively known as the Moors murderers?

10. Who was the fictional 'Barber of Fleet Street'?

11. Name the capital of the Isle of Man

12. Name the fictional town where Dr Finlay lived.

13. Who founded the Monster Raving Loony Party?

14. What is the name given to terrorists using female disguise in Ireland of the 1840's

15. Name the rival sixties teenage styles.

16. Which painter of the industrial northwest is known for his stick-like figures?

17. Which school did Billy Bunter attend?

18. What was thought to be the location of King Arthur's court?

19. Which author lived at Abbotsford, near Melrose on the Tweed?

20. Who became Poet Laureate in 1972?

WHO WERE KNOWN BY THE FOLLOWING NICKNAMES:

1. Brandy Nan

2. The Virgin Queen

3. Father of the English Novel

4. The Welsh Wizard

5. Lord Haw Haw

6. Fluff

7. Father of English printing

8: The Master

9. Parrot Face

10. Vindaloo

11. Madame Sin

12. Doris Karloff

13. Fiery Fred

14. Beast of Bolsover

15. Father of the Detective Story

16. Lord Porn

17. The Wigan Nightingale

18. The Grand Old Man

19. Sooty

20. Father of Steam

1. Name the architect who came to public attention in 1951, when he won the competition to design the new Coventry Cathedral.

2. Who won the Whitbread prize with 'The Curious incident of The Dog in the Night-Time'?

3. Which actors' biography of 2004 by Alan Strachan was entitled 'Secret Dreams'?

4. What did Joseph Cyril Bamford invent?

5. Which family's name do you associate with the Vernons Pools Inheritance?

6. Which couple has a home nicknamed 'Beckingham Palace' in Hertfordshire?

7. Name Margaret Thatchers' twins.

8. What do Erin O'Connor and Karen Elson have in common?

9. Who sailed single-handed round the world in the yacht 'Lively Lady'?

10. Name the Minister of Transport who introduced the breathalyser in 1967.

11. Richard John Bingham, a suspected murderer' is more commonly known by what name?

12. Which canal, with 29 locks links the East and West coasts of Scotland?

13. Where was Oscar Wilde imprisoned for two years?

14. What do John Dryden, William Wordsworth, Robert Bridges and John Masefield have in common?

15. Which impressive 18th century building in London is particularly associated with family records?

16. In which city did the first Body Shop open in 1976?

17. 'Gasping' and 'Silly Cow' are plays by which modern playwright/comedian?

18. Which architect do you associate with the interiors of Harewood House, Syon House and Osterley Park?

19. Name four English counties beginning with the letter N.

20. What is the pseudonym of the writer Franklin Birkinshaw?

GIVE THE FIRST NAMES OF THE FOLLOWING PEOPLE, WHO ARE MORE COMMONLY KNOWN BY THEIR INITIALS:

1.	The poet	W.H. Auden
2.	Irish poet	W.B. Yeats
3.	Welsh rugby player	J.P.R. Williams
4.	Journalist and explorer	H.M. Stanley
5.	English illustrator	E.H. Shepard
6.	Scottish psychiatrist	R.D. Laing
7.	English author	L.P. Hartley
8.	English cricketer	W.G. Grace
9.	Writer	J.G. Ballard
10.	Historian	E.P. Thompson
11.	English newsagent	W.H. Smith
12.	Children's writer	J.K. Rowling

13. British soldier/writer	T.E. Lawrence
14. Economist	J.K. Galbraith
15. Novelist and critic	A.S. Byatt
16. British politician	W.E. Gladstone
17. English author	R.F. Delderfield
18. British politician	R.A. Butler
19. English operetta librettist	W.S. Gilbert
20. Scottish novelist	J.M. Barrie

NAME THE FOLLOWING:

1. The naturalist who made his voyage of discovery in 'H.M.S. Beagle'

2. Person elected Prime Minister in 1979

3. Photographer known for his images of Jean Shrimpton in the sixties

4. He gave the world's first demonstration of television on 26th January 1926

5. He was Prime Minister three times 1923-4, 1924-9 and 1935-7

6. Alexander Plunket Greene married this fashion designer

7. Rock star who died in 1991, a few hours after issuing a statement that he had Aids.

8. Her modelling career ended abruptly in 1993 when she lost part of her leg after being hit by a police motor bike.

9. Oxford mathematician; an international author of two children's books, published 1865 and 1871.

10. Victor Meldrew's wife from 'One Foot in the Grave'

11. Actress/model who became the £1 million-a-year face of Estee Lauder

12. His feast day is celebrated on March 1st

13. He said "Never in the field of human conflict was so much owed by so many to so few"

14. He introduced The Open University in 1969 as a pioneering educational venture

15. Female half of the Eurythmics

16. The name of the ship in the Captain Pugwash books and T.V. series.

17. Scottish architect whose works include Cranston tea-rooms and Hill House in Helensburgh

18. English wood engraver, known for his masterpiece 'History of British Birds'

19. He was appointed Astronomer Royal in 1995

20. The Milburngate shopping centre is in this city

NAME THE LOCATION OF THE FOLLOWING AIRPORTS:

1. Ronaldsway

2. Compton Abbas

3. Grimsetter

4. Aldergrove

5. St. Just

6. Tingwall

7. Rhoose

8. Tiree

9. West Freugh

10. Dalcross

11. Scone

12. Dyce

13. Turnhouse

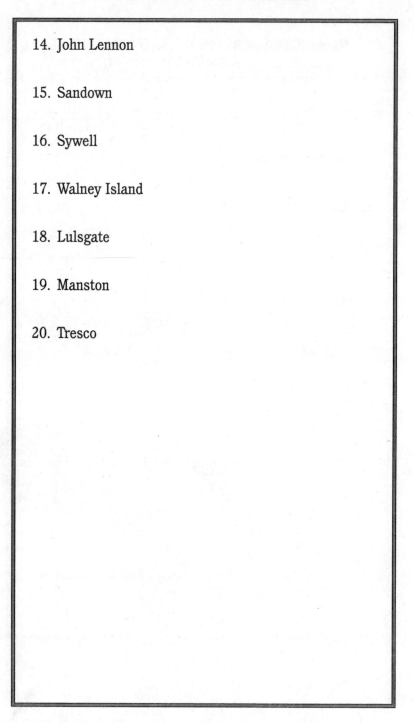

14. John Lennon

15. Sandown

16. Sywell

17. Walney Island

18. Lulsgate

19. Manston

20. Tresco

1. Name the two Scots brothers who created an elegant, neo-classical style of architecture and furniture in the 18th century.

2. Name the fashionable town and former health resort in Gloucestershire, which is famous for its public schools, mineral springs and racecourse.

3. On which London street would you locate Harvey Nichols?

4. Whose fashion designs were the basis of two royal charity galas in 1985 and 1988 to raise money for Barnado's?

5. In what year did Winston Churchill die?

6. Name the villain in Peter Pan.

7. Name the girl prodigy who finished her Oxford University Degree aged 13 on 4 July 1985.

8. Name the uninhabited island in the Hebrides, famous for Fingal's Cave.

9. The actress Glenda Jackson was elected Labour MP for which constituency in 1992?

10. Which mainline terminal is the closest to the centre of London?

11. Who created the Just William books?

12. Who became The Royal Ballet's youngest principal dancer at just 20?

13. What do Donald Coggan, John Habgood and David Michael Hope have in common?

14. Which photographer's book 'Locations' focuses on his wide-ranging international subject matter of the seventies?

15. Which author do you associate with the line, "The female of the species is more deadly than the male"?

16. In 2002, which comedian appeared in a series of television commercials in an attempt to improve flagging interest in the National Lottery?

17. Which clergyman said, "I look upon the world as my parish"?

18. What was the family name of 'The Brothers' in the TV series?

19. What was founded by Wilson Carlile in the slums of London in 1882?

20. How did the Bay City Rollers choose their name?

NAME THE LOCATIONS OF THE FOLLOWING RAILWAY STATIONS:

1. Bank Top

2. Forster Square

3. Snow Hill

4. Mumps

5. Paragon

6. Spa

7. Lime Street

8. Connolly

9. St. Enoch

10. London Road

11. Priory

12. Temple Meads

13. Low Level

14. Foregate Street

15. Citadel

16. St. David's

17. Haymarket

18. Liverpool Street

19. Piccadilly

20. Thorpe

QUOTES

1. Who made the great understatement, "I am just going outside and may be some time"? (1912)

2. Who made the prophetic statement in his maiden speech in parliament, "I will sit down now but the time will come when you will hear me."

3. Who was Lady Caroline Lamb referring to when she described him as 'mad, bad and dangerous to know'?

4. Of whom was it said 'If you seek his monument, look about you'?

5. Which Health Minister created uproar with the remark "good Christians won't get Aids"?

6. Which poet and preacher wrote the lines "No man is an island, entire of itself;...... and therefore never send to know for whom the bell tolls; it tolls for thee."

7. Which opera singer's dying words were "now I'll have eine kleine pause".

8. Which politician coined the phrase "a week is a long time in politics"?

9. Which British politicians dying words were "Am I dying, or is this my birthday"?

10. Who was the Lord Chief Justice, who said on entering office in 1992 that he aimed to "make the judiciary seem more accessible and user-friendly"?

11. Who did Churchill refer to as "bands of determined men armed with shot-guns, sporting rifles, clubs and spears"?

12. Which King on his deathbed apologised to the courtiers attending to him with the words: "I am sorry, gentlemen, for being such a time a-dying".

13. Who wrote 'Confessions of an English Opium Eater'?

14. Which politician in October 2002 said, "Do not underestimate the determination of a quiet man"?

15. Who asked, "Are you sitting comfortably?" on BBC radio's Listen With Mother?

16. Which British novelist's final words were: "God bless you all, I feel myself again."?

17. Whose work ends with the line "The coward does it with a kiss, the brave man with a sword"?

18. Which author said in 1763 "the noblest prospect which a Scotchman ever sees, is the high road that leads him to England"?

19. Who was Winston Churchill referring to when he wrote "Indomitable in retreat; invincible in advance; insufferable in victory."?

20. "Yarooooh, you rotters! Oh Crikey!" are words associated with which fictional schoolboy?

WHO FAMOUSLY SAID:

1. "Buy old masters. They fetch a better price than old mistresses".

2. "Slums have their good points, they at least have a community spirit and solve the problem of loneliness".(1966)

3. "Had we lived, I should have had a tale to tell of the hardihood, endurance and courage of my companions which would have stirred the heart of every Englishman. These rough notes and our dead bodies must tell the tale" (diary entry)

4. "It doesn't matter what you do in the bedroom as long as you don't do it in the street and frighten the horses".

5. "Life is too short to stuff a mushroom".

6. "How horrible, fantastic, incredible it is that we should be digging trenches and trying on gas-masks here because of a quarrel in a faraway country between people of whom we know nothing".

7. "Don't put your daughter on the stage, Mrs. Worthington".

8. "It is a commonplace observation that work expands so as to fill the time available for its completion".

9. "Macmillan's role as a poseur was itself a pose"

10. "The argument of the broken pane of glass is the most valuable argument in modern politics"

11. "Not a penny off the pay, not a minute off the day".

12. "Patriotism is not enough; I must have no hatred and bitterness towards anyone".

13. "There is no terror in a bang, only in the anticipation of it".

14. "Nudge, nudge, wink, wink, say no more, know what I mean........".

15. "The only methods we shall employ will be English ones. We shall rely on the good old English fist".

16. "You can't reheat a souffle".

17. "As long as my picture is on the front page, I don't care what they say about me on page 96".

18. "I'm going to spend, spend, spend!"

19. "It is very good advice to believe only what an artist does, rather than what he says about his work".

20. "Clearly, then, the city is not a concrete jungle, it is a human zoo".

1. Which avant-garde artists are known for painting their faces gold and wearing identical outfits?

2. Name David Niven's final film of 1983.

3. With which Italian fashion house did Stella McCartney sign a £15million deal in 2001?

4. Which philosopher coined the phrase 'better red than dead'?

5. Name the actor who gave £1million to the National Trust in 1998 towards the £3million cost of purchasing land surrounding Snowdon, Wales.

6. Name the oil tanker disaster of 18th March 1967 off the Isles of Scilly.

7. In which year did Queen Elizabeth II agree to pay tax on her private income?

8. Who unveiled the seven-foot bronze statue of John Lennon at Liverpool airport (which is named in his honour)?

9. Name the longest suspension bridge in the UK spanning 4,626 feet.

10. Which comedian developed his own catchphrase of 'Swinging...' (thumb raised) and 'Dodgy' (thumb down)?

11. Which British science fiction writer wrote 'When childhood dies, its corpses are called adults and they enter society, one of the politer names of hell. That is why we dread children, even if we love them. They show us the state of our decay!?

12. Who coined the slogan "Holiday with pay: Holiday with play: A week's holiday for a week's wage"?

13. Name the British Child Psychiatrist who worked from 1923 for 40 years at the Paddington Green Children's Hospital in London and became an immense influence on methods of child analysis and therapy.

14. Name the British radicals who were partners in marriage and who founded the London School of Economics in 1895 and launched the New Statesman in 1913.

15. Who was the comedian who was often referred to as 'Big-Hearted'?

16. Who was the self-styled 'Rimbaud of Cwndonkin Drive'?

17. Who, in his autobiography of 1964 said 'All I need to make a comedy is a park, a policeman and a pretty girl'?

18. Which fictional character of book, stage and screen is invariably portrayed with a Meerschaum pipe?

19. Which British humourist was editor of 'Punch' from 1977 - 1987?

20. Who penned the line "Anyone who has been to an English public school will always feel comparatively at home in prison. It is the people brought up in the gay intimacy of the slums ... who find prison so soul-destroying". (1928)

1. Whose most important contribution to art history is 'The Nude: A Study of Ideal Art' (1953)?

2. Who founded the chain of Habitat stores?

3. Name the poet and writer who created the detective 'Nigel Strangeways'.

4. Which British photographer said, "Perhaps the world's second worst crime is boredom. The first is being a bore".

5. Who or what are 'Trekkies'?

6. Name the steep flight of 322 steps up one face of Cheddar Gorge.

7. Name the best preserved Roman villa in Britain situated north-east of Cirencester.

8. Who was the diarist Harold Nicholson referring to when he said, ".... Is a charming and intelligent man, but as a public speaker he is, compared to Winston, like a village fiddler after Paganini"?

9. Which British essayist, novelist and critic who died in 1936, referred to journalism as "the easiest of all professions".

10. Name the British academic who coined the slogan 'Think Sideways'.

11. By what name were Kingsley Amis, John Wain, John Osborne and Colin Wilson collectively known in the fifties?

12. Name the first 'garden city' founded in 1903.

13. Name the stately home north-west of Lancaster known for its gardens and for housing the Lakeland Motor Museum.

14. Who wrote 'In Memoriam' an elegy for his friend Arthur Hallam?

15. 'The Naked Civil Servant' (1968) was the first volume of whose memoirs?

16. In which city would you find the Welsh Industrial & Maritime Museum?

17. Name the most spectacular of the series of caves worn by the river Axe on its course through the Mendips.

18. Who was the first woman to read the national news on TV?

19. What is the RNLI?

20. Name the gentleman thief who was the hero in several books by E.W. Hornung.

1. This Conservative politician represented Kingston-upon-Thames from 1972. He was a member of the Cabinet in 1989 and in 1990, he succeeded John Major as Chancellor of the Exchequer. He gained much unwanted publicity when it was revealed in the News of the World in 1991 that a tenant of his was a sex therapist. Name him.

2. This author and leader of irregular troops was immortalised in a film directed by David Lean in 1962. He attempted to fade out of fame by joining the RAF as Aircraftsman Ross and after his cover was blown, enlisted with the Royal Tank Corps. He died in a motorcycle accident, near his cottage in Dorset, which is now a museum. Name him.

3. Born in 1951, this footballer was one of the first British players to make his mark playing in Europe. He was named European Footballer of the Year in two successive years (1978-9) while with Hamburg. He returned to English football in 1980 to play for Southampton, before transferring to Newcastle in 1982. Who is he?

4. Born in 1904, he began his career as a photographer in fashionable 'Twenties' London society. His successful 'Book of Beauty' appeared in 1930. He worked for various magazines as well as producing travel books throughout the Thirties. As an official war photographer, he worked in London and the Far East. Name him.

5. This British Journalist joined the 'Observer' as a columnist in 1960. She combined her career in journalism with a number of administrative jobs, notably the Rectorship of St. Andrews University (1982-85). She is known for her statement in 1975 of "The best careers advice to give to the young is 'Find out what you like doing best and get someone to pay you for doing it'." Can you name her?

6. Born in 1933, this footballer and manager began his playing career with Fulham (1950-6, 1962-7) and West Bromwich Albion (1956-62). He managed Ipswich Town from 1969-82 and has also managed PSV Eindhoven in the Netherlands. Name him.

7. Educated at Westminster School and then the London Guildhall School of Music, she performed with her brother Rollo in his band Faithless, before going solo. She is the daughter of an Irish publisher and French poetess. 'Life for Rent' was her second album. Name her.

8. This British poet, born in 1886, began writing poetry in the trenches of World War I and his work illuminates the futility of war and the bravery of the average soldier. He was awarded the Military Cross but threw it away as he found the war so painful and commented'... I believe that the War is being deliberately prolonged by those who have the power to end it'. Name him.

9. Born in 1951, this Scottish footballer and manager was successful in both arenas. In 1985, he became player manager of Liverpool, taking over on the day after the Heysel Stadium tragedy. He retired in 1991 briefly and came back to manage Blackburn Rovers, who he took to promotion in the top division. Who is he?

10. This writer, born 1908, was the second son of a Conservative M.P. He had a traditional upper-class education before joining Reuters, followed by the family Merchant Bank. He worked abroad as a Times reporter and as a member of British Intelligence. He created his celebrated character in his first novel of 1953. Can you name him?

11. This British writer and visionary who died in 1946, began life as an impoverished draper's apprentice but worked his way first to teaching and then to studying science under T.H. Huxley. He was a prolific writer and he often used his scientific knowledge to create bizarre fictional worlds as well as writing comedies and plays. Can you name him?

12. Born in 1945, this composer, singer and guitarist has had an amazing musical career. In 1997, 'Business Age' estimated his personal fortune at £120 million. He has composed for such box office film hits as 'Lethal Weapon' (1987,1989,1992 & 1998), 'The Van' (1996) and 'Nil by Mouth' (1997). He is a former alcoholic and drug addict and in 1998 he set up a clinic in Antigua, 'Crossroads', to treat alcoholism and drug abuse. Name him.

13. This Suffolk trawler skipper's son began racing in 1949. An accident two years later ended his own driving career but he moved to team management and eventually became the ringmaster of the Formula 1 circuit. He is married to Slavica, a Croation-born former model. Name him.

14. She received critical acclaim for 'Dangerous Liaisons'. In 1996, she was nominated for Best Supporting Actress in 'Pulp Fiction' and has since starred in 'The Truth about Cats & Dogs', 'Gattaca' and Woody Allen's 'Sweet & Lowdown'. Name her.

15. Born in 1938, he became the most successful of Britain'sThree-Day-Event riders at the Olympic Games, taking an individual Gold medal in 1972. He was part of the gold-medal winning team at the World Championships of 1967, 1971 and 1981. He also won Badminton in 1970 and 1982. Who is he?

POT LUCK

POT LUCK 1

1. What items of clothing were known as 'brothel creepers' in the fifties?

2. Who wrote 'The Pilgrim's Progress'?

3. Name the BBC's teletext service.

4. With what do you associate the voluntary organisation, known as CAMRA?

5. Who led the SDP from 1983 until it was disbanded in 1990?

6. The Great Exhibition of the Works of Industry of all Nations took place in London in what year?

7. Name the British Prime Minister who negotiated with Ian Smith over Rhodesia, in what came to be known as the 'Tiger Talks'.

8. What do the initials BSI represent?

9. What is a Dandie Dinmont?

10. What name is given to a Scottish flat wool cap, without a brim but with a bobble on the top?

11. What term is used to describe grammatically correct English?

12. Name the open, flat-bottomed boats, which are very popular at Oxford and Cambridge Universities, and are a tourist attraction.

13. Selfridges and John Lewis stand on which crowded London Street?

14. Which charity was founded after an estate agent disappeared in 1986, after showing a property to a Mr Kipper?

15. Which supermarket took its name from its original tea supplier Stockwell and the firm's founder Sir John Cohen?

16. In which children's comic did we meet Desperate Dan?

17. What is Cader Idris?

18. Who wrote 'Tristram Shandy'?

19. Name the only city in England where the entire medieval city wall survives.

20. 'Joey' is often used as a general name for a clown. Which classic English clown is commemorated by this name?

POT LUCK 2

QUICKIES - NAME THE FOLLOWING:

1. A vegetable, an unofficial emblem of Wales

2. In Scotland, an attendant or guide for a person who is hunting or fishing

3. The 24-hour English radio programme, broadcast to overseas countries by the BBC

4. She also writes under the pseudonym Barbara Vine

5. Affectionate name for a person employed to help children cross a busy road

6. London Zoo is situated to the north of this park

7. Lombard Street, London is particularly associated with this activity

8. A florin was worth what sum of money?

9. Heroine of Shakespeare's 'Othello'?

10. Britain's first safari park was established here in 1966.

11. Decimal coinage was introduced in this year.

12. A weekly financial and commercial review founded in 1843.

13. She created the Gothic tale of terror, 'Frankenstein'.

14. Lord Snooty was a character in this comic

15. Complex of flyovers where the M6 motorway links with the A38 and A5127

16. Name of the two northeast towns where the first public railway to use steam locomotion was used

17. Ancient name for Ireland

18. What is the SNP?

19. In which park is Speaker's Corner?

20. Hospital in Buckinghamshire with world-wide reputation for treatment of spinal injuries

21. Area of London associated with strip clubs and sex shops

22. The annual congress of Welsh bards

23. One of the oldest newspapers in Britain, it covers all matters of interest to the insurance industry.

24. Lectures founded and named after the first general manager of the BBC in 1947

25. Playwright of 'Bouncers'

NAME THE ARTISTS RESPONSIBLE FOR THE FOLLOWING WORKS: -

1. Dedham Vale; The Haywain; Salisbury

2. The Hut; My Bed

3. Admiral Lord Anson; Three Ladies Adorning a Term of Hymen; The Montgomerie Sisters

4. The Fall of the Clyde; Battle of Trafalgar; The Field of Waterloo

5. My Parents and Myself; Rocky Mountains and Tired Indians

6. Molly Long Legs with a Jockey; Mares and Foals in a River Landscape

7. King Cophetua and the Beggar Maid; Perseus series; The Legend of the Briar Rose series

8. Harvest Wagon; Portrait of Mary, Countess Howe; The Blue Boy

9. The Light of the World; The Scapegoat;

10. Monarch of the Glen; The Rout of Comus; Shoeing

11. Young Man among Roses; Elizabeth I Playing a Lute; Young Man in a Garden

12. The Blind Girl; Christ in the House of His Parents; Autumn Leaves

13. The Circle of the Lustful; Heads of the Poets

14. Yarmouth Jetty; Marlingford Grove; The Beaters

15. The Rakes's Progress series; Self-portrait with His Pug

POT LUCK 4

1. In what year did the great poet and dramatist, William Shakespeare die?

   a) 1615   c) 1617
   b.)1616   d) 1618

2. What in Scotland may be referred to as 'but and ben'?

   a) A small cottage with two rooms   c) article of clothing
   b) A dance   d) man and wife

3. What was the codename in World War 11 for the Allied Invasion of Normandy?

   a) Overmore   c) Shakleton
   b) Orlando   d) Overlord

4. 'Alas, poor Yorick' is a line from which of Shakespeare's plays?

   a) King Lear   c) Hamlet
   b). Macbeth   d) Measure for Measure

5. A farthing was legal tender until the end of which year?

   a) 1940   c) 1950
   b) 1960   d) 1970

6. What is a Black Maria?

   a) An alcoholic drink   c) a police van
   b) A lady of ill-repute d) a jig

7. Which river rises in Northamptonshire, drains the Fens and enters the Wash at King's Lynn?

    a) The Ouse
    c) The Severn
    b) The Trent
    d) The Avon

8. The Lambeth Walk was a song and dance from which musical?

    a) As time goes by
    c) The Boyfriend
    b) Me and My Girl
    d) Carousel

9. Who wrote the poem The Pobble who has No Toes?

    a) Edward Lear
    c) A.A. Milne
    b) Lewis Carroll
    d) John Burningham

10. What was the Danegeld?

    a) A tax
    c) a coin
    b) An item of headgear
    d) item of clothing

11. Decimalization came into effect in Britain on this date

    a) 15th February 1971
    c) 14th February 1970
    b) 1st April 1970
    d) 9th April 1971

12. What is Bara brith?

    a) A hat
    c) mountain range
    b) Sword
    d) a Welsh bread

13. What is the most popular pub name in Britain?

    a) The Crown   c) The Red Lion
    b) The King's Head   d) The Five Alls

14. Which city uses the STD code 0131?

    a) Birmingham   c) Edinburgh
    b) Durham   d) Cardiff

15. Name Captain Robert Falcon Scott's ship, used on his ill-fated Antarctic expedition of 1910-12.

    a) Quest   c) Challenger
    b) Terra Nova   d) Resolution

16. Where, in London would you locate the bronze statue of Sir Winston and Lady Churchill by Oscar Nemon?

    a) Chelsea Embankment c) Kensington Gardens
    b) Grosvenor Square   d) Park Lane

17. What was Jeeves Christian name?

    a) Peregrine   c) Ronald
    b) Reginald   d) Peirs

18. In which year did the first Premium Bond go on sale?

    a) 1946   c) 1954
    b) 1949   d) 1956

POT LUCK 4

19. In captivity, Mary Queen of Scots complained of being deprived of what sport?

   a) Tennis
   b) Billiards

   c) golf
   d) croquet

20. Clare Balding specialises in commentating on which sport?

   a) Horse Racing
   b) Athletics

   c) Ice-Skating
   d) Swimming

POT LUCK 5

1. Which TV series is centred on Blue Watch B25, Blackwall?

2. Which Scottish essayist and historian was known as 'the sage of Chelsea'?

3. The Pipes and Drums and Military Band of The Royal Scots Dragoon Guards had a No1 hit in 1972. Name it.

4. Who founded London Zoo?

5. Which medical discovery of 1628 is associated with William Harvey?

6. Name the RAF's acrobatic team.

7. In which war did the Battle of Naseby take place?

8. Name the cow in The Magic Roundabout.

9. Who as Poet laureate was entitled to a pitcher of wine every day, under the reign of Edward III ?

10. Name Frazer Hines first wife.

11. What name is given to the adult leader of the junior branch of the scouts?

12. What is the meaning of the word Cymru?

13. Which politician is reputed to have said on his deathbed, "Die, my dear doctor, that's the last thing I shall do!"

14. Which correspondent gave TV's first widely remembered broadcast on the coronation of 1953?

15. Which British football club won the European Cup-Winners' Cup in 1991?

16. The main newspaper of British pop music is known by the letters 'NME'. What do they represent?

17. The Millenium Prayer was a No1 pop hit in 1999. Who sang it?

18. Which Order of Chivalry, instituted in 1902, is limited to 24 British men and women plus an occasionally honorary foreigner?

19. Which children's book do you associate with the phrase 'messing about in boats'?

20. Who in 1987 said "There is no such thing as society, there are individual men and women, and there are families."?

POT LUCK 6

THE ANSWERS TO THE FOLLOWING QUICK QUIZ
ALL BEGIN WITH THE LETTER B
NAME THE FOLLOWING:

1. The nineteenth hole at a golf course

2. A kind of soft, round, flat bread roll

3. The fat greedy boy in the stories about 'Greyfriars'

4. A type of stout walking shoe

5. A dish made from cold cabbage and potato leftovers

6. An alcoholic drink of champagne and orange juice

7. Colloquial name for Buckingham Palace

8. The highest mountain in Britain

9. Trade name of a make of light, good quality raincoat

10. An official in charge of the finances in a school or a college

11. In the North of England, a colloquial name for a sandwich

12. A popular gambling game, 'Eyes down....'

13. A group of shallow navigable lakes and rivers in East Anglia

14. Familiar nickname for the BBC

15. An inhabitant of Birmingham

16. Junior branch of the Girl Guides

17. Fashionable seaside resort in East Sussex famous for its architecture

18. Trade-name of a popular make of ball-point pen

19. A performer who makes money in public places

20. Title given to a poet who wins a competition at an Eisteddfod

POT LUCK 7

1. Name the breed of black hornless beef cattle which takes its name from two Scottish counties

2. Name the government agencies responsible for Britain's security at home and abroad.

3. In which city would you find the Ashmolean Museum?

4. What name is given to two high hills in Powys, South Wales, on which signal fires were lit in medieval times?

5. Which church was founded by John Wesley (1703-91)

6. 'Mad Cow disease' is known by what initials?

7. What term is a conventional indication of an official invitation that evening dress must be worn?

8. Name Winston Churchill's home from 1922 until his death.

9. What term is used for the prosecution in criminal proceedings during the reign of a queen?

10. BUPA is a leading provider of private health insurance in Britain. What do the initials represent?

11. Who wrote 'The Clockwork Orange'?

12. What name is given to the obelisk of pink granite placed on the Thames Embankment in 1878?

13. What was the nickname originally used for soldiers who served with the British 7th Armoured Division in the North Africa campaign of 1941-2?

14. What name is given to the state organisation that manufactures British coins?

15. Name the large country house, near Oxford, built for the Duke of Marlborough in memory of his victory in battle.

16. Name the band Paul McCartney formed after the split of The Beatles.

17. First published in 1864, which well-known reference book is named after a cricketer?

18. What name is given to the seat on which the Lord Chancellor sits in the House of Lords?

19. Name the Derbyshire open tart made from pastry lined with jam and filled with almond-flavoured sponge cake.

20. What name is given to the MP who has sat in the House of Commons for the longest uninterrupted period?

POT LUCK 8

1. Blind Pew appears in which adventure story?

2. Which long-distance path from Helmsley to Filey Brigg is a 110-mile horseshoe-shaped route?

3. St Michael is the trade mark of which company?

4. Antony Hopkins won an Oscar for Best Actor in which film of 1991.

5. Which Van Gogh painting fetched £24.75 million at Christie's in 1987?

6. What colour are the lines painted along the side of a road to indicate waiting restrictions for vehicles?

7. In England, whose feast day is celebrated on April 23rd?

8. Whose 'Book of Household Management '(1861) was an extremely influential collection of recipes and tips on all aspects of housekeeping?

9. Three rivers in Britain share this name - the longest of which rises in the Cairngorm Mountains and enters the North Sea at Aberdeen. Which river is it?

10. Name London's third major airport.

11. What was the value of a half-crown?

12. In which city would you find Strangeways prison?

13. Which entrepreneur gave us the bagless vacuum cleaner and the double drum washing machine?

14. Name the portrait and history painter who was nicknamed 'the Cornish wonder'.

15. In which city would you locate the Bredero shopping Centre?

16. Name the largest castle in Scotland.

17. Name the 17-ton bell of St Paul's Cathedral.

18. What name is given to an MP who does not hold any special office?

19. Name the castle in northeast Scotland which has been a private home of the Royal Family since 1852.

20. Who was the founder of The Body Shop?

POT LUCK 9

QUICKIES - NAME THE FOLLOWING:

1. The group of teenagers who rivalled 'the Mods' in the sixties

2. The annual carnival in London W11

3. The chief residence of the monarch

4. Frances Hodgson Burnett's 'Little Lord...'who?

5. Any idealised old couple, living in marital harmony

6. Area of high moorland in Devon, designated a national park in 1951

7. Famous public school for girls near Brighton, founded in 1885

8. Term for the small-sized paper for popular newspapers

9. The year of The Great Fire of London

10. Defence force of equipped and trained volunteers, who can be called upon during national emergency

11. The capital of Wales

12. Commonly used name for the Central Criminal Court.

13. The plane associated with The Dam Busters.

14. The main event of the canine year.

15. The pseudonym of Eric Blair (1903-50)

16. The county ground of Surrey County Cricket Club

17. Cloth of checked design of contrasting colours used in Highland dress

18. Euphemistic expression for an undertaker's mortuary

19. Group of islands, separated from John O'Groats by The Pentland Firth

20. Britain's largest aid agency, founded in 1942

WHAT DO THE FOLLOWING HAVE IN COMMON?

1. Good Friday; Boxing Day; May Day

2. Brian Turner; Nick Nairn; Paul Rankin

3. Dragon; harp; bulldog;

4. Ermine Street; Fosse Way; Watling Street;

5. Keith Deller; Dennis Priestley; John Lowe

6. Clara Peggotty; Barkis; Steerforth

7. Michaelmas; Hilary; Trinity;

8. Growltiger; Shimbleshanks; Napoleon

9. Anita Lonsbrough; David Wilkie; Adrian Moorhouse

10. Gordon Richardson; Robin Leigh-Pemberton; Eddie George

11. Red; Fallow; Roe

12. Lover's Leap; The Twelve Apostles; Jacob's Ladder

POT LUCK 10

13. Crown Quarto; Demy Octavo; Royal Quarto

14. The Mock Turtle; The Gryphon; The Caterpillar

15. Valerie Singleton; John Noakes; Peter Purves

16. Relatively Speaking; The Norman Conquests; Absurd Person Singular

17. Francis Rossi; Rick Parfitt; Alan Lancaster; John Coghlan

18. William Shepherd Morrison; Horace King; Selwyn Lloyd

19. Harry Wharton; Bob Cherry; Hurree Jamset Ram Singh

20. DBE; DCVO; DCB

1. Where did Billy Butlin open his first holiday camp in 1936?

2. Which furniture maker published his revolutionary pattern book of designs 'The Gentleman and Cabinet Maker's Directory in 1754?

3. Who hosted TV's 'The City Gardener'?

4. St David's and Tenby are in which national park?

5. The annual Race for Life raises funds for which charity?

6. Who played the heroine, the governor's daughter Elizabeth in 'Pirates of the Caribbean'?

7. Which Derbyshire spa town is known for its annual music festival?

8. The tiny green-headed extraterrestrial Mekon was the enemy of which character in 'The Eagle' comic?

9. Which square in London is particularly associated with theatres, cinemas and restaurants?

10. Name the unit of speed of a ship at sea

11. How many fiddlers had 'Old King Cole'?

12. Which organisation, founded in 1965 by John Smith saves unusual buildings threatened with demolition?

13. What is nicknamed 'Alley Pally'?

14. Who played Sergeant Wilson in TV's 'Dad's Army'?

15. Name the organisation set up in 1941 by Kurt Hahn with the purpose of providing physical and mental challenges for young people.

16. What are Oxford Bags?

17. Jasper, a type of hard, unglazed stoneware is associated with which pottery family?

18. By what name are the Yeoman Warders' of the Tower of London more commonly known?

19. Which football team is known as The Gunners?

20. Name three London Boroughs whose name begins with W.

POT LUCK 12

1. What is the popular name for Remembrance Sunday?

2. The logo of a crusader is found on which daily newspaper?

3. What is a Mari Lwyd?

4. Which tangy spread is a by-product from brewing and has been produced since 1902 in Burton-on-Trent?

5. Who took over from Harold Macmillan as Prime Minister of Great Britain in 1963?

6. Who won an Oscar for Best Actor in 'My Left Foot'?

7. In what year did Diana, Princess of Wales give birth to her first child?

8. Who is the narrator of Emily Bronte's 'Wuthering Heights'?

9. Who followed James Callaghan as leader of the Labour Party after their election defeat of 1980?

10. Name Britain's best-known prehistoric site, on Salisbury plain.

11. Name Sir Richard Branson's private Caribbean Island.

12. Name the avant-garde artist known for his use of parts of dead animals preserved in formaldehyde.

13. Name three English counties beginning with the letter W.

14. Which castle is known as 'The key of England'?

15. What is the STD code for Glasgow?

16. Name Britain's first nuclear submarine.

17. Who was Sherlock Holmes domestic servant?

18. What was the nickname of Edward, prince of Wales (1330-76), son of King Edward III.

19. What is the address of the Chancellor of the Exchequer?

20. 'Auntie' is the affectionate name for which organisation?

1. Which newspaper do you associate with the slogan 'all human life is there'?

2. Where in London would you find a bronze statue of Captain James Cook by Sir Thomas Brock (1914)?

3. 'The Tablet' is a newspaper of which christian denomination?

4. Which art gallery in Port Sunlight houses some excellent pre-Raphaelite and Victorian paintings?

5. What is the smallest imperial unit of length?

6. What is Up-Helly-Aa?

7. Which city took the title of European City of Culture in 1990?

8. What is the Granta?

9. In which National Park could you climb to the highest point in England?

10. Who married Jean Armour in the village of Mauchline in 1788?

11. George Romney, the portrait painter, used which Lady with whom he was infatuated, as the model for more than 50 paintings?

POT LUCK 13

12. Billy Smart's name is synonymous with what?

13. Name Katie Price's autobiography of 2004.

14. To what does the word 'Yuppies' refer?

15. Which popular film of 2001 concerned an Indian dance instructor who is mistaken for a mystic?

16. Arthur's seat is the most prominent feature of which city?

17. Who achieved prominence as the 'Director of Architecture' for the Festival of Britain in 1951?

18. The 'Journey of the Magi' is a well-known poem from which poet?

19. Name the channel separating Anglesey from Wales.

20. 'Rum, Bum and Concertina' (1977) is an autobiography of which Jazz singer?

1. Inaugurated in 1984 and sponsored by Channel 4, this award is given to a British Artist under the age of 50. Name it.

2. Name three Scottish Districts, which begin with the word East.

3. The highest pub in England is situated in Arkengarthdale in North Yorkshire. Name it.

4. In Liverpool, what is known as 'Paddy's Wigwam'?

5. What is the STD code for Newcastle?

6. What name is given to the Roman road from London to York?

7. If you were standing on Waverley railway station, where would you be?

8. Whose name do you associate with the yacht 'Lady Ghislaine'?

9. Name Ernest Shackleton's ship on his Antarctic voyage of 1914-16.

10. In which year was the driving test initiated?

11. Name the local pub in radio 4's 'The Archers'.

12. Who launched a seat-belt campaign in 1971, with the slogan 'Clunk, click, every trip'?

13. Name the parliament of the Isle of Man.

14. What are Cromarty, Tyne and Fair Isle?

15. Who became Poet Laureate in 1972 after Cecil Day-Lewis?

16. What is a 'Strathspey'?

17. Which aircraft carrier was the flagship during the Falklands conflict?

18. In Morse code, which letter is represented by dash dash dot dot?

19. What name is given to a breed of draught horse with a powerful body, relatively short legs and chestnut-coloured coat?

20. What is the colloquial term for the Universities of Oxford and Cambridge?

POT LUCK 15

IDENTIFY THESE COMMONLY USED ABBREVIATIONS:

1. A.P.T.

2. B.S.T.

3. C.A.B.

4. D.P.P.

5. E.O.C.

6. F.T.

7. G.C.S.E.

8. H.G.V.

9. I.R.A.

10. J.P.

11. K.G.

12. L.E.A.

13. M.C.C.

14. N.C.P.

15. O.A.P.

16. P.A.Y.E.

17. Q.P.R.

18. R.A.D.A.

19. S.A.S.

20. T.T.F.N.

21. U.C.C.A.

22. V.A.T.

23. W.R.V.S.

24. Y.H.A.

25. Z.P.G.

1. 'An Evil Cradling' was the autobiography of which hostage?

2. Which eighties group named themselves after a Robert Wagner/Natalie Wood film?

3. In what year did 'The Gang of Four' formally launch the Social Democratic Party?

4. In the 2001 World Athletic Championships in Edmonton, Britain came away with only one gold medal. Who won this and for which event?

5. Which British actor won a Golden Globe award as Best Supporting Actor for his portrayal of John Bayley in the film 'Iris'.

6. Which dramatist's final words were "Either this wallpaper goes or I do"?

7. By what name was the first speaking clock known?

8. What is a Glengarry?

9. By what name is the Shaftesbury Memorial Fountain more commonly known?

10. 'Jennifer's Diary' is a regular feature in which women's magazine?

POT LUCK 16

11. Which four scrabble tiles are each valued at 3?

12. Who became a millionaire with her creation of the 'Teletubbies?

13. Name the fourth Harry Potter film.

14. St. Patrick is the patron saint of Ireland. On which date is his feastday celebrated?

15. What was 'Peter Grimes' occupation in the opera of the same name?

16. What or who is Sir Roger de Coverley?

17. In which town was the popular series 'Last of the Summer wine' filmed?

18. Who recorded the Top 10 album 'Heathen Chemistry' in 2002?

19. Who adopted Tom Sharpe's comic novel 'Blott on the Landscape' for TV?

20. Which designer, born 1940, first came to public attention when she opened her Fulham Road clothes shop in 1967?

1. Which medical discovery of 1847 do you associate with James Simpson?

2. 'Rhoda' was a spin-off from which TV series?

3. the Brighouse & Rastrick Brass Band had their first and only hit in 1977. What was its title?

4. Name the Household Cavalry Regiments.

5. Name the ballet dancer who married broadcaster Ludovic Kennedy.

6. Which English cathedral houses the tomb of St. Cuthbert?

7. 'How to be Good' was a best-selling novel for which author?

8. Name Richard Harris's comedy cricketing play.

9. Which actor in the original 'Auf Wiedersehen Pet' series, died whilst filming the follow-up series in Spain?

10. Whose name is forever associated with the magnificent garden at Sissinghurst?

11. Which artist's exhibition of 2004 was entitled 'Can't See Past My Own Eyes"?

12. What do the initials S.E.R.P.S. represent?

13. Which English painter, who died in 1909, became the wealthiest painter of his time by selling both paintings and their copyright?

14. Who was the first British person to make a space flight on 18 May 1991?

15. In which county would you find Dunstanburgh Castle?

16. Which veteran broadcaster hosted his final radio show on 20 December 2002, completing 29 years in the morning slot?

17. Which actor also had a Top 20 hit with the Beatles No. 1 song 'A Hard Day's Night'?

18. Who, at the end of the nightly BBC programme, used to say "and the next 'Tonight' will be tomorrow night"?

19. The British politician, Paul Boateng, was born in which country?

20. What do John Thaw, Spike Milligan, Pat Coombs and Lonnie Donegan have in common?

POT LUCK 18

1. Who was TV's 'Callan'?

2. In which country was the English Prime Minister Andrew Bonar-Law born?

3. 'Dead Famous' was a best-seller for which comedian?

4. What do Peter Purves, Simon Groom, Janet Ellis and Michael Sundin have in common?

5. In what year did National Service commence?

6. Who was the composer of the opera 'Hugh the Droves'?

7. Tim Healy and his wife both play 'Geordie' roles on TV. Name his wife.

8. What was the prize money received by Craig, the first winner of 'Big Brother'?

9. Which comedian had his first and only pop hit in 1975 with 'Funky Moped'?

10. In which building would you find the 'Whispering Gallery'?

11. "Goodnight my darlings, I'll see you tomorrow" were the dying words of which British playwright?

12. In what year was the old age pension introduced in the U.K.?

13. Who was known as the 'Father of the Factory System'?

14. Which weekly magazine was launched by the B.B.C. in 1929 to preserve in print the best of its radio talks?

15. Who, in his early years as Prime Minister, was referred to as 'Supermac'?

16. Which Conservative politician was the last Governor of Hong Kong?

17. What is a 'solar topee'?

18. Name the junior branch of the Scouts.

19. The patriot song 'Heart of Oak' celebrates victories of which war?

20. What is the Christian name of TV's Mr. Rumbold?

POT LUCK 19

1. Name the two actors who had a pop hit in 1990 with 'Kinky Boots'?

2. In what year was National Service abolished?

3. In Britten's opera 'Billy Bud' what was Billy Bud's occupation?

4. Which cricketer was nicknamed 'Kipper'?

5. Name the 'Teletubbies'.

6. Who had a top 10 hit in 2002 with 'Dy-Na-Mi-Tee'?

7. Which wars do you associate with the Battles of Towton and Ferrybridge?

8. Name Andrew Lloyd Webber's second wife.

9. Which portrait painter was knighted for his 'George III and the Prince of Wales Reviewing The Troops'?

10. Who created the TV series 'London's Burning'?

11. Name the sequel to TV's 'Are You Being Served'?

12. Where would you find Carisbrooke Castle?

13. Who wrote 'Five Quarters of the Orange'?

14. Name the final 'Carry On' film of 1992.

15. The British actress Gabrielle Drake was born in which country?

16. In what year was 'Hello!' magazine launched?

17. Name the British architect who turned Lindisfarne Castle into a country house?

18. Which T.V. series featured Father MacAnally, Father Aidan and Father Clifford?

19. In which English cathedral is Edith Cavell buried?

20. Name the character Jill St. John played in the Bond movie 'Diamonds are Forever' (1971)?

WHAT DO THE FOLLOWING HAVE IN COMMON?

1. Acklington, Kirklevington Grange, Belmarsh, Winson Green.

2. Hounds Hill, North Point, St. David's, Wellgate.

3. Akeman Street, Dere Street, Icknield Way, Stone Street.

4. Elizabeth Fry, Charles Dickens, Michael Faraday, Sir Christoper Wren.

5. Shrub Hill, Buchanan Street, High Street, Queen Street.

6. Hamilton Harty, John Barbirolli, James Loughran.

7. Eleanor Burford, Kathleen Kellow, Philippa Car, Victoria Holt.

8. R.A. Butler, Roy Jenkins, Merlyn Rees, David Waddington.

9. Cambridge Utd., Colchester Utd., Oxford Utd.

10. Cougar, Sapphire, Probe, Maverick.

11. Donkey, Napoleon, Pope Joan, Loo.

POT LUCK 20

12. Brian Turner, Philip Harbin, Paul Rankin.

13. Angela Rippon, Hugh Scully, Bruce Parker.

14. Ant & Dec, Lulu, Tears for Fears.

15. Lord Porter, Baroness Thatcher, Dame Joan Sutherland, Dame Ninette de Valois.

16. Rocket, Panther, Rebel, Gold.

17. 'Whole Lotta Love', 'Yellow Pearl', 'The Wizard', 'Get Out of That'.

18. Rowena Johnson, Oliver Heath, Graham Wynne, Laura McCree.

19. Workie Ticket, Old Speckled Hen, Rector's Revenge.

20. Janice Gifford, Rosemary Hunter, Wilf Harvey and Sandy Richardson

POT LUCK 21

WHAT ARE THE MEANINGS OF THE FOLLOWING ABBREVIATIONS?

1. A.K.A.

2. B.Y.O.

3. C.O.D.

4. D.I.N.K.Y.

5. E.T.A.

6. F.Y.I.

7. G.D.P.

8. H.B.

9. I.V.F.

10. J.C.R.

11. K.B.E.

12. L.U.L.U.

13. M.I.R.A.S.

14. N.I.M.B.Y.

15. O.F.S.T.E.D.

16. P.I.N.

17. Q.U.A.N.G.O.

18. R.S.I.

19. S.W.A.L.K.

20. T.E.F.L.

21. U.S.D.A.W.

22. V.H.S.

23. W.Y.S.I.W.Y.G.

24. Y.2K.

25. Z.E.G.

POT LUCK 22

1. Which college is the home of the world-famous 'Book of Kells'?

2. 'Blood and Fire' is the motto of which organisation?

3. Lady Day is celebrated on March 25th; it is also a feast day. Name it.

4. Maudie Littlehampton was one of the upper class characters in which cartoonist's work?

5. What are 'The Mumbles'?

6. 'Jack Ketch' was a common term for which profession?

7. What name is given to the judge who presides over civil cases in the Court of Appeal?

8. Whose name do you associate with the musical work 'The Young Person's Guide to the Orchestra'?

9. Name Glasgow's main shopping street.

10. What was the nickname of the pirate Edward Teach?

11. Name the 1956 biopic of the flying ace Douglas Bader.

12. Name the inlet off the Firth of Clyde, which became the subject of much controversy when U.S. nuclear submarines began using it as a base in 1961.

13. How many tiles are there in a set of dominoes?

14. Which TV series, loosely based on the life of Lynn Franks, gives constant reference to 'Harvey Nichols'?

15. In 'All Creatures Great & Small', what type of 'creature' was Tricki Woo?

16. Name the cheapest property in Monopoly.

17. Name the pressure group formed in 1924 to campaign against all forms of hunting.

18. In which T.V. series did Michael Gambon play Philip E. Marlow?

19. In what year did the Princess of Wales die in a Paris car crash?

20. What name was given to the period of industrial unrest in the U.K., during the severe winter of 1978-9?

POT LUCK 23

WHAT IS THE MEANING OF THE FOLLOWING COCKNEY RHYMING SLANG TERMS?

1. Auntie Nellie

2. Tom Thumb

3. Rosy Lee

4. Mickey Mouse

5. Harry Randall

6. Dicky Dirt

7. Jim Skinner

8. Andy Cain

9. Richard the Third

10. Molly Malone

11. Jack the Ripper

12. Lilian Gish

13. Auntie Ella

14. Tommy Tucker

15. Kate and Sydney

16. Captain Cook

17. Oliver Twist

18. Harvey Nichols

19. Doctor Crippen

20. Lucy Locket

21. Conan Doyle

22. Uncle Bert

23. Jerry O'Gorman

24. Barnaby Rudge

25. Mrs Chant

POT LUCK 24

1. Name the newspaper of 'The Salvation Army'.

2. Who succeeded George Carey as Archbishop of Canterbury in 2002?

3. What is the airport code for Heathrow?

4. Which pop singer in 2002 signed a contract worth up to £70million, the largest ever in British music history?

5. According to the rhyme, who killed Cock Robin?

6. What date is St. Vitus's Day.

7. Name the largest bird of prey in the U.K.

8. What is the Scottish equivalent of the 'Daily Mirror'?

9. On which motorway would you travel from London to Cambridge?

10. 'Card Players' and 'Penny Wedding' are the works of which Scottish artist who painted in the Dutch style?

11. Which organisation is known by its initials F.O.R.E.S.T.?

12. Which sixties film starring Tom Courtenay and Julie Christie, was inspired by 'The Secret Life of Walter Mitty'?

13. Which comedian emerged triumphant from the 'Celebrity Big Brother' house in March 2001?

14. By what other names are McPartlin and Donnelly also known?

15. Which politician said, "How these dukes harass us. They're as expensive to keep as a dreadnought and not half so useful"?

16. Who founded The Salvation Army?

17. What is the English translation of the Latin hymn 'Adeste, fideles'?

18. In what year did the London Marathon first take place?

19. What is the colloquial term for a priest's stiff white collar?

20. Name the London Park famous for the Round Pond and the statue of Peter Pan.

POT LUCK 25

1. BBC2 first went on air in 1964. What was its first programme?

   a) Jackanory
   b) Play School
   c) Open University
   d) What's My Line

2. In which year did the 50p piece replace the ten shilling note?

   a) 1971
   b) 1973
   c) 1965
   d) 1969

3. Lady Churchill destroyed the official portrait of Sir Winston Churchill as she hated it. Who painted this portrait?

   a) Jack Butler Yeats
   b) Lucien Freud
   c) Francis Bacon
   d) Graham Sutherland

4. Hallmarks give information about the metal they are impressed in. Which city has the Assay Office mark of an anchor?

   a) London
   b) Sheffield
   c) Birmingham
   d) Edinburgh

5. Tracy Hilton and Alison Holloway were both married to which comedian?

   a) Jimmy Tarbuck
   b) Jim Davidson
   c) Freddie Starr
   d) Les Dawson

POT LUCK 25

6. Which pioneer of Pop Art in Britain do you associate with 'Just What Is It That Makes Today's Homes So Different'?

   a) Damien Hirst
   b) Lucien Freud
   c) David Hockney
   d) Richard Hamilton

7. Which Norman castle in Northumberland was 'restored' by Lord Armstrong 1894-1905?

   a) Ford
   b) Morpeth
   c) Bamburgh
   d) Norham

8. 'Carry On Emmanuelle' (1978) was the final film for which actor?

   a) Sid James
   b) Kenneth Williams
   c) Bernard Bresslaw
   d) Hatty Jacques

9. Who was the first Conservative Party leader to refuse to join the Carlton Club because it bars women from becoming full members?

   a) Margaret Thatcher
   b) William Hague
   c) Iain Duncan Smith
   d) John Major

10. By what name was TV Gladiator Mike Lewis known?

    a) Shadow
    b) Siren
    c) Fox
    d) Saracen

11. How did the British Statesman Viscount Castlereagh meet his death in 1822?

    a) Stabbed himself with a penknife
    b) Assassinated
    c) Natural causes
    d) Drugs-related illness

12. Radio Caroline began transmissions from a ship in the North Sea in which year?

    a) 1961　　　　　　c) 1963
    b) 1962　　　　　　d) 1964

13. At 404 ft. high, the spire of which cathedral makes it the tallest in England?

    a) Salisbury　　　　c) Wells
    b) Canterbury　　　 d) Durham

14. Who wrote the plays 'Are You Lonesome Tonight?', 'Having a Ball' and 'It's A Madhouse'?

    a) Tom Stoppard　　 c) Brian Friel
    b) John Godber　　　d) Alan Bleasdale

15. What relationship was Virginia Woolf to Vanessa Bell?

    a) Mother　　　　　c) Aunt
    b) Sister　　　　　 d) Niece

16. A flag flown by ships chartered by the government is known as the:

    a) Blue Ensign　　　c) Blue David
    b) Blue Peter　　　 d) Blue Flag

17. Who was the designer who launched the 'Warehouse' chain?

    a) Hardy Amies　　　c) Patrick Cox
    b) Alexander McQueen　d) Jeff Banks

POT LUCK 25

18. Which writer declared "Wine is bottled poetry"?

    a) Robert Louis Stevenson c) William Wordsworth
    b) Oscar Wilde   d) Sir Walter Scott

19. What was Thomas Hardy's final novel?

    a) Tess of the D'Urbervilles c) The Return of the Native
    b) Jude the Obscure   d) Under the Greenwood Tree

20. What is Huckle-my-buff?

    a) A dance   c) A drink of beer, eggs & brandy
    b) A garment   d) A game

1. Which Northumberland village achieved fame as the birthplace of Grace Darling?

2. Which Christian sect did George Fox found in the 1650's?

3. Which film producer do you associate with 'Bugsy Malone' (1976) and 'Midnight Express' (1978)?

4. Name the woman who created a multi-million pound business with her website 'Friends Reunited'.

5. In what year did the General Strike take place?

6. What is Sage Derby?

7. How many favourite pieces of music are castaways on radio's 'Desert Island Discs' allowed?

8. Which brewer's red triangle was the first trademark to be registered in 1875?

9. 'Boom Boom' was the catchphrase of which TV glove puppet?

10. Who killed Hamlet's father in the Shakespearean tragedy?

11. Where does the Lord Mayor's Banquet take place?

12. 'Wynken, Blynken and Nod, one night
Sailed off in a ....' what?

13. Desperate Dan appeared in which children's comic?

14. Which reverend wrote the celebrated 'Railway
Series' of children's books?

15. Which doctor 'stepped in a puddle right up to his
middle'?

16. Name the theme songs recorded by Shirley Bassey
for two James Bond films.

17. Who was known as the 'Bard of Avon'?

18. Name the second largest city in Britain.

19. Which twins edited 'The Guiness Book of Records'?

20. How many yards make a furlong?

THEY SHARE A NAME, WHAT IS IT?

1. A nickname of Queen Mary Tudor and a type of vodka cocktail.

2. A Scottish town in Grampian and marble sculptures from Athens.

3. An elderly female role played by a male in pantomime and the female equivalent of 'Sir' for men.

4. A white, mild, Welsh cheese and a castle which is second only in size to Windsor.

5. A popular blend of tea and the politician who succeeded Charles James Fox as leader of the Whig party in 1806.

6. A parrot in Treasure Island and a character in the 'Swallows & Amazons' books.

7. A sweet plum and a London railway terminus.

8. A top London hotel overlooking Hyde Park and a market town of Dorset.

9. A small beetle and a children's publisher.

10. An extract of beef and the Grand National winner of 1959.

11. A public school dating from 1615 and a London borough.

12. Nickname of a 'Spice Girl' and the nickname of Peterborough United.

13. A novel by Sir Walter Scott and a Scottish football team.

14. A woman's large hat named after a character from a Dickens novel and a flowered dress.

15. A character in 'Jane Eyre' and a city on the river Medway.

16. A peer of the realm and a turboprop civil aircraft.

17. The first speech of an MP in the House of Commons and an Iron Age fort in Dorchester.

18. The county town of West Sussex and the man knighted with the sword of Francis Drake after his solo round the world voyage.

19. Nickname of the football team who play at Meadow Lane and another who play at St. James' Park.

20. The witch in Burn's 'Tam O'Shanter' and a tea and wool clipper ship.

1. Which U.K. International airport is known by the code MME?

2. How many Pilgrim Fathers sailed from Plymouth to Massachusetts in 1620 to found the first New England colony?

3. Which cathedral has three spires named 'The Ladies of the Vale'?

4. Which character from a children's series owned a yacht known as 'FAB 2?

5. Name the largest British bird.

6. Name the only Archbishop of Canterbury to write an autobiography.

7. On which motorway would you travel from Manchester to Hull?

8. Which Yorkshireman designed the Royal Mews in Trafalgar Square, the Treasury buildings and the Horse Guards block in Whitehall (1745)?

9. Which organisation is known by its initials DEFRA?

10. What do David Bowie, Shirley Bassey, Ron Moody and Stephen Hawking have in common?

11. Which poets dying words were: "Is that you Dora?"?

12. Name the Army's officer training school

13. Which Londoner's operas include 'Therese' (1979) and 'Mary of Egypt' (1992)?

14. What is the meaning of the internet abbreviation TPTB?

15. The largest colony of which of Britain's seabirds is found on St. Kilda, West of the Outer Hebrides?

16. Who was Britain's first Christian martyr?

17. Name the largest railway station in the U.K.

18. Name Steve McQueen's final film of 1980.

19. In March 2001, The Post Office changed its name to what?

20. Who is known by the catchphrase 'booyakasha!'?

1. Which British bird has the largest egg?

2. Which British conductor commented "The English may not like music - but they absolutely love the noise it makes"?

3. Name the British writer who took her nom de plume from the heroine of Ibsen's 'Rosmersholm' (1886).

4. Which rock star when asked why he wore so many rings on his fingers replied, "Because I can't get them through my nose"?

5. Which radio programme's panel of experts were Fred Loads, Bill Sowerbutts and Professor Alan Gemmell?

6. 'Gather ye rose-buds while ye may' is the opening line of whose poem?

7. Which politician coined the phrase the 'Gnomes of Zurich'?

8. Which writer and caricaturist did Bernard Shaw refer to as the 'incomparable Max'?

9. 'Their's not to reason why' is a line from which poem?

10. What is Glayva?

11. Which Jack Higgins novel concerned a wartime plot to assassinate Churchill?

12. Name the child murderer who in a statement to the police in 1968 said; "Murder isn't that bad. We all die sometime".

13. Whose first novel was entitled 'Mary Barton: a Tale of Manchester Life' (1848)?

14. What colour is the Welsh dragon?

15. "A man falls in love through his eyes. A woman through her ears", so said which British politician and author in 1981?

16. Who wrote the romantic novel 'Trilby'?

17. Which document is issued to anyone registered as unemployed?

18. Where in the Caribbean did Princess Margaret have a home?

19. Where is the 'Pebble Mill' radio and television studio?

20. Which Irish playwright referred to P.G. Wodehouse in 1941 as 'English literature's performing flea'?

THE FOLLOWING ALL CONCERN 'NATIONAL INSTITUTIONS'

1. Location of the National Railway Museum.

2. State scheme providing old-age pensions and sickness and support for families.

3. Area given the status of a National Park in 1992?

4. Directors have included Peter Hall and Richard Eyre.

5. Total amount of money borrowed at any time by the government.

6. Location of the National Exhibition Centre.

7. New government department set up in 1992, nicknamed the 'Ministry of Fun'.

8. Organisation founded in the East End of London in 1956 by Michael Croft.

9. Britain's foremost conservation body.

10. Building adjacent to the National Gallery designed by Ewan Christian.

11. Location of the National Museum of Photography, Film and Television.

12. Established by Act of Parliament in 1934 and opened in 1937 in the Queen's House.

13. Body set up in 1962, bringing together government, management and trade unions to discuss matters of economic growth.

14. Britain's largest art charity founded in 1903.

15. Stately home location of the National Motor Museum.

16. Organisation founded in 1947 by Ruth Railton for teenagers.

17. Location of the custom-built National Army Museum (1971).

18. Group of ten 'foundation' subjects established by Act of Parliament 1988.

19. National Horseracing Museum was opened in the Regency Subscription Rooms in 1983 in which town?

1. Name the ventriloquist's dummy you would associate with the name of Peter Brough and Max Bygraves.

2. Which British writer coined the phrase and book title 'The Rise of the Meritocracy'?

3. Which British theatre manager's slogan of the Windmill Theatre 1939-45 was 'We Never Closed'?

4. Name the disc jockey who compered 'Ready, Steady, Go'.

5. Name the character Marlon Brando played in 'On The Waterfront'.

6. Which divorcee did Princess Margaret wish to marry in 1953?

7. Which British scientist commented, "A genius is a man who has two great ideas"?

8. Name the most common British bird.

9. Who in 1905 wrote the hugely successful 'The Four Just Men' and went on to write a further 170 books, 17 plays and a regular horseracing column for the newspapers?

10. In which TV programme would you hear the line '... to boldly go where no man has gone before....'?

11. On its first publication, 'The Well of Loneliness' was banned for obscenity. Who was its author?

12. Which comedian commented in 1977 "That's what show business is - sincere insincerity"?

13. Born John Ravenscroft in 1939, by what name was this disc jockey more commonly known?

14. Name the British architect whose crusading zeal on behalf of modern architecture earned him the nickname 'Saint Basil'.

15. Which playwright reflecting on death in his sixties' play wrote "The bad end unhappily, the good unluckily. That's what tragedy means"?

16. Which snooker player won the European Open Championship in 1989 and again in 1990 and followed it with the Embassy World Professional Championship in 1991?

17. What is the Scottish name for Lowlands?

18. What is the meaning of HMV?

19. What is the official name of the Royal Court of Britain?

20. Who at the London Palladium in 1963 said, "Will people in the cheaper seats clap your hands? All the rest of you, if you'll just rattle your jewelry":

POT LUCK 32

1. Complete the following slogan, which is a summary of the private soldier's best policy - 'If it moves, salute it; ....'

2. The jockey Mark Dwyer rode which two horses to victory in the 1985 and 1993 Cheltenham Gold Cup?

3. What was the stage name of Ronald Wycherley 1941-83?

4. 'Awakenings' and 'The Man who Mistook His Wife for a Hat' are works by which neurologist?

5. Identify the classic TV series from the line "I am not a number - I am a free man!"

6. Name the famous herd of wild white cattle, which take their name from a castle in Northumberland where they have lived for 700 years.

7. Name the British actor and comedian who said in 1980 "There used to be a me, but I had it surgically removed".

8. Who was Lloyd George referring to when he remarked "When they circumcised him, they threw the wrong part away"?

9. Name the British sexologist who wrote a no-nonsense DIY sex manual entitled 'The Joy of Sex'.

10. Which author created the academic Philip Swallow of Rummidge University?

11. Who famously said in 1966, "Christianity will go. It will vanish and shrink...... We're more popular than Jesus now. I don't know which will go first - rock and roll or Christianity"?

12. Name the British psychiatrist whose first major work was 'The Divided Self'.

13. By what name was the British writer Hector Hugh Munro more commonly known?

14. Who played Jack & Harriet Boult in the TV drama series 'Forever Green'?

15. What is the meaning of the abbreviation NAAFI?

16. In which city did the first National Garden Festival take place in 1984?

17. Who was the first Secretary of State for the Department of National Heritage, set up in 1992?

18. Name the Cathedral town on the river Usk in Gwent.

19. On New Year's Eve crowds gather in which square in Glasgow?

20. Name the Edinburgh- born actress who played Thelma in 'Whatever Happened to the Likely Lads?'.

1. Who are referred to as SLF?

2. 'The most FANTASMAGORICAL stage musical in the history of everything!" proclaims the publicity for which musical?

3. In which Alan Ayckbourn comedy do a young woman and her friend embark on a desperate plan to save their upmarket lifestyle?

4. Name the area of England associated with the 'Five Towns'.

5. What name is given to the period of architecture 1603-25?

6. Who won the Whitbread prize for his autobiography 'Under the Eye of the Clock'?

7. Name Britain's leading dealers in stamps whose annual catalogue is the Philatelist's bible.

8. In what year were the railways nationalised?

9. 'The Times' leader of 11 June 1963, declared, 'It is a moral issue'. What was it referring to?

10. Where in Britain could you ride on the Pepsi Max Big One?

11. What title did Harold Macmillan take?

12. The archaeologist Howard Carter declared in 1923, "Surely never before in the whole history of excavation has such an amazing sight been seen". What was he referring to?

13. The film 'Blind Flight' (2003) concerned the captivity of which two men?

14. In what year did the Brighton bombing at the Grand Hotel take place?

15. Who wrote the multi-award winning play 'Democracy'?

16. In which town would you locate the RHS garden of Harlow Carr?

17. Name the rail union in Britain.

18. What do Liz McColgan, Paul Gascoigne and Fatima Whitbread have in common?

19. What was Betty Boothroyd's earlier occupation prior to 'Speaker of the Commons'?

20. What is William Grundy's occupation on radios 'The Archers'?

1. Name the former head of MI5 whose first novel 'At Risk' was published in 2004.

2. Which British University conferred an honorary doctorate on Bob Dylan in June 2004?

3. Name the architect who you would associate with the iconic apartment building Montevetro in Battersea.

4. Who voiced the courtier bird Zazu in the film of 'The Lion King'?

5. Which epic vengeance thriller of 2004, directed by Tony Scott, starred Denzel Washington?

6. Name Sir Paul McCartney's youngest child.

7. What are 'Samurai', 'Dragon's Fury' and 'Spinball Whizzer'?

8. 'The Big Chill' music festival celebrated its tenth birthday in 2004. Where is it held?

9. Name the capital of the island of Mull.

10. Which musical is billed 'A mother. A daughter. Three possible dads. And a trip down the aisle you'll never forget!?

11. Which agony aunt's autobiography was entitled 'How did I get here from there'?

12. Its highlights include St. Boniface Kirk, one of the oldest Christian sites in Scotland and the knap of Howar, the oldest house in Western Europe. Where are you?

13. Where are the headquarters of Aston Martin vehicles?

14. 'A Chef For All Seasons', 'Just Desserts' and 'Secrets' are books by which chef?

15. Who was Harold Macmillan referring to when he said 'He is forever poised between a cliché and an indiscretion'?

16. Name the writer who joined Queen to produce the musical 'We Will Rock You'.

17. What do Leslie Crowther, The Krankies, Ed Stewart, Michael Aspel and Stu Francis have in common?

18. Name the English dancer who, with Markova formed several companies, the most notable becoming the English National Ballet.

19. Who established himself as the ideologist of the Labour Party's social democratic wing with the publication of the book 'The Future of Socialism'?

20. What name is given to the events in Ireland between 24-29 April 1916?

THE ANSWERS TO ALL OF THE FOLLOWING QUESTIONS CONTAIN THE WORD 'BRITISH'

1. The national airline of Britain.

2. Local time in the UK from the last Sunday in March to the Sunday following the fourth Saturday in October.

3. National collection of antiquities is found in this building which dates from 1753.

4. Alberto Ascari, Jim Clark and Carlos Reutemann all won this race

5. Motor manufacturing group formed in 1968

6. Name used for the first British army sent to the continent in each of the World Wars

7. Independent airline, formed in 1970, taken over in 1987

8. Name for the Falkland Islands

9. Body established after World War I to represent the interests of ex-service men and women

10. Designed by Eric Bedford and stands 580 feet high

11. Order of chivalry, known as the BEM

12. Colony also known as Belize

13. Name of the store first opened in 1928 as a more up-market Woolworths

14. A neo-Nazi party

15. Independent public body with the purpose of representing British culture abroad

ROYALTY
&
TRADITION

1. Name the largest castle in Wales.

2. What title did George Thomas, the Speaker of the House of Commons become known by?

3. Which King died on the toilet?

4. Who wrote the biography, 'Diana: Her True Story'?

5. In 1993 it was announced that Buckingham Palace would be opened for tourists, the money being used to pay for the fire damage to Windsor Castle. What was the charge for entry?

6. Who did Princess Alexandra marry on 24th April 1963?

7. Name Prince Philip's father.

8. Who did the Liberal leader, Jeremy Thorpe marry in March 1973?

9. Who was the first royal to abdicate?

10. In what year were £10 bank notes first issued?

11. The Prince of Wales escaped death in a skiing accident in 1988. Name the member of the royal party, a former equerry to the Queen, who was killed in the avalanche.

12. Balliol, Merton and Brasenose are colleges of which university?

13. Who was murdered in Berkeley Castle, possibly with a red-hot poker, at the instigation of his wife Isabella and her lover Roger de Mortimer?

14. In which year did Queen Elizabeth II give birth to her third son?

15. Prince Charles and Lady Diana Spencer announced their engagement in February 1981. How old was the prince at this time?

16. Old Boys of which school are known as Old Alleynians?

17. Lord Mountbatten was killed by an IRA bomb in which year?

18. Who was the first member of the royal family to become a Roman Catholic in modern times (1994)?

19. What are Prince Andrew's other Christian names?

20. At the Queen's Golden jubilee concert at Buckingham Palace, Sir Paul McCartney closed the proceedings with which song?

1. Ian Ball attempted to kidnap which royal in 1974?

2. Which King did HenryIV of France refer to as the 'wisest fool in Christendum'?

3. Who was Prince Philip's mother?

4. Name the palatial mansion in the stable yard of St James's Palace, which takes its current name in honour of Lord Leverhulme's county of birth.

5. Name the Scottish school attended by Princes Charles, Andrew and Edward.

6. Who was the first Royal to marry a commoner?

7. Which King was nicknamed 'Farmer George'?

8. Which royal did the Honourable Serena Stanhope marry?

9. When was the coronation of Queen Elizabeth II?

10. Name the five Royal Dukes.

11. Who did George VI marry?

12. What is Princess Anne's Gloucestershire address?

13. Name Britain's oldest regiment.

14. Which royal married Birgitte Eva Van Deurs?

15. Which royal holds the titles of Earl of Inverness and Baron Killyleagh?

16. Name the oldest royal residence.

17. What title do the wives of knights, baronets and barons use?

18. Who did Prince Edward marry on 19th June 1999?

19. Which town in Warwickshire was designated a royal spa in 1838?

20. Lady Davina and Lady Rose are the daughters of which royal?

1. What do you have to do to get the 'gift of the gab'?

2. Who said, "He speaks to me as if I were a public meeting"?

3. In the nursery rhyme, on what day did Solomon Grundy marry?

4. Who became King of Scotland in 1057 on the death of Macbeth?

5. Who was born at 17 Brunton Street, London on 21 April 1926?

6. Who was the eldest son of Victoria and Albert?

7. In what year did Prince Andrew and Sarah Ferguson marry?

8. What name is given to the assembly of bishops in the world-wide Anglican Communion under the chairmanship of the Archbishop of Canterbury?

9. The actress Lillie Langtry became the mistress of which royal?

10. Which city became home of the Royal Armouries in 1996?

11. Who was the first member of the British Royal Family since henry VIII to divorce?

12. Name the sovereign's mounted bodyguard.

13. Which monarch made cricket illegal in 1477?

14. 'A Royal Duty' was which butler's story of his relationship with Princess Diana?

15. Where did Queen Victoria die?

16. What relationship is Princess Alexandra to the current Queen?

17. Give Princess Anne's full Christian names.

18. The royal christening robe is made from what type of lace?

19. What is the courtesy title for the sons and daughters in the peerage?

20. Name the Queen's official residence in Edinburgh.

1. 'Grey', 'Hatfield', St. Chad's, and 'Van Mildert', are colleges of which university?

2. Which royal died peacefully in her sleep at 6.30 a.m. on February 9 2002, in the King Edward VII Hospital, London?

3. The birth of a royal infant is marked by a gun-salute at the Tower of London and Hyde Park. How many guns salute?

4. Born 23 June 1894, he became known as the 'People's King'. Name him.

5. Name Prince Andrew's Ascot address.

6. What name is given to the Act which bars Catholics from succession to the throne?

7. Lord Frederick Michel George David Louis Windsor is the eldest child of which Prince?

8. In which year did Princess Anne take the title Princess Royal?

9. Which royal died of smallpox at Kensington on 28 December 1694?

10. Which university did Prince William attend?

11. Which king traditionally burnt the cakes?

12. Name Prince Charles' Gloucestershire home.

13. Who was the last Roman Catholic monarch?

14. Name the ancestral home in Scotland of the Earl of Strathmore

15. Which King in 1533 organised the dissolution of the monasteries?

16. Name the Scottish castle, which was used as an island prison for Mary Queen of Scots in 1567.

17. What is Prince Harry's full Christian name?

18. Which grandson of George V has three children, Alexander, Davina and Rose?

19. Which royal ceremony has its roots in a medieval church ritual commemorating the Last Supper and the washing of his disciples' feet by Jesus?

20. By what title is the Prince of Wales officially known when in Scotland?

1. Which royal lives at Bagshot Park, Surrey?

2. Who are the Crown jewellers?

3. Who became Archbishop of Canterbury in 2002?

4. Which female is fifth in line in the order of succession to the British throne?

5. Which Lady created the character 'Jemima Shore'?

6. Which royal was killed in 1972 when his Piper Cherokee aircraft crashed during the Goodwood Trophy air race?

7. In what year was the Royal Yacht Britannia launched?

8. Who was the last Sovereign to be buried in Westminster Abbey?

9. In what year did the Duke of Windsor die?

10. Name the four Inns of Court at London.

11. Which royal said in 1977 "When I appear in public, people expect me to neigh, grind my teeth, paw the ground and swish my tail - none of which is easy"?

12. Which classic British car was promoted in 1958 with the slogan, 'At 60 miles an hour the loudest noise in this new .... comes from the electric clock'?

13. Wren House, Palace Green, London, is the address of which royal?

14. Who reigned for 77 days in 1483?

15. What date is Grandparent's Day in the UK?

16. Finish the slogan campaign of 1954, 'Top People Take ....'.

17. Which Queen was rumoured to have an extra breast and extra finger?

18. Which royal was nicknamed 'Dickie'?

19. What is the equivalent rank in the navy to Field Marshall?

20. Which British aristocrat said of David Lloyd George in her autobiography of 1927, "He could not see a belt without hitting below it"?

KINGS & QUEENS
NAME THE FOLLOWING;

1. The first Plantagenet King of England.

2. He was nicknamed Rufus after his ruddy complexion.

3. Less than a year old when he became King of England and just over a year when he became King of France.

4. He was a Knight of the last Crusade of 1270.

5. Forced to abdicate because of his Catholic sympathies; he was succeeded by William of Orange.

6. She ruled for 9 days and was beheaded on 12 February 1554.

7. He came to the throne after his mother, Mary Queen of Scots, was forced to abdicate.

8. He had long periods of insanity and is said to have fathered a child with Hannah Lightfoot.

9. She said that when she died, Calais would be found writ on her heart.

10. He was called the Sailor King.

11. He became Governor of the Bahamas in World War II.

12. He had a famous victory at Agincourt in 1415.

13. In 1301, he became the first English Prince of Wales.

14. He was excommunicated by Pope Innocent III in 1209.

15. He was the first Tudor monarch of England.

16. She set up a fund to benefit the poorer clergy in 1704.

17. The first monarch to live in Buckingham Palace.

18. He played in the Wimbledon Championships of 1926.

19. He was cited in a divorce scandal in 1870.

20. He instigated the Christmas Day broadcast to the nation in 1932.

1. What is the familiar name for the 'Peerage and Baronetage' which is a reference work on Britain's titled families?

2. Which formal ceremony is held every morning in the forecourt of Buckingham Palace?

3. Name Princess Ann's two children.

4. Who in the House of Commons is appointed to keep party discipline and encourage active support for the party and its policies?

5. In which palace was Queen Victoria born?

6. Name Britain's oldest Sunday newspaper, founded in London in 1791 by the Irishman W.S. Bourne.

7. Name the property Queen Victoria purchased on the Isle of Wight, which she described as "a place of one's own, quiet and retired".

8. Which coin was given to each new recruit in the British army until 1879 and became a term for enlisting?

9. Which phrase is used to mean the length and breadth of the land?

10. The Babington Plot was an incompetent conspiracy to assassinate whom?

11. Where did the second marriage of the Princess Royal take place in 1992?

12. Name the two luxury liners built by Cunard in the 1930's, each launched by a queen and named after her.

13. Which former BBC Royal Correspondent displayed nerves of steel in TV's 'I'm A Celebrity Get Me Out Of Here'?

14. Who married the second son of George V in Westminster Abbey in 1923?

15. Who was the first king of the House of Lancaster

16. Which government department, formed in 1964, is responsible for the armed forces?

17. Which aristocratic photographer, born 1939, made his reputation from royal photographs and his nude calendars?

18. Which royal is President of Save the Children Fund?

19. Who was the last British sovereign to lead an army into battle?

20. What is the actual date of the Queen's birthday?

NAME THE FOLLOWING WHOSE ANSWERS ALL BEGIN WITH THE WORD 'ROYAL'

1. Britain's oldest museum.

2. This organisation's first home was in Somerset House and is now in Burlington House.

3. Golf course in Lancashire founded in 1886.

4. Annual show to raise funds for the Entertainment Artiste's Benevolent Fund.

5. Adrian Noble followed Trevor Nunn as artistic director of this enterprise.

6. Golf club at St. Andrews.

7. The final stage in the passage of a bill before it becomes an Act of Parliament.

8. Established in 1828 by the surgeon William Marsden.

9. Traditionally, the central trading place for London's merchants and bankers.

10. Institution founded in 1830, which has sponsored expeditions since its inception.

11. One of the oldest units in the armed forces, formed in 1664, as 'land soldiers prepared for sea service'.

12. Annual showjumping competition first staged at Olympia in 1907.

13. Forces known in World War II as the 'Wavy Navy'.

14. Pressure group founded in Manchester in 1889 by Mrs Robert Williamson and a group of ladies who pledged not to wear feathers in their hats.

15. An appointment as supplier of goods to the immediate Royal Family.

16. Military display now held in Earl's Court.

17. Walter Welles became musical director in 1992.

18. Formed in 1939 to combine the mechanised units of the army under central control.

19. A theatre in the round in Manchester.

20. Established at Greenwich by Charles II in 1675.

1. What was Princess Diana's name and title before her marriage to Prince Charles?

2. Who gave birth to the future Edward VI in October 1537 and died 12 days later?

3. How many sides has a 50p?

4. Which government department collects VAT?

5. Which school did Henry VI found as a preparatory school for King's College, Cambridge in 1440?

6. Who became engaged to Princess Margaret in 1960?

7. Who was Speaker of the House of Commons before Betty Boothroyd?

8. Who was the father of Mary Queen of Scots?

9. Give Prince William's other two Christian names.

10. Who summons the Commons to join the Lords to hear the Queen's Speech?

11. Name the stately home of the Duke of Bedford.

12. Which duke sold Raphael's masterpiece 'The Madonna of the Pinks' for £22 million (it now can be seen in the National Gallery)?

13. Which royal is portrayed in artist Graham Dear's work 'Refugee from England?

14. Which London street do you associate with Asprey the jeweller?

15. Which Earl wrote a book about the Duke of Marlborough's victory at Blenheim?

16. The White Lion is a popular pub name. It is named after whose heraldic symbol?

17. Which Welsh castle was Edward II born in on 25 April 1284?

18. Which royal married Daniel Chatto?

19. Which King was known as 'Old Rowley'?

20. King George VI died in 1952 of what complaint?

1. Name the music festival in Suffolk, which was started by Benjamin Britten in 1948?

2. In Scotland, what is the title given to the leader or hereditary head of a clan?

3. Which grandson of George V married Marie-Christine von Reibritz, a divorcée and Roman Catholic, in 1978?

4. What was the London residence of the Queen Mother?

5. Which former member of the Royal Family became a spokeswoman for Weight Watchers?

6. Who is the religious head of the Church of England?

7. What festival day for Christians is celebrated on the 40th day after Easter?

8. Which young royal created interest when she had her tongue pierced?

9. Who was Disraeli referring to when he said "everyone likes flattery and when it comes to royalty, you should lay it on with a trowel"?

10. 'Zadok the Priest' was written for the coronation of George II and has been performed at every coronation since. Who composed it?

11. The Duke of Rutland inherited his title and which castle in 1999?

12. Which Norman Castle has been the seat of the Percy family since 1309?

13. What name is given to the representative of the sovereign in a county?

14. Who was the monarch from 1910-1936?

15. What royal occasion took place on 6 September 1997 in Westminster Abbey?

16. Name the Scottish Quarter Days of 28 February/28 May/28 August/28 November.

17. The mnemonic 'Did Mary ever visit Brighton Beach' is used to remember the order of nobility. Name them in order.

18. Which royal has been nicknamed 'Princess Pushy'?

19. Which royal married Mrs. Maria Fitzherbert?

20. Name Prince Andrew's daughters.

1. Name the designers who made the wedding dress of Diana, Princess of Wales

2. Which royal was fined £400 in March 2001 for driving a Bentley at 93 m.p.h. on the A417 dual carriageway?

3. Which royal did the Queen appoint to the exclusive Order of Merit on 26 June 2002?

4. What name is given to formal academic dress, especially at Oxford University?

5. Which King did James Hadfield attempt to assassinate in 1800?

6. Name Edward and Sophie Wessex's daughter.

7. Which reward for conspicuous bravery is the most highly coveted of British Military decorations?

8. Name the oldest city in the UK - its original charter being granted in 886.

9. Charles and Diana announced their separation and Windsor Castle was damaged by fire. What year was this?

10. Who, when faced with a barrage of questions during the Abdication Crisis of 1936 said, "My lips are sealed. I am bound to keep silence"?

11. In what year was the Cunard liner 'Queen Elizabeth II' launched?

12. What is the slang term used by British servicemen abroad to refer to Britain?

13. Complete the line, 'Land of Hope and Glory, Mother of the Free ....'

14. Who died after bearing the future Edward VI?

15. Who reputedly said, "You can never be too rich or too thin"?

16. In what year did Her Majesty Queen Elizabeth the Queen Mother die, aged 101?

17. What do Blenheim Palace, Hadrian's Wall, Stonehenge and the Giant's Causeway have in common?

18. Which King said, "Never miss an opportunity to relieve yourself; never miss a chance to sit down and rest your feet"?

19. Which city is referred to as the 'Queen of the North'?

20. Which journalist and broadcaster said of Edward VIII? "The most damning epitaph you can compose about Edward - as a prince, as a king, as a man - is one that all comfortable people should cower from deserving: he was at his best only when the going was good".

1. Who was known as the 'queen of people's hearts"?

2. What is meant by the term 'the fourth Estate'?

3. In what year did Princess Margaret divorce?

4. What are ceremoniously searched by the Yeoman of the Guard before the State Opening of Parliament?

5. Name the Derbyshire seat of The Duke of Devonshire.

6. Which common pub name is named after Richard II's heraldic symbol?

7. Who was executed at Fotheringhay Castle on 8 February 1587?

8. The mnemonic 'No plan like yours to study history wisely' is used to remember the British ruling houses. Name them.

9. In what year was the House Of Lords first televised?

10. Who was referred to in 'Private Eye' as Brenda?

11. By what brief name is David Albert Charles Armstrong Jones known?

12. Name Henry VIII's favourite ship which sank in 1545.

13. Which royal resigned from the Royal Marines on 12 January 1987?

14. Which building's extension was Prince Charles referring to when he described it as "a monstrous carbuncle on the face of a much-loved friend"?

15. Which year did the Queen describe as her 'Annus Horribilis"?

16. Who was Britain's first communist peer to sit in the House of Lords in 1963?

17. Which member of the Royal Family made an appearance in radio 4's 'The Archers' for a fashion show in 1984?

18. What was Prince Philip's name and title at the point of his engagement to Princess Elizabeth?

19. Which King's dying words were "It came with a lass and it will go with a lass"?

20. In what year did Queen Elizabeth II make her first Christmas speech?

1. Which royal founded Westminster school?

2. In which year did Princess Margaret marry?

3. Which royal ruled from 1727-60?

4. Which Queen's Consort's dying words were, "The executioner is, I believe, very expert; and my neck is very slender"?

5. Who was the first Prince of Wales?

6. Name Princess Anne's second husband.

7. Who was Lady Antonia Fraser's father?

8. Which British King married the German noblewoman Princess Adelaide of Saxe-Coburg Meiningen?

9. Which royal said, "I know I have the body of a weak and feeble woman, but I have the heart and stomach of a King"?

10. According to the rhyme, when did the Queen of Hearts make some tarts?

11. Who was the first Pope to visit Britain?

12. The Bishops' Wars of 1639-40 were provoked by which King's attempts to impose Anglicanism on Scotland?

13. Where is George VI buried?

14. Which royal's residence is Thatched House Lodge, Richmond Park, Surrey?

15. In what year did Prince Charles have the title Prince of Wales bestowed upon him?

16. What name is given to the royal allowance?

17. Which King was the father of two Queens?

18. Name the Archbishop of Canterbury who crowned Elizabeth II.

19. Which duke said, "Publish and be damned"?

20. Who is fourth in line of the order of succession to the British throne?

1. Which traditional song is especially sung as midnight strikes on New Year's Eve?

2. Name given to a stiff straw hat with a low, flat crown, straight brim and broad band around it, still worn at some public schools.

3. Who stole the tarts in the 'Queen of Hearts' nursery rhyme?

4. What is the schoolroom mnemonic for the fate in sequence of the wives of King Henry VIII?

5. According to tradition, a true Londoner is a person born within the sound of which bells?

6. The most effective way of giving money to charity, making the gift tax-free is known as what?

7. In which castle was Prince Charles; Prince of Wales invested in 1969?

8. What geographical feature has acquired great symbolic status as the first and last glimpse of England?

9. Whose feast day of July 15th is particularly associated with the weather?

10. Which trade union founded in 1922 comprises a range of industrial groups, including engineers, drivers, dockers and clerical workers?

11. In what year was Prince Harry born?

12. Which actress and royal mistress said, "Pray, good people, be civil, I am the Protestant whore"?

13. Two of the best known works of British genealogy take their name from their first author in 1826. Name him and them.

14. Which grandson of George V (and leading British Freemason) married Katharine Worsley in York Minster in 1961?

15. In which year did Edward VII come to the throne?

16. In which year did Princess Diana and Prince Charles divorce?

17. Name the home of the Marquess of Bath

18. In which castle was Mary Queen of Scots imprisoned when she first entered England?

19. What do Scots everywhere celebrate annually on January 25?

20. Who did George V marry in 1893?

SPORTS &
PASTIMES

1. In snooker, who won the women's Embassy World Champion title in 2002?

2. Name the Colonel, Professor and Reverend in Cluedo.

3. Name the National Centre for Mountain Activities in Gwynedd.

4. The names of the cricketers, Jack Hobbs, Jim Laker and Peter May are associated with which country cricket club?

5. Who won Rugby League's Challenge Cup in 1993?

6. Which snooker-based game show was hosted by Jim Davidson and John Virgo?

7. Which footballer joined Lindisfarne on their Top 10 hit of 1990?

8. Name the female presenter of TV's 'A Question of Sport'.

9. Which sports stadium was opened for the 1970 Commonwealth Games?

10. What name is given to the annual round of international matches in Rugby Union football between England, Ireland, Scotland, Wales, France and Italy?

11. In what year did the England World Cup Squad have a No. 2 hit with 'This Time (We'll Get It Right)/England We'll Fly the Flag'?

12. He began his career with Leicester City (1978-85), was briefly with Everton (1985-6), before joining Barcelona (1986-9). Name him.

13. What name is given to rugby teams representing the British Isles?

14. Name Edinburgh's oldest surviving football club, dating from 1874.

15. The swimmer, Sharon Davies was one of TV's Gladiators. What was her assumed name?

16. Which football club teamed up with The Boot Room Boyz on the 1996 hit 'Pass and Move'?

17. Name the four corners on a Monopoly board.

18. Name the goalkeeper who survived the Manchester United air disaster.

19. English cricketers Adam and Ben Hollioake were born in which country?

20. Which sports' commentators autobiography was entitled 'Unless I'm Very Much Mistaken'?

WHICH FOOTBALL LEAGUE CLUBS PLAY AT THE FOLLOWING GROUNDS?

1. Ewood Park

2. Reynolds Stadium

3. Dens Park

4. Bootham Crescent

5. Easter Road

6. The Stadium of Light

7. Gigg Lane

8. Vicarage Road

9. Prenton Park

10. Griffin Park

11. The Reebok Stadium

12. Whaddon Road

13. Molineux

14. Brunton Park

15. Ibrox Stadium

16. The Britannia Stadium

17. Deepdale

18. Kassam Stadium

19. Riverside Stadium

20. Balmoor Stadium

21. St. Mary's Stadium

22. Portman Road

23. Gayfield Park

24. London Road

25. Spotland

1. Which flat race for 3-yr. old colts and fillies is run over 1.5 miles at Epsom on the first Wednesday in June?

2. Name the location of the annual TT Races.

3. Where was the location of the first British Grand Prix in 1926?

4. Which figure skater won the European Championship, the World Championship and a gold medal in the Olympics in 1976?

5. Jackie Stewart won the World Championship in 1969, 1971 and 1973. Name the company he drove for.

6. Which sport do you associate with Welshman Dominic Dale?

7. Which annual event takes place on a course from Greenwich to the Mall?

8. The wealthiest man in Britain in 2004 is a hero to Chelsea fans. Name him.

9. With which team did David Coulthard begin his Formula 1 career in 1994?

10. Who is known as the 'Clones Cyclone'?

11. Which 40-1 outsider won the Grand National in 1995?

12. Who was the first Briton to win the coveted US Masters Championship title?

13. Who was the first woman to train a Grand National winner and with what horse?

14. Which sportsman says "bet you can't eat three" in a TV advertisement?

15. Which millionaire boxer promoters 'Fubu' clothing?

16. Which jockey rode the Derby winners Henbit (1980) and Nashwan (1989)?

17. Which athlete won the annual Woman of the Year Outstanding Achievement Award in October 2002?

18. Name the oldest professional football club in Britain.

19. Name the sport played for the Strathcona Cup.

20. Which sport do you associate with Neil Adams, Craig Fallon and Dave Starbrook?

1. Who is known as 'Chairman Mo' by Fulham F.C. fans?

2. He made his Formula 1 debut driving for Eddie Jordan in 1993, switched to Ferrari in 1996 and joined Jaguar in 2000. Name him.

3. Who rode Nashwan to win the Derby in June 1989?

4. Why was horse-racing suspended on 27 February 2001?

5. Who came second to Roger Bannister in the four-minute mile?

6. Which two horse races are referred to as the 'Spring Double'?

7. In Formula 1 motor racing, what is the meaning of the black flag?

8. How many hoops are used in croquet?

9. Who won the Super Heavyweight boxing gold medal for Britain in the 2000 Summer Olympics?

10. Which title did Gary Taylor take for Great Britain in 1993?

11. In bowls, who became the World Indoor Champion in 2002?

12. In darts, who sponsors the BDO World Championship?

13. By what nickname are Warrington Rugby League team known?

14. Name the three female characters in Cluedo.

15. Who won the title of European Footballer of the Year in 1966?

16. Scotland beat Sweden 6-5 in which world championships in 2002?

17. Where is the Welsh Grand National run?

18. Forthbank Stadium is the ground of which Scottish League club?

19. What was Harvey's occupation in the TV series 'Shine on Harvey Moon'?

20. Which Everton player won the 1986 Football Writers' Player of the Year Title?

SPORTING TROPHIES

1. Bologna Trophy

2. Westchester Cup

3. Talbot Handicap

4. Queen's Prize

5. America's Cup

6. Curtis Cup

7. Dewar Cup

8. George Hearn Cup

9. Camanachd Cup

10. Lonsdale Belt

11. Wyfold Challenge Cup

12. Queen Elizabeth II Cup

13. Ashes

14. Doggetts Coat & Badge

15. Harry Sunderland Trophy

16. Goldberg-Vass Memorial Trophy

17. Iroquois Cup

18. Henry Benjamin Trophy

19. Londonderry Cup

20. Calcutta Cup

1. Which boxer came out of retirement in 1992 to defeat Pierre Coetzer in what was seen to be an eliminator for another world title attempt?

2. Brian Gamlin, of Bury in Lancashire devised the scoring system of which popular game in 1896?

3. What name is given to the notorious sharp bend before the final straight on Epsom race course?

4. Colin Cowdrey, Leslie Ames and Alan Knott, were among which club's best-known players?

5. Sally Gunnell took Gold for Britain in the Barcelona Olympics of 1992 in which event?

6. Name the two most regular locations for Test Matches.

7. With which sport do you associate the name of Steve Backley?

8. Who in the 1982 Lada Classic, became the first man to achieve the perfect score of 147 while being televised?

9. The first Test Match was played in 1877 between England and which other team?

10. Name Scotland's oldest football club founded in 1867.

11. Known as 'The First Lady of Football', she became Managing Director of Birmingham City Football Club. Name her.

12. Which football club, formed in 1884, is known as the 'Rams'?

13. Which grey gelding had more than 30 victories as a steeplechaser, including the Cheltenham Gold Cup (1989) and the King George VI Chase three times (1986,88,89)?

14. Which boxer achieved fame at 21 years of age when he took Henry Cooper's British, Commonwealth and European titles in 1971, before losing them by the end of the year?

15. Which sport do you associate with the Grand Challenge Cup, first held in 1839?

16. In the 2000 Olympics, Denise Lewis won gold in which event?

17. In horse racing, what are known as the 'Autumn Double'?

18. Charlotte Brew achieved fame in 1977 when she became the first woman to do what?

19. What is the height of the stumps in cricket?

20. In which city did Roger Bannister run the first four-minute mile?

1. In track & field, what is the weight of the hammer?

2. What name is given in cricket to a googly bowled by a left-hander?

3. Which player won the 2001 Football Writer's Player of the Year?

4. Which sport is played for the Solheim Cup?

5. Which jockey rode 'Casual Look' to take the Oaks in 2003?

6. Who did Celtic beat to take the 2001 Scottish Cup final title?

7. Which classic horse race was inaugurated by Sir Charles Bunbury?

8. In motor racing, what is the meaning of the flag of yellow and red diagonal stripes?

9. In the Summer Olympics 2000, Stephanie Cook was the British Gold Medal winner in which event?

10. Who in 1966 became the first world champion in bowls?

11. Give the season for grouse shooting.

12. Which martial arts name can be translated as 'way of the empty hand'?

13. Which football club was the first to use artificial turf in 1981?

14. Name the four exercises for women in gymnastics.

15. Which sport has the largest pitch - 300 yds x 200 yds?

16. The origins of squash are associated with which school?

17. Name the six weapons in Cluedo.

18. Who were the presenters of TV's 'Fantasy Football'.

19. Who was the first Black English international football player?

20. Who won the title of European Footballer of the Year in 1964?

1. Name the events in the heptathlon.

2. Who won the cricketing County Championship in 2002?

3. What do the initials BDO stand for?

4. Which player won the Football Writers' Player of the year, for the second time in 1983?

5. What is the maximum number of clubs allowed in golf?

6. Who was the first jockey to be knighted?

7. In ten-pin bowling, what is the maximum score in one game?

8. Which TV series was set in Whitbury Newtown Leisure Centre?

9. Which football club was the founder of the Premier League in 1992?

10. What is the distance for the completion of a run in cricket?

11. Who won the World Professional Snooker Championship in 1986?

12. Name the national sports centre in Shropshire, run by the Sports Council.

13. Which competition equestrian event in October receives television coverage when it is staged at the Empire Pool, Wembley?

14. Which footballer had the first £1 million transfer in 1979?

15. Name the four stations on a Monopoly board.

16. What do the initials MCC stand for?

17. What name is the Tour of Britain cycle race more commonly known by?

18. Which racing motorist has the unique distinction of having been World Champion on two wheels and four?

19. What value has the scrabble tile J?

20. Who were Scottish Cup Final winners in 1982, 83, 84, 86 and 1990?

**WHO WERE THE DIVISION 1 FOOTBALL ENGLISH
LEAGUE WINNERS IN THE FOLLOWING DECADES?**

1. 1890

2. 1900

3. 1910

4. 1920

5. 1930

6. 1940

7. 1950

8. 1960

9. 1970

10. 1980

11. 1990

12. 2000

1. The annual Devizes-Westminster is a race in which sport?

2. In which race might you fall at Becher's Brook?

3. Which sport do you associate with the name the 'Royal and Ancient'?

4. In which month is Royal Ascot held?

5. What is the top score for a single dart?

6. Which flat race for 3-year-old fillies (over 1.5m) is held at Epsom in early June, three days after the Derby?

7. What is meant by an 'Old Firm Match'?

8. With which sport do you associate the names of Jonny Searle and Greg Searle?

9. Who won the 100m Gold for Britain in the 1992 Olympics?

10. The Uber cup is awarded to women in which sport?

11. In which year did Roger Bannister run the first four-minute mile?

12. Which sport is governed by the Queensberry Rules?

13. At the age of 24 she took on the 94-day solo Vendée Globe yacht race round the world. Name her.

14. Which athlete won gold at the 1986 Commonwealth Games in the 5000 metres?

15. Who won the World Professional Darts Championship five times in the eighties?

16. The G.Melville Clark Trophy is awarded to England's most successful club in which sport?

17. Who were Rugby League Challenge Cup winners 1988-1995?

18. In which Olympics Event did Jonathan Edwards take Gold in the year 2000?

19. Name the course where all of the Irish Classic horse races are run.

20. Who were Scottish League Champions in 2003 and what was the score?

WHAT ARE THE NICKNAMES OF THE FOLLOWING FOOTBALL LEAGUE CLUBS:

1. Albion Rovers

2. Ayr United

3. Birmingham City

4. Blackpool

5. Cowdenbeath

6. Cardiff City

7. Crew Alexandra

8. Crystal Palace

9. Darlington

10. Dundee Utd

11. Exeter City

12. Fulham

13. Falkirk

14. Grimsby Town

15. Hull City

16. Heart of Midlothian

17. Luton Town

18. Livingston

19. Northampton Town

20. Sheffield Wednesday

21. St. Johnstone

22. Stenhousemuir

23. Walsall

24. Wimbledon

25. York City

1. Where is the regular location for the British Motorcycle Grand Prix?

2. What is the national game of the republic of Ireland?

3. How many Lonsdale Belts did Henry Cooper win?

4. Opened in 1965 as Britain's first long distance walking route from the Peak District to the Scottish Borders. Name it.

5. Which country won Football's World Cup in 1978 and again in 1986?

6. Who won the Formula 1 World Car Championship in 1996?

7. Who were Rugby League Challenge Cup winners in 1996 and 97?

8. In which years has London hosted the Summer Olympic Games?

9. Name Scotland's national football stadium.

10. Name the two clubs who played in the final of football's FA Cup in 1997.

11. Which British ice skating duo won an Olympic Gold Medal in 1984?

12. The game of squash began at which public school in the first half of the nineteenth century?

13. Who in 1970, became the first British player to win the US Open for 70 years?

14. Who won the Scottish FA Cup in 1997?

15. 15 April 1989 saw Britain's worst sporting disaster when 96 were killed. Where was this?

16. Who was the first woman to sail single-handed round the world Sept 1977-June 1978?

17. Which daily newspaper founded in 1859 is primarily concerned with horse racing?

18. In which county is Lilleshall National Sports Centre?

19. Who were Football League Champions 1996-97?

20. Who was the first snooker player to make 147 in the World Championships?

NAME THE SPORTS PERSONALITIES WHO WROTE THE FOLLOWING AUTOBIOGRAPHIES:

1. Facing the Music (sporting pair)

2. Eye of the Tiger (boxing)

3. Courting Triumph (tennis)

4. The Good, the Bad and the Bubbly (football)

5. Born Lucky (horse racing)

6. Testing Times (cricket)

7. Taking on the World (sailing)

8. Safe Hands (football)

9. Glorious Uncertainty (horse racing)

10. Allis in Wonderland (golf)

11. Opening up (cricket)

12. Lions, Tigers & Roses (rugby)

13. Walking on Water : My Life (football)

CAN YOU IDENTIFY THE YEAR BY THE FOLLOWING EVENTS?

1. Len Hutton scored his 100th century; Randolph Turpin defeated Sugar Ray Robinson to take the World Crown; Richards rode his 200th winner of the season for the 7th season in succession.

2. John Francome entered a select club of jockeys on having ridden 1000 winners in hurdles and steeplechases; Daley Thompson retained his Decathlon title; Oxford won the Boat Race in a record 16mins 45 secs.

3. Football legend Bobby Moore died; Eamonn Martin won the 13th London Marathon, his first such race; The Grand National ended in chaos and officials declared the race void after demonstrators ran onto the course.

4. Joe Davis achieved snooker's first official highest break of 147; Newcastle United appeared in a record 10th FA Cup Final, beating Manchester City 3-1; Stirling Moss won his first Grand Prix, beating World Champion Fangio in the British Grand Prix.

5. The 200th Derby was won by Troy with the biggest winning margin in 54 years; Sebastian Coe completed a hat trick of athletics records, aged 22; Essex became County Cricket Champions for the first time.

6. Torvill & Dean won the British ice-dancing championship with nine perfect sixes for their free-style routine; Castleford thrashed Wigan 33-2 to win the Rugby League Regal Trophy; Sir Matt Busby died.

7. Liverpool won the League Championship for the tenth time; Manchester United beat Liverpool 2-1 in the FA Cup Final; Lester Piggott had his eighth Derby win on Minstrel.

8. West Ham beat Preston North End 3-2 to win the FA Cup Final; Jackey Scobie Breasley won the Derby at the 13th attempt on Santa Claus; Team Spirit won the Grand National at the fifth attempt.

9. Steve Davis beat Doug Mountjoy 18-12 to win the World Championship aged 23; Torvill and Dean won their first European title; the first woman cox in the history of the Boat Race, steered her crew to victory.

10. Wolverhampton Wanderers beat Blackburn Rovers 3-0 in the FA Cup Final; Francis Chichester set a new record for crossing the Atlantic solo in Gypsy Moth II; Lester Piggott won his 1000th race.

1. Which boxer's autobiography was entitled Zero to Hero?

2. Which 800 metres Commonwealth Gold medallist was barred for four years after failing a drug test in December 1994?

3. Which jockey achieved a record 200 victories in a season in 1989?

4. Which sport do you associate with the names Trina Gulliver and Mandy Solomons?

5. Who became the fastest woman and youngest person to circumnavigate the world in a single-handed race when she finished second in the 24,000 mile Vendée Globe race in 2001?

6. In which game is a player out if struck by a thrown ball when running between bases?

7. What is the weight of the men's and women's discus in kg.?

8. On what race course is the Scottish Grand National run?

9. In the 2000 Summer Olympics, Jason Queally won Gold for Britain in which sport?

10. Who were Rugby League Challenge Cup winners in 2001?

11. The official title of which sporting trophy is The International Men's Team Championship of the World?

12. What is meant by the sporting term 'a garryowen'?

13. Mississippi, sans égal and cannon game are all variations of which game?

14. In men's gymnastics, six exercises are used. Name them.

15. In 2002, Samantha Lowe was British Open Champion in which Sport?

16. Which Rugby League team are nicknamed Chemics?

17. Which rugby commentator's voice became synonymous with the phrase 'up and under'?

18. Who was the first professional footballer to be knighted, and in what year?

19. Who became Wimbledon's Ladies Champion in 1977?

20. Who was the reigning Embassy World Darts Champion, who on 7 January 2001, won his first round match, despite a 20-minute interruption for a female streaker?

IN THE GAME OF BINGO WHAT NUMBERS WOULD YOU ASSOCIATE WITH THE FOLLOWING CALLS?

1. Jump and Jive

2. Harry Tate

3. Sunset strip

4. Torquay in Devon

5. Tom's tricks

6. Royal Salute

7. Bull's eye

8. Christmas cake

9. Doctor's orders

10. Bang on the drum

11. Gandhi's breakfast

12. Time for fun

13. End of the line

14. Rise and Shine

15. Winnie the Pooh

16. Burlington Bertie

17. Was she worth it?

18. Debbie McGee

19. All but one

20. Tickety boo

1. Which team did Denis Law play with in the final year of his career (1973-4)?

2. Who gained her 5th London Marathon victory in the women's wheelchair race in 2001?

3. Name the UK's first motor racing circuit.

4. The Yeaden Memorial Trophy is awarded in which sport?

5. Who said, "There are two things no man will admit he can't do well: drive and make love".

6. Which footballer has a son by Jordan aka Katie Price?

7. Cyril Washbrook and Brian Statham are among which club's best known players?

8. Who was penalised two strokes in the final round of the 2001 British Open for having 15 clubs in his bag?

9. Name Britain's oldest and most prestigious rowing club, dating from 1818?

10. Which cricketer had a three-year gap in his Test career, the result of being banned after leading a rebel tour to South Africa in 1982?

11. Name the country ground of Gloucestershire Country Cricket Club.

12. Who overcame cancer and went on to win the Grand National on Aldanih in 1981?

13. From which game does the term 'grand slam' derive?

14. W.G. Grace is probably the best-known player in the history of cricket. What was his other profession?

15. Name Scotland's national stadium.

16. Which swimmer, born 1957 won the Gold medal in the 100m breaststroke in the 1980 Olympics?

17. Mike Hailwood won the Isle of Man Senior TT in 1979 riding for which team?

18. Name the two courses at Gleneagles.

19. Name the ground of Durham County Cricket Club.

20. What do the initial PDC stand for?

1. Goodwood's name is associated with horse racing. Which other sport was it associated with 1948-66?

2. Which horse won the Irish 1000 Guineas and the Oaks at Epsom in 2001?

3. Name the county ground of Leicestershire County Cricket Club.

4. Name the Queen Mother's horse, which collapsed on 50 yards from the winning post in the 1956 Grand National.

5. Which cross-country sport is also referred to as a paper chase?

6. With which club did Stanley Matthews play his first League game in 1931?

7. Which cricket commentators were affectionately known as 'Johnners' and 'Blowers'?

8. Name the Rugby Union Football club, formed in 1866 and based in Twickenham.

9. Name the three-day event rider who won individual bronze in the Olympics of 1984 and 88 and was also a member of the teams, which won Silver on these occasions?

10. Which 'royal' golf course on the West Coast of England was founded in 1897?

11. Name the world's oldest auction house for thoroughbred racehorses, which takes its name from its founder.

12. Which sport do you associate with the following names: Dave Ropner, Tom Pickering and Bob Nudd?

13. Who won Silver for Great Britain in the 400m in the 1996 Olympics?

14. Name the events of the decathlon.

15. Which county joined the other 17 cricketing counties in 1992?

16. Who was named European Footballer of the year 2001?

17. Who were runners-up to Rangers in the 2003 Scottish Cup Final?

18. Which golfer won the British Open in 1992?

19. Dettori won the St. Leger in 1995 and 1996 on which horses?

20. Which horse won the 2003 Grand National?

IN THE CGU NATIONAL LEAGUE, WHAT NICKNAMES ARE GIVEN TO THE FOLLOWING CRICKET TEAMS?

1. Derbyshire

2. Durham

3. Essex

4. Glamorgan

5. Gloucestershire

6. Hampshire

7. Kent

8. Lancashire

9. Leicestershire

10. Middlesex

11. Northamptonshire

12. Nottinghamshire

13. Somerset

14. Surrey

15. Sussex

16. Warwickshire

17. Worcestershire

18. Yorkshire

1. Name the events of the modern pentathlon.

2. Which team won the 2002 Benson & Hedges Cup?

3. Who was the 1997 News of the World Champion darts player?

4. Which creatures are the nicknames of the following football teams: Brentford, Bristol City and Derby County?

5. How many fences has The Grand National?

6. In Formula 1 motor racing, what colour flag is used to indicate danger and therefore no overtaking?

7. In which event did Louis Attrill take Gold for Britain in the 2000 Summer Olympics?

8. Which Arsenal player won, in 2002, Football Writers' Player of the Year award?

9. Which billiards player became the 1998 World Matchplay champion when he defeated Peter Gilchrist 8-5?

10. Sarah Clark, Georgina Singleton and Craig Fallon are top sportspeople in which sport?

11. Which scrabble tile has a value of 5?

12. Which footballer had the first £10 million transfer fee?

13. Which tennis player appeared in TV commercials in 2004 for Ariel Soap powder?

14. Which football club formed in 1867 is nicknamed the Owls?

15. Who won the World Professional Snooker championship in 1991?

16. In Monopoly, what is the most expensive property?

17. Who were runners-up to Chelsea in the 1998 European Cup Winners' Cup?

18. What colour jerseys do the Welsh Rugby Union team wear?

19. What score do you get from a Q or Z in Scrabble?

20. In which year did the Heysel Stadium disaster take place?

WHICH FOOTBALL CLUBS DO YOU ASSOCIATE WITH THE FOLLOWING MILLIONAIRES?

1. Trevor Hemmings

2. Harry Dobson

3. Steve Morgan

4. Brian Kennedy

5. Danny Fiszman

6. Stewart Milne

7. Paul Gregg

8. Sir Tom Farmer

9. Nigel Doughty

10. Sir Richard Storey

11. Jamie Moffat

12. Steve Gibson

13. Dave Allen

14. Fergus McCann

15. Simon Jordan

1. Which sport can be attributed to an English barrister named John MacGregor who founded the Royal Club for this sport in 1866?

2. Name the lightest boxing weight under WBC rules.

3. Name the heaviest weapon used in fencing.

4. Which British boxer, quoted in 1902 said, "The bigger they come, the harder they fall"?

5. Who wrote 'The Theory and Practice of Gamesmanship, or the Art of Winning Games without Actually Cheating'?

6. Which writer declared in 'The Sporting Spirit' (1945), 'Serious sport has nothing to do with fair play. It is bound up with hatred, jealousy, boastfulness, disregard for all rules and sadistic pleasure in witnessing violence: in other words, it is war minus the shooting"?

7. Which jockey rode Desert Orchid to victory in the 1989 Cheltenham Gold Cup?

8. Name the Scottish athlete who won the 100 metres in the 1982 Commonwealth Games and shared his 200 metres title in a dead heat with Mike McFarlane.

9. Name the national daily newspaper launched in 1986 as a rival to 'Sporting Life'.

10. Who was TV's 'Sports Personality of the Year' in 2001?

11. Who hosted 'Fantasy Football - Euro 2004'?

12. With which sport is the presenter Suzi Perry most associated?

13. Name the football team, who in 1988 had a Top 10 hit with 'Red Machine in Full Effect'.

14. Which light-hearted soccer quiz show has been presented by David Vine, Barry Davies and Stuart Hall?

15. Name the sportsman who took up residence in the 'Big Brother' house in the celebrity edition for Comic Relief in 2001.

16. Born Gwaun-cae-Gurwen in 1947, this rugby player was first capped for Wales aged 19. Name him.

17. Name the birthplace of Bobby Charlton.

18. Who was the English billiards and snooker champion who had made his first break of 100 aged 12.

19. Which sportsman was nicknamed 'Zap'?

20. Whose autobiography of 2003 was entitled, 'Flat Out, Flat Broke : Formula 1 the Hard Way'?

1. Name the three former England Managers who joined Des Lynam and Gabby Logan to present TV's Euro 2004

2. Who succeeded David Vine as presenter of 'A Question of Sport' in 1979?

3. Name the footballer whose autobiography was called 'After the Ball'.

4. Which famous road in London was closed on July 6 2004 to allow Formula One drivers to race along it?

5. Which sporting superstar, who is featured in advertisements for cosmetics, said about the England locker room in 2004, "People don't bat an eyelid about using moisturisers"?

6. Which sport featured in the sitcom. 'The Upper Hand'?

7. Which sport presenter's inspirational fight against cancer, was recognised with a new Award for Inspiration at the BBC's Sports Review of the Year ceremony in 1999?

8. Whose portrait at the Royal Academy in London had 'You Loosers' (sic) scrawled over it in retaliation for England's defeat in Euro 2004?

9. Who, in June 2004, became the youngest Wimbledon Champion since Martina Hingis?

10. Which sportsman was nicknamed 'The Long Fellow'?

11. Name the sports you would link to each of the following names: Martin Johnson, Colin Jackson, Alec Stewart and David James

12. This Scottish jockey, born 1942, had his first classic success on 'High Top' in the 2,000 Guineas (1972); won his first Derby on 'Troy '(1979), then on 'Henbit' (1980). Name him.

13. Who took the TV title of 'Sports Personality of the Year' in 2000?

14. Which football club did the Dutch international, Michael Reiziger sign up to in July 2004?

15. Who became Britain's youngest Formula 1 driver in 2000?

16. Name the course on which the 2004 Open Golf Championship was held.

17. Where is Sportcity Arena located?

18. What was the venue for the 2004 UK Download Festival which saw extreme BMX and Skateboarding action?

19. Name the teenager who Sir Geoff Hurst correctly tipped as the key player in England's Euro 2004 team.

20. Which football manager said, "Some people think football is a matter of life or death. I don't like that attitude. I can assure them it is much more serious than that"?

AUTHORS & LITERATURE 1/ANSWERS

1. PENGUIN

2. THE LAKE POETS

3. TUBERCULOSIS

4. TALBOT

5. MASQUUERADE

6. BILL CULLEN

7. THE TWO GENTLEMEN OF VERONA

8. JOANNE HARRIS

9. KATE ADIE

10. NORTHANGER ABBEY

11. REBECCA BY DAPHNE DU MAURIER

12. ANOREXIA

13. WILLIAM COWPER

14 THE LORD OF THE RINGS

15 BARONESS SUSAN GREENFIELD

16 ALZHEIMER'S DISEASE

17 THOMAS GRAY

18 THE IMPORTANCE OF BEING EARNEST

19 MIDDLEMARCH BY GEORGE ELIOT

20 MURDER IN THE CATHEDRAL

AUTHORS & LITERATURE 2/ANSWERS

1. JM BARRIE

2. PETER SHAFFER

3. ARNOLD WESKER

4. WILLY RUSSELL

5. BRIAN FRIEL

6. ALAN AYCKBOURN

7. JOHN GODBER

8. NOEL COWARD

9. RICHARD BRINSLEY SHERIDAN

10. JOHN OSBOURNE

11. TOM STOPPARD

12. ALAN BLESDALE

13. JOE ORTON

14. ALAN BENNETT

15. DYLAN THOMAS

16. GEORGE BERNARD SHAW

17. HAROLD PINTER

18. GORDON STEELE

19. OSCAR WILDE

20. BEN JOHNSON

AUTHORS & LITERATURE 3/ANSWERS

1. AGATHA CHRISTIE

2. PERSUASION

3. JOHN BURNINGHAM

4. THOMAS DE QUINCEY

5. WUTHERING HEIGHTS

6. A.S. BYATT

7. NICHOLAS NICKLEBY

8. THE TEMPEST

9. ANTHONY TROLLOPE

10. TERRY PRATCHETT

11. MACBETH

12. PUBLISHING

13. COLIN

14. ANNE FINE

15. LAURIE LEE

16. THE PILGRIM'S PROGRESS

17. EDNA O'BRIEN

18. JOHN MILTON

19. THORNFIELD

20. PRIDE AND PREJUDICE

AUTHORS & LITERATURE 4/ANSWERS

1. DR JEKYLL AND MR HYDE by Robert Louis Stevenson

2. SONS AND LOVERS by D. H. Lawrence

3. LITTLE LORD FAUNTLEROY by Frances Hodgson Burnett

4. LUCKY JIM by Kingsley Amis

5. THE MOONSTONE by Wilkie Collins

6. BARCHESTER TOWERS by Anthony Trollope

7. THE JUNGLE BOOK by Rudyard Kipling

8. GOODBYE, MR CHIPS by James Hilton

9. OF HUMAN BONDAGE by William Somerset Maugham

10. THE HITCHHIKERS GUIDE TO THE GALAXY by Douglas Adams

11. FAR FROM THE MADDING CROWD by Thomas Hardy

12. BRIDESHEAD REVISITED by Evelyn Waugh

13. TOM BROWN'S SCHOOLDAYS by Thomas Hughes

14. PICKWICK PAPERS by Charles Dickens

15. UNDER MILK WOOD by Dylan Thomas

16. REBECCA by Daphne du Maurier

17. GULLIVER'S TRAVELS by Jonathan Swift

18. MANSFIELD PARK by Jane Austen

19. THE PICTURE OF DORIAN GRAY by Oscar Wilde

20. TRISTRAM SHANDY by Laurence Stern

AUTHORS & LITERATURE 5/ANSWERS

1. JOHN KEATS

2. RUDYARD KIPLING

3. GEORGE ORWELL

4. DAVID LODGE

5. JOHN BUCHAN

6. JOHN GALSWORTHY

7. JEFFREY ARCHER

8. JOHN OSBORNE

9. RAYMOND BRIGGS

10. RODDY DOYLE

11. AGATHA CHRISTIE

12. GRAHAM GREENE

13. VIRGINIA WOOLF

14. JOANNA TROLLOPE

15. H.G. WELLS

16. TOM STOPPARD

17. D.H. LAWRENCE

18. FAY WELDON

19. ARNOLD BENNETT

20. ARTHUR CONAN DOYLE

AUTHORS & LITERATURE 6/ANSWERS

1. ALL'S WELL THAT ENDS WELL

2. THE TEMPEST

3. AS YOU LIKE IT

4. MACBETH

5. KING LEAR

6. OTHELLO

7. JULIUS CAESAR

8. THE TAMING OF THE SHREW

9. A MIDSUMMER NIGHT'S DREAM

10. MERCHANT OF VENICE

11. ROMEO AND JULIET

12. LOVE'S LABOUR'S LOST

13. MUCH ADO ABOUT NOTHING

14. HAMLET

15. TWELFTH NIGHT

16. ANTONY AND CLEOPATRA

17. RICHARD 111

18. THE TWO GENTLEMEN OF VERONA

19. THE COMEDY OF ERRORS

20. CYMBELINE

21. THE MERRY WIVES OF WINDSOR

22. TROILUS AND CRESSIDA

23. MEASURE FOR MEASURE

24. THE WINTER'S TALE

25. CORIOLANUS

AUTHORS & LITERATURE 7/ANSWERS

1. ALEXANDER POPE 'A LITTLE LEARNING'

2. WILLIAM SHAKESPEARE (A SONG SUNG IN ARDEN)

3. DEN JONSON 'TO CELIA'

4. DYLAN THOMAS

5. CHRISTOPHER MARLOW 'THE PASSIONATE SHEPHERD TO HIS LOVE'

6. A.A. MILNE 'THE KING'S BREAKFAST'

7. EDWARD LEAR 'THE JUMBLIES'

8. RUDYARD KIPLING 'THE HUMP'

9. LEWIS CARROLL 'THE LOBSTER QUADRILLE'

10. ROBERT BROWNING 'THE PIED PIPER OF HAMELIN'

11. ROBERT LOUIS STEVENSON 'HAPPY THOUGHT'

12. T.S. ELIOT 'THE SONG OF THE JELLICLES'

13. A.A. MILNE 'VESPERS'

14. WALTER DE LA MARE 'THE LISTENERS'

15. W.B. YEATS 'THE LAKE ISLE OF INNISFREE'

16. RUPERT BROOKE 'THE SOLDIER'

17. WILLIAM BLAKE 'THE TIGER'

18. ROBERT LOUIS STEVENSON FROM A RAILWAY CARRIAGE'

19. JOHN KEATS 'THERE WAS A NAUGHTY BOY'

20. CHARLES WESLEY 'GENTLE JESUS, MEEK AND MILD'

AUTHORS & LITERATURE 8/ANSWERS

1. RICHARD DUKE OF GLOUCESTER IN 'RICHARD III'

2. ROMEO IN 'ROMEO AND JULIET'

3. MALVOLIO IN 'TWELFTH NIGHT'

4. ARIEL IN 'THE TEMPEST'

5. HELEN IN 'ALL'S WELL THAT ENDS WELL

6. KING HARRY IN 'HENRY V'

7. MISTRESS QUICKLY IN 'HENRY IV PART 2'

8. ROSALIND IN 'AS YOU LIKE IT'

9. KING CLAUDIUS IN 'HAMLET'

10. CAESAR IN 'JULIUS CAESAR'

11. THE WITCHES IN 'MACBETH'

12. PORTIA IN 'THE MERCHANT OF VENICE'

13. MARIANA IN 'MEASURE FOR MEASURE'

14. RICHARD IN 'RICHARD II'

15. LYSANDER IN 'A MIDSUMMER NIGHT'S DREAM'

16. CLAUDIO IN 'MUCH ADO ABOUT NOTHING'

17. DEMETRIUS IN 'TITUS ANDRONICUS'

18. HOST IN 'THE TWO GENTLEMEN OF VERONA'

19. KATHERINE IN 'THE TAMING OF THE SHREW'

20. IAGO IN 'OTHELLO'

AUTHORS & LITERATURE 9/ANSWERS

1. PICKWICK PAPERS

2. HUGH LOFTING

3. DORCHESTER

4. SIR WALTER SCOTT

5. LICHFIELD

6. TED HUGHES

7. LEWIS CARROLL

8. ALDOUS HUXLEY

9. 84 CHARING CROSS ROAD

10. THE OOMPA-LOOMPAS

11. GREAT EXPECTATIONS

12. JOHN LE CARRE

13. THE FELLOWSHIP OF THE RING, THE TWO TOWERS, THE RETURN OF THE KING

14. ROBERT HERRICK

15. ALAN ALEXANDER

16. WINSTON CHURCHILL

17. EDWARD LEAR

18. LONGFELLOW

19. C.P. SNOW

20. LYNNE TRUSS

AUTHORS & LITERATURE 10/ANSWERS

1. BARBARA TAYLOR BRADFORD (A Woman of Substance)

2. FLAMINGOES

3. QUENTIN BLAKE

4. ALAN BENNET

5. NANA

6. JIMMY PORTER

7. THE WATER BABIES

8. LONDON & PARIS

9. PHYLLIS DOROTHY

10. MUCH ADO ABOUT NOTHING

11. IRENE

12. BROTHER & SISTER

13. KATE LONG

14. ANGEL CLARE

15. ROBERTA, PETER, PHYLLIS

16. RATS

17. MIDDLEMARCH

18. JOANNE ROWLING

19. MR. JONES

20. WUTHERING HEIGHTS

AUTHORS & LITERATURE 11/ANSWERS

1. JULIAN AND DICK

2. JANE AUSTEN

3. P.G . WODEHOUSE

4. 221B BAKER STREET

5. SHIRLEY HUGHES

6. A CHRISTMAS CAROL

7. RUTH RENDELL

8. HAWORTH

9. THACKERAY

10. DEERSTALKER

11. DANIEL DEFOE

12. RUDYARD KIPLING

13. MR BROWNLOW

14. GULLIVERS TRAVELS

15. DUSTMAN

16. THE RIVALS

17. A STATELY PLEASURE-DOME DECREE

18. THE MAYOR OF CASTERBRIDGE

19. ROGER HARGREAVES

20. COLD COMFORT FARM

AUTHORS & LITERATURE 12/ANSWERS

1. KING LEAR, HAMLET, OTHELLO, MACBETH.

2. SIR WALTER SCOTT

3. SECRETARY OF THE BANK OF ENGLAND

4. TENNYSON

5. GERVASE PHINN

6. REBUS

7. A SEVERE STAMMER

8. OLIVER TWIST by Charles Dickens

9. RICKY TOMLINSON

10. A STUDY IN SCARLET

11. A DIAMOND

12. FATHER BROWN

13. ANIMAL FARM by George Orwell

14. THE COMEDY OF ERRORS

15. LORD BYRON

16. WILFRED OWEN

17. COBWEB, MOTE, MUSTARD SEED, PEASE BLOSSOM

18. THE LADY OF SHALOTT

19. MUNCHAUSEN SYNDROME BY PROXY

20. DYLAN THOMAS

AUTHORS & LITERATURE 13/ANSWERS

1. FALSTAFF

2. SUICIDE - HE STABS HIMSELF

3. DENMARK

4. GERTRUDE

5. THOU ART MORE LOVELY AND MORE TEMPERATE

6. ARIEL

7. BALTHAZAR

8. 1564

9. ALL'S WELL THAT ENDS WELL

10. JAQUES

11. BIANCA

12. RICHARD III

13. CORDELIA

14. THE MERCHANT OF VENICE

15. THE MERRY WIVES OF WINDSOR

16. MESSINA IN SICILY

17. EMILIA

18. A MIDSUMMER NIGHT'S DREAM

19. JULIET IN ROMEO AND JULIET

20. CYMBELINE, KING OF BRITAIN

AUTHORS & LITERATURE 14/ANSWERS

1. AN IDEAL HUSBAND

2. CHESHIRE CAT (From Alice's Adventures in Wonderland)

3. KIDNAPPED

4. SHELLEY

5. THE OLD CODGERS

6. OLD POSSOM'S BOOK OF PRACTICAL CATS

7. JACK DAWKINS

8. LEN DEIGHTON

9. WALTER DE LA MERE

10. HELEN FIELDING

11. PAT BARKER

12. THE BIBLE AND THE COMPLETE WORKS OF SHAKESPEARE

13. WIMPOLE STREET

14. MARGARET DRABBLE

15. THE DIARY OF A NOBODY

16. IRIS MURDOCH

17. PRIDE AND PREJUDICE BY JANE AUSTEN

18. E.H .SHEPARD

19. BECKY SHARP

20. ANNE ROBINSON

AUTHORS & LITERATURE 15/ANSWERS

1. THE JUNGLE BOOKS by Rudyard Kipling

2. BALLET SHOE by Noel Streatfield

3. THE WATER BABIES by Charles Kingsley

4. THE ONE HUNDRED AND ONE DALMATIONS by Dodie Smith

5. CHITTY CHITTY BANG BANG by Ian Fleming

6. THE LION, THE WITCH AND THE WARDROBE by C.S. Lewis

7. THE TALE OF TWO BAD MICE by Beatrix Potter

8. THE HOBBIT AND LORD OF THE RINGS by J.R.R. Tolkien

9. WATERSHIP DOWN by Richard Adams

10. THE WILLIAM STORIES by Richmal Crompton

11. HARRY POTTER BOOKS by J.K. Rowling

12. PETER PAN by J.M. Barrie

13. TOM BROWN'S SCHOOLDAYS by Arthur Hughes

14. TREASURE ISLAND by R.L. Stevenson

15. DOCTOR DOOLITTLE by Hugh Lofting

16. THE HEART OF MIDLOTHIAN by Sir Walter Scott

17. THE WIND IN THE WILLOWS by Kenneth Grahame

18. THE TREASURE SEEKERS by E. Nesbit

19. CHARLIE AND THE CHOCOLATE FACTORY by Roald Dahl

20. THE BORROWERS by Mary Norton

AUTHORS & LITERATURE 16/ANSWERS

1. SIR JOHN BETJEMAN

2. THE SHELL SEEKERS

3. THE CAMOMILE LAWN

4. DAPHNE DU MAURIER

5. AGATHA CHRISTIE

6. JANE AUSTEN

7. RICHARD DODDRIDGE

8. R .F. DELDERFIELD

9. WESTWARD HO!

10. JOHN GAY

11. THE OLD CURIOSITY SHOP

12. JOHN BRAINE

13. ANITA BROOKNER

14. RICHARD HANNAY

15. BULL-DOG DRUMMOND

16. MURIEL SPARK

17. PETER PAN BY J.M .BARRIE

18. WAYNE SLEEP

19. HEFFALUMPS

20. WOMEN IN LOVE

AUTHORS & LITERATURE 17/ANSWERS

1. EVELYN WAUGH

2. H.G. WELLS (Kipps: the story of a simple soul)

3. OZ

4. PROFESSOR HENRY HIGGINS

5. TENNYSON (Charge of the Light Brigade.)

6. CARPENTER

7. COLERIDGE

8. CARTHORSE

9. SYLVIA PLATH

10. JANE, ELIZABETH, MARY, KITTY, LYDIA

11. BRIDESHEAD REVISITED

12. MISS ELIZABETH MAPP AND MRS EMMELINE 'LUCIA' LUCAS

13. ADRIAN HENRI, ROGER MCGOUGH, BRIAN PATTEN

14. ULYSSES

15. LYME REGIS

16. WINIFRED HOLTBY

17. HELEN FORRESTER

18. TENNYSON

19. NINA BAWDEN

20. BRIGHTON ROCK

AUTHORS & LITERATURE 18/ANSWERS

1. THE WINTER'S TALE ARCHIDAMUS.

2. MACBETH SPOKEN BY THE FIRST WITCH

3. THE MERCHANT OF VENICE SPOKEN BY ANTONIO

4. AS YOU LIKE IT SPOKEN BY ORLANDO

5. THE TWO GENTLEMEN OF VERONA SPOKEN BY VALENTINE

6. MUCH ADO ABOUT NOTHING SPOKEN BY LEONATO

7. ROMEO AND JULIET SPOKEN AS A PROLOGUE

8. TWELFTH NIGHT SPOKEN BY ORSINO

9. A MIDSUMMER NIGHT'S DREAM SPOKEN BY THESEUS

10. KING LEAR SPOKEN BY EARL OF KENT

11. THE COMEDY OF ERRORS SPOKEN BY EGEON

12. ALLS WELL THAT ENDS WELL SPOKEN BY DOWAGER COUNTESS OF ROUSSILLON

13. JULIUS CAESAR SPOKEN BY FLAVIUS

14. THE TEMPEST SPOKEN BY MASTER OF A SHIP

15. TROILUS AND CRESSIDA PROLOGUE

16. CYMBELINE, KING OF BRITAIN SPOKEN BY FIRST GENTLEMAN

17. ANTONY AND CLEOPATRA SPOKEN BY PHILO

18. HAMLET SPOKEN BY BERNARDO

19. LOVE'S LABOUR'S LOST SPOKEN BY K FERDINAND

20. THE MERRY WIVES OF WINDSOR SPOKEN BY SHALLOW

AUTHORS & LITERATURE 19/ANSWERS

1. CHRISOPHER MARLOWE

2. JOHN MORTIMER

3. DANIEL DEFOE

4. BRAM STOKER

5. ROBERT GRAVES

6. J.R.R. TOLKEIN

7. ANNE BRONTE

8. A.J .CRONIN

9. R.B. SHERIDAN

10. SIR WALTER SCOTT

11. CHARLES DICKENS

12. HENRY FIELDING

13. GEORGE BERNARD SHAW

14. SUE TOWNSEND

15. JANE AUSTEN

16. JOSEPH CONRAD

17. JAMES JOYCE

18. GEORGE ELIOT

19. ARNOLD WHESKER

20. EDITH WHARTON

AUTHORS & LITERATURE 20/ANSWERS

1. JAMES BARRIE ('Peter Pan')

2. DYLAN THOMAS

3. STEPHEN SPENDER

4. SIR ARTHUR CONAN DOYLE (Holmes referring to Moriarty)

5. MALCOLM BRADBURY

6. JACK STORY

7. E.M. FORSTER ('Howard's End')

8. GEORGE BERNARD SHAW

9. SAMUEL BECKETT

10. BRENDAN BEHAN

11. STEVIE SMITH

12. CHRISTOPHER FRY ('The Lady's Not for Burning')

13. KENNETH GRAHAME ('The Wind in the Willows')

14. FRANK RICHARDS ('Billy Bunter's Last Fling')

AUTHORS & LITERATURE 20/ANSWERS cont

15. STELLA GIBBONS ('Cold Comfort Farm')

16. DOROTHY L. SAYERS

17. ARTHUR RANSOME ('Swallows & Amazons')

18. GRAHAM GREENE ('The Power & the Glory')

19. BEATRIX POTTER ('The Tales of the Flopsy Bunnies')

20. ROBERT GRAVES

AUTHORS & LITERATURE 21/ANSWERS

1. JOHN BERGER

2. DAVID STOREY

3. IRIS MURDOCH

4. WILLIAM GOLDING

5. THOMAS KENEALLY

6. ANITA BROOKNER

7. KINGSLEY AMIS

8. PENELOPE LIVELY

9. PETER CAREY

10. A.S. BYATT

11. BARRY UNSWORTH

12. RODDY DOYLE

13. PAT BARKER

14. GRAHAM SWIFT

15. IAN McEWAN

AUTHORS & LITERATURE 22/ANSWERS

1. KATHY REICHS

2. PHILIPPA GREGORY

3. JANET STREET PORTER

4. SUSAN, PETER, LUCY, EDMUND

5. GERMAINE GREER

6. DON JUAN

7. MR. TOAD (Kenneth Grahame)

8. GRAHAM GREENE

9. CRANFORD

10. WALTER DE LA MARE

11. JOHN GALSWORTHY

12. A TURKISH SLIPPER

13. GEORGE ORWELL

14. FRANCES MAYES

15. AGATHA CHRISTIE

16. SOPHIE KINSELLA

17. GERTRUDE LAWRENCE

18. PICKWICK PAPERS

19. CRIME WRITERS ASSOCIATION

20. TRACY CHEVALIER

AUTHORS & LITERATURE 23/ANSWERS

1. WILLIAM WORDSWORTH

2. RUDYARD KIPLING

3. LORD ALFRED TENNYSON

4. EVELYN WAUGH

5. SIR WALTER SCOTT

6. JOHN DONNE

7. OSCAR WILDE

8. HENRY WADSWORTH LONGFELLOW

9. ALEXANDER POPE

10. FRANCIS BACON

11. W.H. AUDEN

12. ALAN AYCKBOURNE

13. GEORGE BERNARD SHAW

14. CHRISTOPER ISHERWOOD

15. GEORGE ORWELL

16. ROBERT BROWNING

17. L.P. HARTLEY

18. ADRIAN HENRY

19. JAMES HILTON

20. DAVID LODGE

AUTHORS & LITERATURE 24/ANSWERS

1. IAN RANKIN

2. TERRY PRATCHETT

3. CHARLOTTE BINGHAM

4. EMILY BARR

5. MARIAN KEYES

6. ANITA BROOKMER

7. HELEN FIELDING

8. BEN RICHARDS

9. SUSAN HILL

10. ADELE PARKS

11. PATRICIA SCANLAN

12. ERICA JAMES

13. ANDREW COLLINS

14. LESLIE THOMAS

15. KEVIN LEWIS

16. TONY PARSONS

17. HOWARD JACOBSON

18. MAGGIE O'FARRELL

19. MELVYN BRAGG

20. ANNE DONOVAN

ENTERTAINMENT 1/ANSWERS

1. A) BAYLEAF
    B) HYPER
    C) SICKNOTE
    D) VASELINE
    E) RECALL

2. A) JEAN MARSH
    B) JACQUELINE TONY
    C) JOHN ALDERTON
    D) CHRISTOPHER BEENY
    E) PAULINE COLLINS

3. A) ERIN
    B) MARY ELLEN
    C) JIM BOB
    D) ELIZABETH
    E) JOHN BOY
    F) BEN
    G) JASON

4. A) CARDIAC ARREST
    B) PEAK PRACTICE
    C) POLICE SURGEON
    D) MEDICS
    E) THE PRACTICE
    F) DON'T WAIT UP

5. A) ANGELS
    B) ARE YOU BEING SERVED
    C) CASUALTY
    D) CHEF!
    E) HOWARD'S WAY
    F) JULIET BRAVO

6. A) JOHN SULLIVAN
    B) LUCY GANNON
    C) LANCE PERCIVAL
    D) JEAN MARSH, EILEEN ATKINS
    E) JACK ROSENTHAL
    F) JAMES MITCHELL

7. A) 1960
    B) 1996
    C) 1972
    D) 1984
    E) 1979
    F) 1982

8. A) SCOOP
   B) DIZZY
   C) MUCK
   D) LOFTY
   E) ROLEY

9. A) SIDNEY CHARLES 'POP' LARKIN
   B) JACK FROST
   C) DEL BOY TROTTER
   D) TOAD
   E) GRANVILLE

10. A) BIRDS OF A FEATHER
    B) THE LIVER BIRDS
    C) MAPP & LUCIA
    D) THE MONSTERS
    E) JOHN STEED'S HOME IN 'THE AVENGERS'

ENTERTAINMENT 2/ANSWERS

1. LIBERACE

2. LAURENCE OLIVIER

3. DAVY JONES, MIKE NESMITH, PETER TURK & MICKY DOLENZ

4. AUNT SALLY

5. TOP GEAR

6. AND MOTHER MAKES THREE

7. ZOO TIME

8. DAVID EDWARDS

9. CAMBERWICK GREEN

10. HANNIBAL HEYES / JOSHUA SMITH / JED 'KID' CURRY / THADDEUS JONES

11. KENNETH BRANAGH & EMMA THOMPSON

12. ANNE WOOD

13. BAD ATTITUDE

14. ANIMAL MAGIC

15. DANDY NICHOLS

16. WHAT'S MY LINE

17. GEORGE PEPPARD

18. ERIC THOMPSON & NIGEL PLANER

19. NICE TIME

20. THE DUCHESS OF DUKE STREET

ENTERTAINMENT 3/ANSWERS

1. BOTTOM

2. ABSOLUTELY FABULOUS

3. ER

4. THE NEW STATESMAN

5. CAMBERWICK GREEN

6. THE OFFICE

7. PERFECT SCOUNDRELS

8. BOYS FROM THE BLACKSTUFF

9. IT AIN'T HALF HOT MUM

10. 'ALLO 'ALLO

11. LAST OF THE SUMMER WINE

12. MAKING OUT

13. THE DUKES OF HAZZARD

14. THE PROFESSIONALS

15. ALLY McBEAL

16. LOVEJOY

17. MOONLIGHTING

18. ON THE BUSES

19. THE KUMARS AT NO. 42

20. BAYWATCH

21. MAY TO SEPTEMBER

22. NEW AVENGERS

23. CHIGLEY

24. DRAGNET

25. BALLY KISSANGEL

ENTERTAINMENT 4/ANSWERS

1. JAMES NESBITT

2. MARTIN CLUNES

3. GEOFFREY HUGHES

4. PENELOPE KEITH

5. LYNDA BELLINGHAM

6. PAULINE QUIRKE

7. JAMES BOLAM

8. TONY BRITTON

9. PETER DAVISON

10. WILL MELLOR

11. JULIA SAWALHA

12. GORDEN KAYE

13. ALUN ARMSTRONG

14. LOVE IN A COLD CLIMATE

15. WENDY RICHARDS

16. TIM HEALEY

17. PETER BOWLES

18. JOHN NETTLES

19. NICHOLAS LYNDHURST

20. MARTIN JARVIS

ENTERTAINMENT 5/ANSWERS

1. JONATHAN

2. NED SHERRIN

3. STEVIE SMITH

4. ERIC ROBSON

5. A.J. CRONIN

6. BUNN AND CO.

7. MAMMA MIA

8. DR. SEUSS

9. THE MIKADO

10. BEAUTIFUL AND DAMNED

11. CAPTAIN 'LUCKY' JACK AUBREY

12. GERVASE PHINN

13. JOANNE HARRIS

14. RORY AND RITA

15. THE PRIME OF MISS JEAN BRODIE

16. ERIC IDLE

17. MANCHESTER

18. HOLBY CITY HOSPITAL

19. JON PERTWEE

20. PHIL REDMOND

ENTERTAINMENT 6/ANSWERS

1. AFTER HENRY

2. RICK (The Young Ones)

3. DRACULA, FRANKENSTEIN'S MONSTER, WOLFMAN

4. ASSUMPTA FITZGERALD

5. DAVID CARRADINE

6. ADRIAN EDMONDSON

7. STEPHANIE BEACHAM

8. ANNA RAEBURN

9. MIRANDA RICHARDSON

10. DENNIS POTTER

11. THE FOOTBALL FACTORY

12. GORDON RAMSAY

13. JENNY & WILLY

14. 'HANDY' ANDY KANE

15. TV GARDENERS

16. ANGUS DEAYTON

17. WORZEL GUMMIDGE

18. THE VICAR OF DIBLEY

19. OASIS

20. TOM STOPPARD

ENTERTAINMENT 7/ANSWERS

1. READY STEADY GO!

2. JUST A MINUTE (Radio)

3. ABSOLUTELY FABULOUS

4. MASTERMIND

5. HORSE OF THE YEAR SHOW

6. THE ARCHERS (Radio)

7. DAD'S ARMY

8. BLUE PETER

9. DESERT ISLAND DISCS

10. TINKER, TAILOR, SOLDIER, SPY

11. THE OFFICE

12. MONTY PYTHON'S FLYING CIRCUS

13. AUF WIEDERSEHEN PET

14. TEST MATCH SPECIAL

15. THE SOUTH BANK SHOW

16. JUKE BOX JURY

17. BRAIN OF BRITAIN (Radio)

18. THE LONE RANGER

19. MINDER

20. THE SNOWMAN

ENTERTAINMENT 8/ANSWERS

1. PAUL GAUGUIN

2. THE FALKLANDS CONFLICT

3. TEACHER

4. YOSSER HUGHES

5. PETER SELLERS

6. NIGEL BENN, TONY BLACKBURN, RHONA CAMERON, DARREN DAY, URI GELLER, CHRISTINE HAMILTON, NELL McANDREW AND TARA PALMER-TOMKINSON

7. TERRY WOGAN

8. SIR DAVID FROST

9. ROSENCRANTZ AND GUILDENSTERN ARE DEAD

10. 2,000 ACRES OF SKY

11. ORLANDO BLOOM

12. NATIONWIDE

13. SPIKE MILLIGAN, PETER SELLERS., HARRY SECOMBE & MICHAEL BENTINE

14. HENRY HALL

15. JULIANNE MOORE

16. COLIN WELLAND

17. 1972

18. SIR IAN McKELLEN

19. SUPERSONIC

20. HARRY POTTER & THE PRISONER OF AZKABAN

ENTERTAINMENT 9/ANSWERS

1. HELEN MIRREN (Prime Suspect)

2. DAVID JASON (Frost)

3. KEVIN WHATELY (Morse)

4. BERNIE NOLAN (The Bill)

5. STRATFORD JOHNS (Z Cars)

6. DAVID YIP (The Chinese Detective)

7. WARREN CLARKE (Dalziel & Pascoe)

8. DENNIS WATERMAN (The Sweeney)

9. STEPHANIE TURNER (Juliet Bravo)

10. DEREK FOWLDS (Heartbeat)

11. ANGIE DICKINSON (Police Woman)

12. GEORGE SEWELL (Special Branch)

13. PATRICK MALAHIDE (Minder)

14. DON JOHNSON (Miami Vice)

15. LESLIE ASH (Merseybeat)

16. STRATFORD JOHNS (Softly Softly)

17. PATRICK MOWER (Special Branch)

18. SEAN ARNOLD (Bergerac)

19. MARK McMANUS (Taggart)

20. NICK BERRY (In Deep)

ENTERTAINMENT 10/ANSWERS

1. SIR ANTHONY HOPKINS

2. LENNY HENRY

3. LESLIE ASH

4. PAUL MERTON

5. ANNEKA RICE

6. CHRISTOPHER BEENY

7. JAMES NESBIT

8. PATSY KENSIT

9. STEPHANIE BEACHAM

10. PENELOPE KEITH

11. JIM DALE

12. FRANK FINLAY

13. ALBERT FINNEY

14. ANGUS DEAYTON

15. BARRY FOSTER

ENTERTAINMENT 11/ANSWERS

1. HOWARD'S END

2. ALEC LEAMAS

3. START THE WEEK

4. MAN & SUPERMAN

5. JACK & THE BEANSTALK

6. LARKHALL

7. LONDON MINICAB DRIVER

8. LAST OF THE SUMMER WINE

9. THE KUMARS AT NO. 42

10. NELSON MANDELA HOUSE

11. SUE LIMB

12. NEW TRICKS

13. YOUNG ADAM

14. BILLY CONNOLLY

15. KATE WINSLET

16. ANNE ROBINSON

17. NICHOLAS PARSONS

18. LORD REITH

19. SUNHILL

20. KELLY & JACK

ENTERTAINMENT 12/ANSWERS

1. FRY'S TURKISH DELIGHT

2. WONDERLOAF

3. BLUEBAND MARGARINE

4. OPAL FRUITS

5. COKE (Coca-Cola)

6. BRITISH GAS

7. PHYLLOSAN

8. ABBEY NATIONAL

9. ESSO

10. MAXWELL HOUSE COFFEE

11. AUTOMOBILE ASSOCIATION

12. KODAK

13. PLEDGE

14. BOVRIL

15. SMARTIES

16. HOMEPRIDE

17. ANADIN

18. CAMAY SOAP

19. PHILIPS

20. TV TIMES

ENTERTAINMENT 13/ANSWERS

1. THE WOMAN IN WHITE

2. SOFTLY, SOFTLY

3. LARRY FORTENSKY

4. HANNIBAL LECTER

5. CITIZEN SMITH

6. ANTONY SHER

7. MONSOON

8. IAN HISLOP & PAUL MERTON

9. ALL OUR YESTERDAYS

10. BRUCE WAYNE

11. BILLY CRYSTAL & MEG RYAN

12. GORDEN KAYE

13. IAN WRIGHT

14. 15

15. ANGELS

16. HONOR BLACKMAN

17. DAVINA McCALL

18. ABOUT A BOY

19. JIMMY NAIL

20. JACK FORD

ENTERTAINMENT 14/ANSWERS

1. KENNETH BRANAGH

2. ALEC GUINESS

3. DAVID NIVEN

4. LYNN REDGRAVE

5. PATRICK MOORE

6. BRIAN RIX

7. ANTHONY HOPKINS

8. LEO McKERN

9. MICHAEL BENTINE

10. STEPHEN FRY

11. DAVID NIVEN

12. JEAN ALEXANDER

13. TERENCE STAMP

14. JOANNA LUMLEY

15. MICHAEL YORK

16. MICHAEL CAINE

17. KENNETH WILLIAMS

18. RONNIE BARKER

19. DENNIS WATERMAN

20. BRIAN BLESSED

ENTERTAINMENT 15/ANSWERS

1. ANTHONY WEDGEWOOD BENN

2. ITMA

3. KENNETH CLARK

4. JIM DAVIDSON

5. THE BULL

6. DRAGNET

7. MICHAEL FRAYN

8. SUPERMAN

9. 2.4 CHILDREN

10. MARTY FELDMAN

11. THE POET AND WRITER STEVIE SMITH

12. ARTHUR C. CLARKE

13. ROWAN AND MARTIN'S LAUGH-IN

14. THE CLITHEROE KID (Jimmy Clitheroe)

15. 77 SUNSET STRIP

16. ALFRED HITCHCOCK

17. SIMON CALLOW

18. THE HERBS

19. GRIFF RHYS JONES

20. IDIOT BOARD

ENTERTAINMENT 16/ANSWERS

1. THE BANANA SPLITS

2. JOHNNY SPEIGHT

3. EWAN McGREGOR

4. VALERIE HARPER

5. PATRICK TROUGHTON

6. TRIANGLE

7. JENNIFER PATERSON & CLARISSA DICKSON WRIGHT

8. RISING DAMP

9. OLIVER POSTGATE

10. ROBERT OF HUNTINGDON

11. LINDA ROBSON

12. THE SIMPSONS

13. ELLY MAY

14. BILL BAILEY

15. NIGEL HAWTHORNE

16. JOHN STEED

17. VYVYAN

18. BUFFAY

19. ROBERT LINDSAY & ZOE WANAMAKER

20. BMW

ENTERTAINMENT 17/ANSWERS

1. ROMEO AND JULIET

2. ACHILLES

3. STAN LAUREL

4. ALISTAIR COOKE'S 'LETTER FROM AMERICA'

5. FELICITY KENDAL & RICHARD BRIERS, PENELOPE KEITH & PAUL EDDINGTON

6. TONY HANCOCK

7. RELAX

8. DAVID LEAN

9. WE WILL ROCK YOU

10. JONATHON ROSS

11. RIK MAYALL, ADRIAN EDMONDSON, CHRISTOPER RYAN & NIGEL PLANER

12. ALISON STEADMAN

13. JANE HORROCKS

14. ANIMAL HOSPITAL

15. 2000

16. THE OFFICE

17. GOMEZ

ENTERTAINMENT 18/ANSWERS

1. BE COOL

2. THE MATRIX

3. DIANA QUICK

4. BAFTA's

5. TOY STORY

6. SCHINDLER'S LIST

7. INTO THE WEST

8. TOM CRUISE

9. RONNI ANCONA

10. THE 51ST STATE

11. CLAIRE SWEENEY

12. KATE WINSLET

13. ELIZABETH ARDEN

14. INMAN

15. JAMIE OLIVER

16. MICHAEL

17. PETER KAY

18. DANIEL RADCLIFFE

19. ROWAN ATKINSON

20. NEWCASTLE

ENTERTAINMENT 19/ANSWERS

1. IAN FLEMING

2. PETER O'TOOLE

3. MICHAEL CAINE

4. JESSIE WALLACE

5. GOODNESS GRACIOUS ME

6. KAY MELLOR

7. DAVID PUTTNAM

8. BEND IT LIKE BECKHAM

9. FIONA BRUCE

10. A FINE ROMANCE

11. ROY PLOMLEY

12. WAR OF THE WORLDS (Orson Welles)

13. CAROLINE AHERNE

14. BRIAN FRIEL

15. NEIL PEARSON

16. THE DETECTIVES

17. DINO

18. ALL HOSTED 'THE GENERATION GAME'

19. FLASH

20. BOSS CAT

ENTERTAINMENT 20/ANSWERS

1. KENNY EVERETT

2. MICHAEL BARRYMORE

3. HUGHIE GREEN

4. JIMMY SAVILE

5. JULIAN CLARY

6. BRUCE FORSYTH

7. LORRAINE CHASE

8. FRANK CARSON

9. MAX BYGRAVES

10. ALI G

11. ERIC MORECAMBE

12. TONY HANCOCK

13. BOBBY BALL

14. PAUL DANIELS

15. BOB MONKHOUSE

16. RONNIE BARKER & RONNIE CORBETT (The two Ronnies)

17. GEORGE FORMBY

18. DEL BOY (in Only Fools and Horses)

19. LARRY GRAYSON

20. ALAN FREEMAN

21. NORMAN VAUGHAN

22. NICHOLAS PARSONS (in Just A Minute)

23. DAVID FROST

24. JIMMY YOUNG

25. TOMMY TRINDER

ENTERTAINMENT 21/ANSWERS

1. HILDA

2. 50:50; PHONE A FRIEND; ASK THE AUDIENCE

3. THE FOUR FEATHERS

4. FAB 1

5. EWAN McGREGOR

6. DAVID DICKINSON

7. NOAH WYLE

8. SANTA'S LITTLE HELPER

9. HOBSON'S CHOICE

10. LINDA THORSON

11. CARRIE BRADSHAW

12. LEE MAJORS

13. BILLY ELLIOT

14. JESSICA

15. SURGICAL SPIRIT

16. NICK ROSS & FIONA BRUCE

17. RUPERT

18. DROWNED IN A SWIMMING POOL

19. ANTHEA TURNER

20. SUGGS (of Madness)

ENTERTAINMENT 22/ANSWERS

1. JACK

2. ARCHIE

3. DOROTHY

4. STEPHEN

5. MONTGOMERY

6. ENDEAVOUR

7. THOMAS

8. JOHN

9. TONY

10. JAMES

11. RUTH

12. ERIC

13. DAVID

14. EVADNE & HILDA

15. MONTAGUE

16. REGINALD

17. BERNARD

18. RICHARD

19. BETTY

20. WILLIAM & RAY

ENTERTAINMENT 23/ANSWERS

1. JOHN CLEESE

2. ANT & DEC

3. HARRY CORBETT

4. MELVYN BRAGG

5. JULIET STEVENSON

6. TALLY HARPER

7. PHYL

8. FRANK SKINNER

9. DENNIS WATERMAN

10. HAVE I GOT NEWS FOR YOU

11. BILLY CONNOLLY

12. UMA THURMAN

13. GRAHAM NORTON

14. NADIA SAWALHA

15. BRIGHT YOUNG THINGS

16. PAUL ABBOTT

17. "PERFICK"

18. DROP THE DEAD DONKEY

19. THE FLOWERPOT MEN

20. JILL GASCOIGNE

ENTERTAINMENT 24/ANSWERS

1. MICHAEL PARKINSON

2. MICHAEL CAINE

3. THE SAINT

4. VIVIEN LEIGH

5. LONNIE DONEGAN

6. GEORGE SMILEY

7. DENNIS POTTER

8. PAUL EDDINGTON

9. DICK BARTON

10. LIVE AND LET DIE

11. WARREN MITCHELL

12. HARRY ENFIELD

13. LOOBY LOO

14. BANKS

15. J.M. BARRIE

16. SEAMUS HEANEY

17. CECIL DAY LEWIS

18. ROBBIE COLTRANE

19. JOHN MORTIMER

20. THE DARLING BUDS OF MAY

ENTERTAINMENT 25/ANSWERS

1. HUGH SCULLY

2. VIRGINIA, CHARLOTTE, SARAH

3. HAPPY DAYS

4. KEN DODD

5. CARLA LANE

6. CAMBERWICK GREEN

7. DOWN AT THE OLD BULL AND BUSH

8. RICHARD BECKINSALE & PAULA WILCOX

9. GRACE JONES

10. PAUL HEINEY & CHRIS SEARLE

11. PETER SKELLERN

12. MISSION IMPOSSIBLE

13. JOHN THAW

14. LAURENCE OLIVIER

15. Z CARS

16. EMMA CHAMBERS

17. PAUL SHANE & BOB MONKHOUSE

18. MUTTLEY

19. COVERT ACTIVITIES THAMES SECTION

20. WHAT THE PAPERS SAY

ENTERTAINMENT 26/ANSWERS

1. MICHAEL ELPHICK

2. MICHAEL BRANDON & GLYNIS BARBER

3. KELSEY GRAMMER

4. JOHN THAW

5. PETER DAVISON

6. IAN CARMICHAEL OR LATER EDWARD PETHERBRIDGE

7. BARRY NEWMAN

8. EDWARD WOODWARD

9. TELLY SAVALAS

10. RICHARD CHAMBERLAIN

11. ALAN DAVIES

12. ADAM FAITH

13. EDWARD ASNER

14. SEAN BEAN

15. TYNE DALEY (Cagney), MEG FOSTER & SHARON GLASS (Lacey)

16. JACK SHEPHERD

17. LEONARD ROSSITER

18. RICHARD HEARNE

19. HARRY H. CORBETT & WILFRED BRAMBLE

20. JIM BROADBENT

21. ROBERT YOUNG

22. JAMES DRURY

23. RAYMOND BURR

24. LAURENCE PAYNE

25. DENNIS WEAVER

ENTERTAINMENT 27/ANSWERS

1. PATRICIA ROUTLEDGE & PRUNELLA SCALES

2. JONATHAN ROSS

3. MARTIN CLUNES

4. MARTIN FREEMAN

5. BILL NIGHY

6. CAROL SMILLIE

7. PAUL DANIELS

8. LORD VOLDEMORT

9. SIMON COWELL

10. ALI G

11. 1982

12. JULIE WALTERS

13. JOAN BAKEWELL

14. ERIC MORECAMBE

15. ROY PLOMLEY, MICHAEL PARKINSON, SUE LAWLEY

16. ROBIN DAY

17. GAME FOR A LAUGH

18. CAPTAIN PUGWASH

19. GEOFFREY PALMER

20. JIMMY McGOVERN

ENTERTAINMENT 28/ANSWERS

1. ME AND MY GIRL

2. ON THE BUSES

3. TAXI

4. THE DUCHESS OF DUKE STREET

5. MOONLIGHTING

6. THE RISE & FALL OF REGINALD PERRIN

7. DROP THE DEAD DONKEY

8. EVER DECREASING CIRCLES

9. FAME

10. CLOCKING OFF

11. CUTTING IT

12. EXECUTIVE STRESS

13. DIAMONDS

14. FRIENDS

15. EVERY SILVER LINING

ENTERTAINMENT 29/ANSWERS

1. CARTWRIGHT

2. ANDY KANE

3. CRANE

4. JEREMY BEADLE

5. ROBERT HARDY

6. THE DUSTBINMEN

7. PEGGY ASHCROFT

8. ARTHUR LOWE

9. THE BOSWELLS

10. NEIL MORRISEY

11. THE ADDAMS FAMILY

12. RICHARD GORDON

13. FRED ALLEN

14. HYLDA BAKER

15. TOMMY COOPER

16. JIM HENSON

17. SIR ALEC GUINNESS

18. THE KRYPTON FACTOR

19. ARTHUR ASKEY

20. JOHNNY MORRIS, RINGO STARR

ENTERTAINMENT 30/ANSWERS

1. DENTIST

2. UNDERTAKER

3. NURSE

4. CHEF & DETECTIVE

5. VET

6. MATHS TEACHER

7. PATHOLOGIST

8. BARBER

9. HOLIDAY REP.

10. ACCOUNTANT

11. TAXIDERMIST

12. TORY M.P.

13. PUBLICAN

14. PROSTITUTE

15. TAXI-DRIVER

16. LAWYER

17. TV REPAIR MAN

18. MANAGEMENT CONSULTANT

19. KITCHEN ASSISTANT

20. MODEL

ENTERTAINMENT 31/ANSWERS

1. B)   GLENDA JACKSON

2. A)   PAUL ABBOTT

3. B)   MICHAEL FRAYN

4. A)   BOB MONKHOUSE

5. D)   BILLY CONNOLLY

6. C)   JULIE WALTERS

7. B)   JUDI DENCH

8. A)   1947

9. D)   BILLINGSGATE FISH PORTER

10. C)   JIM DAVIDSON

11. B)   JOHN LENNON

12. B)   ROCKY HORROR SHOW

13. C)   PRUNELLA SCALES

14. C)   DOROTHY

15. A)   KITT

16. D)   THE MEN'S ROOM

17. D)   AUF WIEDERSEHEN, PET

18. A)   CHRISTOPHER ECCLESTON

19. C)   ST JOSEPH'S

20. A)   DENNIS WATERMAN

ENTERTAINMENT 32/ANSWERS

1. WAKEY-WAKEEEYYY!

2. NOEL COWARD

3. GOLDFINGER

4. PORTMEIRON, WALES

5. MAVIS RILEY/WILTON IN 'CORONATION STREET'

6. MICHAEL BATES

7. LESLEY DUNLOP

8. RUGBY

9. PATRICK DUFFY

10. J.B. PRIESTLEY

11. ADRIAN EDMONDSON

12. L.A. LAW

13. RICHARD O'BRIEN

14. DAVID JASON

15. SIMON DEE

16. MRS. DOYLE

17. THE TROTTERS ('Only Fools & Horses')

18. DUBOIS

19. BRENDA BLETHYN

20. SANDY POWELL

ENTERTAINMENT 33/ANSWERS

1. RICHARD WHITELEY

2. BRUCE FORSYTH

3. WILLIAM G. STEWART

4. CHRIS TARRANT

5. MARTYN LEWIS

6. STEPHEN FRY

7. JEREMY HAWK

8. NICKY CAMPBELL

9. NICHOLAS PARSONS

10. BAMBER GASCOIGNE, JEREMY PAXMAN

11. EAMONN ANDREWS

12. PAUL DANIELS

13. DALE WINTON

14. CLIVE ANDERSON

15. KIRSTY YOUNG

16. MELANIE SYKES

17. BRUCE FORSYTH

18. VERNON KAY

19. MATTHEW BANNISTER & MISHAL HUSAIN

20. ANNE ROBINSON & PHILLIP SCHOFIELD

ENTERTAINMENT 34/ANSWERS

1. A) THE AIDENSFIELD ARMS
   B) THE ROVERS RETURN
   C) BRIDEHAVEN ARMS
   D) THE NAGS HEAD
   E) JUBILEE SOCIAL CLUB

2. A ROY FIGGIS
   B) JACK FORD
   C) TREVOR CHAPLIN
   D) BILL MACGREGOR
   E) TERRY COLLIER

3. A) PHILADELPHIA
    B) MANCHESTER
    C) BRADFORD
    D) LOS ANGELES
    E) NEWCASTLE

4. A) MICHAEL CRICHTON
    B) LYNDA LA PLANTE
    C) JIMMY McGOVERN
    D) PHIL REDMOND
    E) IAN LA FRENAIS

5. A) MAJOR PAT REID
    B) H.E. BATES
    C) WILLIAM F. NOLAN
    D) W.J. BURLEY
    E) DOROTHY L. SAYERS

6. A) PHOEBE BUFFAY
    B) MONICA GELLER / BING
    C) JOEY TRIBBIANI
    D) RACHEL GREEN
    E) ROSS GELLER
    F) CHANDLER BING

7. A) TRACEY ULLMAN
    B) RUBY WAX
    C) JENNIFER SAUNDERS
    D) DAWN FRENCH

8. A) ALAN PLATER
    B) CLIVE DUNN
    C) CARLA LANE
    D) DAVID RENWICK

9. A) BERNARD CRIBBINS
    B) RICHARD BRIERS
    C) KENNETH BRANAGH
    D) KENNETH WILLIAMS
    E) TIM BROOKE TAYLOR

10. A) A YEAR IN PROVENCE
    B) GOODNIGHT MR. TOM
    D) HOME TO ROOST
    E) REDCAP

11. A) VAN DER VALK
    B) M.A.S.H.
    C) PRISONER CELL BLOCK H
    D) CAPTAIN PUGWASH
    E) FRIENDS

12. A) MARGI CLARKE
    B) CAROL SMILLIE
    C) DAVINA McCALL
    D) DAVE LEE TRAVIS
    E) PHIL SPENCER & KIRSTIE ALLSOPP

13. A) LOVEJOY
    B) THE DUKES OF HAZZARD
    C) LOTUS ELAN
    D) FAB 1
    E) FIREMAN SAM

14. A) WHERE THE HEART IS
    B) OH DOCTOR BEECHING!
    C) THE PETER PRINCIPLE
    D) THE PLANE MAKERS / THE POWER GAME
    E) WHEN THE BOAT COMES IN

15. A) LOVE HURTS
    B) MOONLIGHTING
    C) NICE WORK
    D) OUR FRIENDS IN THE NORTH
    E) WIDOWS

ENTERTAINMENT 35/ANSWERS

1. JASPER CARROTT

2. KATHY STAFF

3. DR. EVADNE HINGE

4. MYSTIC MEG

5. BRUCE FORSYTH

6. VIC REEVES

7. TOM JONES

8. M.C. HAMMER

9. BARBARA WINDSOR

10. ROBBIE COLTRANE

11. LILY SAVAGE

12. FRANK SKINNER

13. MICHAEL CRAWFORD

14. JOHNNY VEGAS

15. TWIGGY

FOOD & DRINK 1/ANSWERS

1. PONTEFRACT

2. ISLE OF SKYE

3. UB 40

4. ELIZABETH DAVID

5. 9 GALLONS

6. DEREK COOPER

7. RICK STEIN

8. HUGH FEARNLEY-WHITTINGSTALL

9. GARY RHODES

10. DR. SAMUEL JOHNSON

11. SAINSBURY'S

12. ROSE GRAY & RUTH ROGERS

13. KENTUCKY FRIED CHICKEN

14. CAROL VORDERMAN

15. FAY WELDON

16. JILLY GOOLDEN & OZ CLARKE

17. CORNED BEEF

18. WHISKY

19. WHOLE MILK

20. WILLIAM BLACK

FOOD & DRINK 2/ANSWERS

1. YORKSHIRE PUDDING

2. WENSLEYDALE

3. SEAWEED

4. HAGGIS

5. BREAKFAST

6. COW PIES

7. A HERRING

8. 'QUORN'

9. VERY SPECIAL OLD PALE

10. FANNY CRADDOCK

11. GARY RHODES

12. LAMB

13. BUBBLE & SQUEAK

14. ULTRA HEAT TREATED

15. BUTTERBEANS

16. JUNIPER

17. MARTINI

18. BEEF WELLINGTON

19. TURNIP

20. MAX BEERBOHM

FOOD & DRINK 3/ANSWERS

1. BLACK PUDDING

2. COCK-A-LEEKIE

3. SYLLABUB

4. WELSH RAREBIT

5. PORK PIE

6. KENDAL MINT CAKE

7. BETTYS TEAROOMS

8. CULLEN SKINK

9. TOAD IN THE HOLE

10. KIPPER

11. LOGANBERRY

12. COLCANNON

13. LIQUORICE CAKE

14. MONOSODIUM GLUTAMATE

15. HAGGIS

16. SALLY LUNN

17. DUNLOP

18. ECCLES CAKES

19. HERRING

20. NORTHUMBERLAND FRUIT LOAF

FOOD & DRINK 4/ANSWERS

1. DRAMBUIE

2. LAMB

3. GARIBALDI

4. SPOTTED DICK

5. TEXTURED VEGETABLE PROTEIN

6. PRUE LEITH

7. 2 OZ PER WEEK

8. FOOL

9. SIMON BATES & GILLIAN MILES

10. SOPHIE GRIGSON

11. GUINNESS

12. HEINZ

13. HAROLD WILSON

14. NIGELLA LAWSON

15. GORDON RAMSEY

16. STIRRUP CUP - SLOE GIN

17. SAKI

18. YORKSHIRE PUDDING

19. MAGNUS PYKE

20. MARKS & SPENCER

FOOD & DRINK 5/ANSWERS

1. CORK

2. OYSTERS WRAPPED IN BACON

3. CLEMENT ATTLEE

4. NIGEL SLATER

5. CORNISH CHEESE WRAPPED IN NETTLES

6. FORTNUM & MASON

7. ANTONY WORRALL THOMPSON

8. BANNOCK

9. JOSCELINE DIMBLEBY

10. DRINKA PINTA MILKA DAY

11. KATHERINE WHITEHORN

12. CLEMENT FREUD

13. CLAUDIA RODEN

14. SAINSBURY

15. DELIA SMITH

16. MARCO PIERRE WHITE

17. WALLS ICE CREAM

18. ANTONY WORRALL THOMPSON

19. P.G. WODEHOUSE

20. HEATHER HONEY

HISTORY 1/ANSWERS

1. C. ARTHUR PEARSON

2. EDWARD I

3. HAROLD WILSON

4. CHESHIRE HOMES

5. ARTHUR MICHAEL RAMSEY

6. 6TH JUNE 1944

7. HENRY VII

8. CLEMENT ATTLEE

9. A1

10. OLIVER TWIST

11. GEORGE V

12. ELIZABETH GARRETT ANDERSON

13. HENRY VII

14. CARLTON CLUB

15. ANNE BOLEYN

16. H.H. ASQUITH

HISTORY 2/ANSWERS

1. CHARLES II

2. 1900

3. BEAGLE

4. DOUGLAS HAIG

5. LOUISE WOODWARD

6. JAMES CALLAGHAN

7. JEREMY THORPE

8. EMPRESS MAUD

9. RICHARD I

10. THE GUILDFORD FOUR

11. ROBERT THE BRUCE

12. 1837

13. ROBERT GRAVES

14. 67

15. THE ARREST OF KEITH RICHARDS, MICK JAGGER AND ROBERT FRASER ON CHARGES OF POSSESSION OF DRUGS

16. 'IN PLACE OF STRIFE'

17. THE LEVELLERS

18. SHERIFF

19. SUFFRAGETTE MOVEMENT (Votes for Women)

20. 1963

HISTORY 3/ANSWERS

1. 1987	6. 1995	11. 1988	16. 1971
2. 1982	7. 1989	12. 1941	17. 1928
3. 1937	8. 1963	13. 1968	18. 1977
4. 1951	9. 1947	14. 1954	19. 1990
5. 1984	10. 1973	15. 1965	20. 1978

HISTORY 4/ANSWERS

1. MARGARET BECKETT

2. WILLIAM HAGUE

3. ARCHIE NORMAN

4. JOHN PRESCOTT

5. ANN WIDDECOMBE

6. ROBIN COOK

7. MICHAEL HOWARD

8. TONY BLAIR

9. KENNETH CLARKE

10. DR. KIM HOWELLS

11. GLENDA JACKSON

12. CHARLES KENNEDY

13. DIANE ABBOTT

14. GORDON BROWN

15. IAIN DUNCAN-SMITH

16. JOHN REDWOOD

17. TAM DALYELL

18. MICHAEL PORTILLO

19. HARRIET HARMAN

20. DON FOSTER

HISTORY 5/ANSWERS

1. HENRY I

2. ROUNDHEADS

3. CHARLES II

4. BEVERIDGE REPORT

5. KIM PHILBY

6. ROBERT II

7. HERMAN'S HERMITS

8. EDWARD III

9. CATHERINE OF ARAGON

10. KEIR HARDIE & RAMSAY MACDONALD

11. 27 OCTOBER 1986

12. BISLEY

13. PETER NISSEN

14. OSCAR WILDE

15. 4TH CENTURY ROMAN SILVER (first discovered during ploughing of a field in Suffolk)

16. ELIZABETH I AND MARY QUEEN OF SCOTS

17. JOHN NOTT

18. APSLEY HOUSE

19. SIR ROBERT WALPOLE

20. LORD SHAFTESBURY

HISTORY 6/ANSWERS

1. HENRY IV

2. LORD BEAVERBROOK

3. JOHN

4. HENRY II

5. THE INDEPENDENT

6. CHARLES II

7. THE PLYMOUTH BRETHREN

8. £2

9. MICHAEL HESELTINE

10. BERTRAND RUSSELL

11. JEFFREY ARCHER

12. BLACK FRIDAY

13. H.H. ASQUITH

14. MURPHY'S LAW

15. THE WOMEN'S SOCIAL AND POLITICAL UNION

16. SIR GEOFFREY HOWE

17. MALCOLM MUGGERIDGE

18. GEORGE V

19. THOSE WHO DIED IN WWI AND THOSE WHO BEING TOO YOUNG TO FIGHT HAD SURVIVED THE SLAUGHTER

20. MARGARET THATCHER

HISTORY 7/ANSWERS

1. MARGARET THATCHER

2. BENJAMIN DISRAELI

3. EDWARD HEATH

4. HAROLD WILSON

5. CLEMENT ATTLEE

6. STANLEY BALDWIN

7. ANTHONY WEDGEWOOD BENN

8. JEREMY THORPE

9. EDITH SUMMERSKILL

10. HAROLD MACMILLAN

11. WINSTON CHURCHILL

12. ARTHUR BALFOUR

13. JAMES CALLAGHAN

14. NORMAN TEBBIT

15. BARBARA CASTLE

16. ANEURIN BEVAN

17. ANTHONY CROSLAND

18. LORD HAILSHAM

19. LORD CURZON

20. ALEC DOUGLAS-HOME

HISTORY 8/ANSWERS

1. THE SOVIET UNION

2. EDDIE SHAH

3. WILLIAM I (the Conqueror)

4. 1958

5. NICHOLAS BREAKSPEAR (Adrian IV 1154-1159)

6. BETTY BOOTHROYD

7. BENJAMIN DISRAELI

8. QUEEN VICTORIA

9. 13

10. NANCY ASTOR

11. ARNOLD TOYNBEE

12. TO RECRUIT FOR WORLD WAR I

13. ANEURIN BEVAN

14. HENRY CAMPBELL-BANNERMAN

HISTORY 8/ANSWERS CONT

15. PHILIP SNOWDEN

16. A.J.P. TAYLOR

17. STANLEY BALDWIN

18. VICKY (Victor Weiss)

19. R.H. TAWNEY

20. S.S. TITANIC HIT AN ICEBERG (it sank 2 hours later)

HISTORY 9/ANSWERS

1. 1983	6. 55	11. 1987	16. 1957
2. 1970	7. 1979	12. 1912	17. 1973
3. 1919	8. 1930	13. 1963	18. 1988
4. 1926	9. 1980	14. 1936	19. 1910
5. 1985	10. 1999	15. 1945	20. 1990

HISTORY 10/ANSWERS

1. MICHAEL FOOT (on the Profumo scandal)

2. CLEMENT FREUD

3. ENOCH POWELL

4. EDWARD GREY (British Foreign Secretary)

5. ARTHUR GEDDES

6. ANTHONY EDEN

7. HUGH GAITSKELL

8. LORD HAILSHAM

9. EDWARD HEATH

10. HAROLD NICOLSON

HISTORY 11/ANSWERS

1. ROBERT MAXWELL

2. ROSEMARY WEST

3. BRIAN KEENAN

4. THE 'BIRMINGHAM SIX'

5. MARY ROBINSON

6. DIANA, PRINCESS OF WALES

7. HONG KONG

8. POSH / BABY / SPORTY / SCARY / GINGER (THE SPICE GIRLS)

9. LOUISE WOODWARD

10. EDWINA CURRIE

11. EDWARD HEATH

12. FREDERICK WEST

13. 1988

14. 'THE MARCHIONESS'

15. HMS SHEFFIELD

16. PETER MANDELSON

17. ANN WINTERTON

18. SIR RICHARD BRANSON

19. JOHN STONEHOUSE

20. DAVID STEEL

MUSIC 1/ANSWERS

1. ERIC CLAPTON

2. STING

3. GENESIS

4. U2

5. GEORGE HARRISON

6. PINK FLOYD

7. KATE BUSH

8. CHRIS REA

9. THE ROLLING STONES

10. DAVID BOWIE

11. SIMPLY RED

12. ROD STEWART

13. ROXY MUSIC

14. PHIL COLLINS

15. DIRE STRAITS

16. QUEEN

17. ELTON JOHN

18. ERASURE

19. WET WET WET

20. EURYTHMICS

MUSIC 2/ANSWERS

1. KATE BUSH

2. KATIE MELUA

3. GARY JULES

4. ANDREW DAVIS

5. NIGEL KENNEDY (with the English Chamber Orchestra)

6. THE EXORCIST

7. IAN GILLAN

8. THE LARK ASCENDING

9. DIRE STRAITS

10. THE HUMAN LEAGUE

11. JOHN BONHAM

12. MORRISSEY

13. NORAH JONES

14. ALANIS MORISSETTE

15. BOB GELDOF AND MIDGE URE

16. JEMINI

17. GLOUCESTER, HEREFORD AND WORCESTER

18. LONDON PHILHARMONIC ORCHESTRA

19. ERIC BURDON

20. PETE BEST

MUSIC 3/ANSWERS

1. ALL SAINTS

2. WET WET WET

3. SHAKESPEAR'S SISTER

4. LEVEL 42

5. PET SHOP BOYS

6. MOTORHEAD

7. SOFT CELL

8. ART OF NOISE

9. COLDCUT

10. FINE YOUNG CANNIBALS

11. ERASURE

12. HEAVEN 17

13. MUNGO JERRY

14. THE STRANGLERS

15. TROGGS

16. TEARS FOR FEARS

17. WHAM!

18. TEN YEARS AFTER

19. SMITHS

20. THE BACHELORS

MUSIC 4/ANSWERS

1. RONNIE WOOD (of The Rolling Stones)

2. QUEEN

3. SIMON COWELL

4. JAY KAY

5. CLIFF RICHARD

6. COLDPLAY

7. CHISHOLM AND GULZAR

8. GARETH GATES

9. BROOKLYN AND ROMEO

10. TRAVIS

11. CREAM

12. JOE STRUMMER

13. JOHN GORMAN, MIKE MC GEAR AND ROGER MCGOUGH

14. MELANIE C

15. WESTLIFE

16. DAVID BOWIE

17. VINCE CLARKE AND ALISON MOYET

18. SHAKIN' STEVENS

19. LED ZEPPELIN

20. ELTON JOHN AND BERNIE TAUPIN

MUSIC 5/ANSWERS

1. HELEN REDDY

2. SUGGS AND LOUCHIE LOU AND MITCHIE ONE

3. GILBERT O'SULLIVAN

4. THE BACHELORS

5. THE DAMNED

6. HOT CHOCOLATE

7. THE HOLLIES

8. DONOVAN

9. COCKNEY REBEL

10. KENNY

11. LINDISFARNE

12. THE BEATLES

13. THE KINKS

14. ROD STEWART

15. BLONDIE

16. ELTON JOHN

17. DON PARTRIDGE

18. SHAKIN' STEVENS

19. FOCUS

20. ROXY MUSIC

MUSIC 6/ANSWERS

1. DAVID BOWIE

2. GARY GLITTER

3. ANNIE LENNOX

4. ALISON MOYET

5. MIKE OLDFIELD

6. ADAM AND THE ANTS

7. PHIL COLLINS

8. THE CURE

9. WET WET WET

10. UB40

11. PET SHOP BOYS

12. ROXY MUSIC

13. THE SEX PISTOLS

14. POLICE

15. THE ROLLING STONES

16. SIMPLY RED

17. U2

18. DEPECHE MODE

19. HOT CHOCOLATE

20. HUMAN LEAGUE

MUSIC 7/ANSWERS

1. DUSTY SPINGFIELD

2. SHAKIN' STEVENS

3. PRINCE

4. HUMPHREY LYTTELTON

5. EVITA

6. CATHY DAVEY

7. GEORGE MICHAEL

8. DAVID BOWIE

9. DEPECHE MODE

10. BAD MANNERS

11. JOHNNY DANKWORTH

12. THE HUMAN LEAGUE

13. GIVE PEACE A CHANCE

14. ROBSON GREEN AND JEROME FLYNN

15. CAT STEVENS

16. PET SHOP BOYS

17. DAN LENO

18. HELEN SHAPIRO

19. ROXY MUSIC

20. ULTRAVOX

MUSIC 8/ANSWERS

1. CHRIS DE BURGH'S DAUGHTER ROSANNA

2. COVENTRY CATHEDRAL

3. KATE BUSH

4. ELTON JOHN AND TIM RICE

5. VESTA TILLEY

6. GAELIC FOR 'FAMILY'

7. ALANNAH CURRIE

8. CULTURE CLUB

9. 1952

10. GEORGE FORMBY

11. BENJAMIN BRITTEN

12. BLUR

13. MARC BOLAN

14. SIR CLIFF RICHARD

15. MS DYNAMITE

16. SHELLY PRESTON

17. THE EURYTHMICS

18. GEORGE MICHAEL

19. EVERYTHING BUT THE GIRL

20. THE YARDBIRDS

MUSIC 9/ANSWERS

1. CHRIS DE BURGH

2. ERROL BROWN

3. ERIC CLAPTON

4. STING

5. ROGER TAYLOR

6. MALCOLM MCLAREN

7. ADAMS

8. TAKE THAT

9. GRACIE FIELDS

10. JOHN LENNON

11. D.I.V.O.R.C.E.

12. THE KINKS

13. MEL AND KIM

14. 5-4-3-2-1

15. ADAM ANT

16. SAMANTHA FOX

17. BRYAN FERRY

18. SARAH BRIGHTMAN AND HOT GOSSIP

19. MELANIE C

20. THE TEARDROP EXPLODES

<u>MUSIC 10/ANSWERS</u>

1. JIMMY NAIL

2. SUGABABES

3. PET SHOP BOYS

4. BEAUTIFUL SOUTH

5. DAVID BOWIE AND MICK JAGGER

6. EMMA BUNTON

7. FREDDIE MERCURY

8. SLADE

9. SANDIE SHAW

10. U2

11. ALL SAINTS

12. LIBERTY X

13. S CLUB 7

14. BUCKS FIZZ

15. BOYZONE

16. THE SPICE GIRLS

17. EUROPE

18. GARY BARLOW

19. OASIS

20. BLUR

21. WHAM!

22. CORRS

23. WET WET WET

24. ADAM FAITH

25. SMALL FACES

MUSIC 11/ANSWERS

1. GLASTONBURY

2. THE KINKS

3. QUEEN

4. KERRY MC FADDEN

5. GARETH GATES

6. STATUS QUO

7. WILLY RUSSEL

8. LIFT ME UP

9. TOM JONES

10. DHANI

11. DAVID BOWIE

12. JETHRO TULL

13. THE TEMPEST

14. JOHN BONHAM

15. SANDIE SHAW

16. RONAN KEATING

17. DAVE GILMOUR

18. TELL ME ON A SUNDAY

19. ARTHUR SULLIVAN

20. KEN DODD

MUSIC 12/ANSWERS

1. CLIFF RICHARD AND THE SHADOWS

2. THE BEATLES

3. TOM JONES

4. SLADE

5. MUD

6. JOHNNY MATHIS

7. WINGS

8. BONEY M

9. PINK FLOYD

10. ST WINIFRED'S SCHOOL CHOIR

11. FLYING PICKETS

12. SHAKIN' STEVENS

13. PET SHOP BOYS

14. BAND AID

15. QUEEN

16. MR BLOBBY

17. SPICE GIRLS

18. WESTLIFE

19. BOB THE BUILDER

20. GIRLS ALOUD

MUSIC 13/ANSWERS

1. KURT COBAIN

2. THE KINKS

3. HENRY LAUDER

4. JOHANN CHRISTIAN BACH (youngest son of Johann Sebastian Bach)

5. THE GONDOLIERS

6. DIDO

7. SIR JOHN BARBIROLLI

8. CANDLE IN THE WIND '97 ELTON JOHN

9. OZZY OSBOURNE

10. ALL HAVE BEEN KNIGHTED AND ALL MUSIC MILLIONAIRES

11. CHICAGO

12. HEAR'SAY

13. DEACON BLUE

14. CLEO LAINE

15. EVERY 3 YEARS

16. W.S. GILBERT (OF GILBERT AND SULLIVAN)

17. WELSH (LAND OF MY FATHERS)

18. I'M ALIVE

19. FRANKIE GOES TO HOLLYWOOD

20. ROBBIE WILLIAMS

MUSIC 14/ANSWERS

1. THE HUMAN LEAGUE

2. MAKING YOUR MIND UP

3. SHARLEEN SPITERI

4. DAVE EVANS

5. THE TRAVELLING WILBURYS

6. ROBBIE WILLIAMS

7. OLIVER

8. ROBBIE WILLIAMS AND NICOLE KIDMAN

9. ALISON MOYET

10. GINGER BAKER, JACK BRUCE AND ERIC CLAPTON

11. MS DYNAMITE

12. 1969

13. BRIAN ENO

14. OASIS

15. MOYA BRENNAN

16. LULU

17. GARY BARLOW

18. ALL SAINTS

19. MOVE

20. DAVID JACOBS, NOEL EDMONDS AND JOOLS HOLLAND

MUSIC 15/ANSWERS

1. THE ROLLING STONES

2. SIMPLE MINDS

3. WESTLIFE

4. BONO AND THE EDGE

5. THE DAMNED

6. IAN CRAIG MARSH AND MARTYN WARE

7. TONY HADLEY

8. LOVE SHINE A LIGHT

9. HOLLY JOHNSON

10. 1997

11. SIMPLY RED

12. THE DAMNED

13. LE ANN RIMES

14. MATT GOSS

15. CLANNAD

16. NICKY BYRNE

17. THOMPSON TWINS

18. CHRISSIE HYNDE

19. RINGO STARR AND GEORGE HARRISON

20. FREEDOM

MUSIC 16/ANSWERS

1. DESTINY'S CHILD

2. FIVE

3. MANIC STREET PREACHERS

4. GERRI HALLIWELL

5. LISA LEFT EYE LOPES

6. HEAR'SAY

7. WESTLIFE

8. BLUE (FEATURING ELTON JOHN)

9. SONIQUE

10. GABRIELLE

11. RONAN KEATING

12. GIRLS ALOUD

13. ATOMIC KITTEN

14. DESTINY'S CHILD

15. ALL SAINTS

16. WILL YOUNG

17. STEPS

18. BLACK LEGEND

19. A1

20. WILL YOUNG AND GARETH GATES

MUSIC 17/ANSWERS

1. CILLA BLACK

2. BENJAMIN BRITTEN

3. THANK YOUR LUCKY STARS

4. DAVID BOWIE

5. ERIC CLAPTON

6. NEWCASTLE

7. CASTLE DONINGTON

8. DONOVAN

9. LAND OF HOPE AND GLORY

10. CHELTENHAM

11. THE SCAFFOLD

12. HAROLD WILSON

13. ARNOLD BOX

14. PETE TOWNSEND (THE WHO)

15. THE BEATLES

16. 'PRIVATE LIVES'

17. WASHINGTON

18. SIR ANTHONY HOPKINS

19. BOB GELDOF

20. BRIAN EPSTEIN

MUSIC 18/ANSWERS

1. B) NERD

2. C) JOHN TAVENER

3. B) SIX-FIVE SPECIAL

4. D) HE AIN'T HEAVY, HE'S MY BROTHER

5. C) ELAINE PAIGE & BARBARA DICKSON

6. B) MIDGE URE

7. B) THE TURN OF THE SCREW

8. D) IVOR NOVELLO

9. B) SUGGS

10. D) THE MERRY WIVES OF WINDSOR

11. A) I ONLY WANT TO BE WITH YOU

12. B) SARAH BRIGHTMAN

13. B) JOHN BLOW

14. C) JOHN WILLIAMS

15. D) BRYAN ADAMS

MUSIC 19/ANSWERS

1. ADAM FAITH

2. NIGEL KENNEDY

3. SIR HARRY SECOMBE

4. EVELYN GLENNIE

5. ROY CASTLE

6. BOY GEORGE

7. MICHAEL TIPPET

8. VICTORIA BECKHAM

9. STING

10. TIM RICE

MUSIC 20/ANSWERS

1. BOB GELDOF

2. READY STEADY GO

3. A HARD DAY'S NIGHT

4. BARBARA DIXON

5. CHRISSIE SHRIMPTON

6. FINE YOUNG CANNIBALS

7. SHAZNAY LEWIS

8. TABOO

9. LULU

10. 1970

11. PAN'S PEOPLE

12. KID

13. ELKIE BROOKS

14. BIG BROTHER

15. SAMANTHA FOX

16. NATALIE & NICOLE APPLETON

17. NORAH JONES

18. PRODIGY

19. FREDERICK BULSARA

20. 1964

PEOPLE & PLACES 1/ANSWERS

1. TINTAGEL CASTLE

2. MOUSEHOLE

3. MISS MARPLE

4. BATH

5. FORD MADOX BROWN

6. JOHN KAY

7. FYLINGDALES

8. BROOKLANDS

9. GOWER PENINSULA

10. THE DAM BUSTERS

11. CANTERBURY

12. 1965

13. AUCTIONEERS

14. CECIL DAY-LEWIS

15. ISAMBARD KINGDOM BRUNEL

16. WOBURN ABBEY

17. OLD CONTEMPTIBLES

18. DANIEL O'CONNELL

19. SUE LAWLEY

20. OXFORD

PEOPLE & PLACES 2/ANSWERS

1. PAUL GASCOIGNE (GAZZA)

2. BENJAMIN BRITTEN

3. FRANCIS BACON

4. DAME CECILY SAUNDERS

5. FREDERICK DELIUS

6. DAME ALICIA MARKOVA

7. ST CUTHBERT

8. ROBERT SOUTHEY

9. AGATHA CHRISTIE

10. CAPABILITY BROWN

11. WILLIAM MORRIS

12. ROALD DAHL

13. JOHN DANKWORTH

14. BEAU BRUMMELL

15. GEORGE STEPHENSON

16. INIGO JONES

17. PETER COOK

18. LORD MOUNTBATTEN

19. ELAINE PAIGE

20. SIR HUMPHREY DAVY (DAVY SAFETY LAMP)

PEOPLE & PLACES 3/ANSWERS

1. COVENT GARDEN

2. LONDON EYE

3. MILLBANK

4. BIG BEN

5. CONGESTION CHARGE

6. WESTMINSTER ABBEY

7. STRAWBERRY HILL

8. PETTICOAT LANE

9. WHITEHALL PALACE

10. BILLINGSGATE

11. FULHAM PALACE

12. HAMPTON COURT

13. IMPERIAL WAR MUSEUEM

14. GREENWICH PALACE

15. ALEXANDRA PALACE

16. CANARY WHARF TOWER

17. DENMARK STREET

18. SMITHFIELD

19. HIGHGATE HILL

20. ST PANCRAS

PEOPLE & PLACES 4/ANSWERS

1. TYNE

2. IRWELL

3. SPEY

4. STOUR

5. KENNET

6. ORWELL

7. SEVERN

8. FIRTH OF FORTH

9. GREAT OUSE

10. DEE

11. TEES

12. NITH

13. WITHAM

14. TAWE

15. DERWENT

16. TAY

17. EX

18. WYE

19. DONN

20. WEAR

PEOPLE & PLACES 5/ANSWERS

1. 1951

2. ALL DIED IN 1984

3. HENRY IRVING

4. NEWCASTLE

5. DOCTOR

6. MARK CHAPMAN

7. JOHN LEWIS PARTNERSHIP

8. 2002

9. TAFF

10. WHITE DIAGONAL CROSS OF ST ANDREW ON A BLUE BACKGROUND

11. ALL SERVED PRISON SENTENCES

12. BAKER DAYS

13. CAULDRON SNOUT

14. JOHN MAJOR

15. ST GILES

16. SUSANNA, JUDITH AND HAMNET

17. FLORENCE NIGHTINGALE

18. KATIE PRICE

19. FREDDIE LAKER

20. 1979

PEOPLE & PLACES 6/ANSWERS

1. TONY HANCOCK

2. DEER

3. THE PEAK DISTRICT

4. RONNIE KRAY

5. SHE WON THE MISS WORLD CONTEST

6. AIRE

7. THE LAW COURTS

8. NOAH'S ARK

9. PROCURATOR FISCAL

10. HAREFIELD HOSPITAL

11. JEAN ROOK

12. SHE FELL DOWN THE STAIRS AT HER DAUGHTERS' COTSWOLD COTTAGE

13. THE SEX PISTOLS

14. ALAN BENNETT

15. ROTTEN ROW

16. LORD YOUNG

17. JUDGE JEFFREYS

18. ANTHONY HOPE

19. ALBERT HALL, LONDON

20. CHESTNUT

1. ST TRINIANS

2. ST ALBANS

3. ST MICHAEL'S MOUNT

4. ST GILES' CATHEDRAL

5. ST LEGER

6. ST DAVID'S

7. ST ANDREWS

8. ST PANCRAS

9. ST JAMES'S PALACE

10. ST CLEMENT DANES

11. ST MARGARET'S, WESTMINSTER

12. ST JOHN AMBULANCE BRIGADE

13. ST KILDA

14. ST PAUL'S CATHEDRAL

15. ST THOMAS'S HOSPITAL

16. ST IVES

17. ST DUNSTAN'S

18. ST JAMES'S HOSPITAL, LEEDS

19. SAINT JOAN

20. ST JAMES'S PARK

PEOPLE & PLACES 8/ANSWERS

1. 1845

2. HORATIA

3. ALL LONDON THEATRES.

4. SIR CLIVE SINCLAIR

5. SIR PATRICK MOORE

6. MICHAEL BOND

7. HADRIAN'S WALL

8. HENRY FIELDING

9. SISSINGHURST CASTLE

10. MICHAEL MARKS (MARKS AND SPENCER)

11. SIR ANTHONY EDEN

12. 1996

13. CHRIS PATTEN

14. SIR BOB GELDOF AND MIDGE URE

15. 1987

16. LOCKERBIE

17. 43

18. LISA RATCLIFFE

19. EDINBURGH

20. ROBIN KNOX JOHNSTON

PEOPLE & PLACES 9/ANSWERS

1. BURGHLEY HOUSE

2. GRACE DARLING

3. TATE

4. 1975

5. CHARING CROSS

6. BALLET DANCER

7. RICHARD BURTON

8. DARTMOOR

9. CARNABY STREET

10. RUDYARD KIPLING

11. VIRGIN

12. SIR LAURENCE OLIVIER

13. BURKE AND HARE

14. 1908

15. CINQUE PORTS

16. BUSH HOUSE

17. NICK LEESON

18. FOREST OF DEAN

19. WALES

20. THE ROYAL MEWS

PEOPLE & PLACES 10/ANSWERS

1. REBEKAH WADE

2. THE BEANO

3. DERWENTWATER

4. CHARLES DICKENS

5. MICHAEL CAINE

6. BIRMINGHAM (NOW KNOWN AS 'THE ROYAL BALLET')

7. JANET

8. JERRY HALL

9. STELLA RIMINGTON

10. LORD DENNING

11. WILLIAM HOLMAN HUNT

12. JULIA NEUBERGER

13. THE HUNGERFORD MASSACRE

14. SOLWAY FIRTH

15. (6) CHARLOTTE SQUARE

16. WHISTLEBLOWERS

17. DAVID LLOYD GEORGE

18. ADMIRALTY ARCH

19. KING'S CROSS

20. CHELSEA FLOWER SHOW

PEOPLE & PLACES 11/ANSWERS

1. LEEDS

2. GLASGOW

3. COVENTRY

4. WINDSOR

5. FOSSE WAY

6. MARYLEBONE

7. ABERDEEN

8. HALIFAX

9. DORSET

10. EDINBURGH

11. BRISTOL

12. LERWICK

13. HARLEY STREET

14. CAMBRIDGE

15. CHELTENHAM

16. STOKE MANDEVILLE

17. CRANWELL

18. HATCHARDS

19. CHESTER

20. JEDBURGH

PEOPLE & PLACES 12/ANSWERS

1. ELIZABETH BARRETT BROWNING

2. SIR JOSHUA REYNOLDS

3. ALASDAIR MILNE

4. ANTI SMOKING GROUP

5. FRANKIE HOWERD AND BENNY HILL

6. RUGBY

7. CHRISTOPHER EWART-BIGGS

8. EDWARD HEATH

9. VIRGINIA WOOLF

10. MARGARET BONDFIELD

11. 5

12. HAIRDRESSING

13. CHILTERNS

14. HENRY VI

15. LILLIE LANGTRY

16. GLASGOW

17. GRAND UNION CANAL

18. NORMAN TEBBIT

19. HOLLOWAY

20. HONOURABLE MEMBER / HONOURABLE FRIEND

PEOPLE & PLACES 13/ANSWERS

1. GP

2. GUSTAV HOLST

3. DAVID MELLOR

4. CHARLOTTE

5. BENJAMIN DISRAELI

6. GLASGOW

7. EDWARD JENNER

8. RED DEVILS

9. ELTON JOHN

10. DANIEL RADCLIFFE

11. DAVID JENKINS

12. ROB ROY

13. RICHARD O' BRIEN

14. VARIETY CLUB OF GREAT BRITAIN

15. GERTRUDE JEKYLL

16. ROEDEAN

17. RALPH VAUGHAN WILLIAMS

18. GILBERT ROBERTS

19. SPIKE MILLIGAN

20. PORTMEIRION

PEOPLE & PLACES 14/ANSWERS

1. LOCH LOMOND

2. BRIDLEWAY / PATH

3. THE CHEVIOTS

4. OFFICE FOR STANDARDS IN EDUCATION

5. MILTON KEYNES

6. LAND GIRLS

7. BARONESS AMOS

8. LAND'S END

9. MARTHA LANE FOX

10. CHARLES DICKENS

11. ST PAUL'S CATHEDRAL

12. LAST POST

13. EDINBURGH CASTLE

14. SEVEN

15. THE OWL AND THE PUSSYCAT

16. FRANK MCCOURT

17. JOHN GODBER

18. WINSTON CHURCHILL

19. THE SAMARITANS

20. HALF A SIXPENCE

1. RICHARD BURTON

2. ANITA RODDICK

3. GEORGE DIXON

4. CAIRNGORMS

5. DOVE COTTAGE, GRASMERE

6. SWANSEA

7. SWAM THE ENGLISH CHANNEL

8. SIR FRANCIS DRAKE

9. MYRA HINDLEY AND IAN BRADY

10. SWEENEY TODD

11. DOUGLAS

12. TANNOCHBRAE

13. SCREAMING LORD SUTCH

14. MOLLY MAGUIRES

15. MODS AND ROCKERS

16. L.S. LOWRY

17. GREYFRIARS

18. CAMELOT

19. SIR WALTER SCOTT

20. SIR JOHN BETJEMAN

PEOPLE & PLACES 16/ANSWERS

1. QUEEN ANNE

2. ELIZABETH I

3. HENRY FIELDING

4. DAVID LLOYD GEORGE

5. WILLIAM JOYCE

6. ALAN FREEMAN

7. WILLIAM CAXTON

8. NOEL COWARD

9. FREDDIE DAVIS

10. EDWINA CURRIE

11. CYNTHIA PAYNE

12. ANN WIDDECOMBE

13. FRED TRUMAN

14. DENNIS SKINNER

15. EDGAR ALLAN POE (WILKIE COLLINS IS ALSO GIVEN THIS NICKNAME)

16. LORD LONGFORD

17. GEORGE FORMBY SNR

18. WILLIAM GLADSTONE

19. RUSSELL HARTY

20. JAMES WATT

PEOPLE & PLACES 17/ANSWERS

1. SIR BASIL SPENCE

2. MIKE HADDON

3. MICHAEL REDGRAVE

4. JCB (MECHANICAL DIGGER, FROM HIS INITIALS)

5. SANGSTER (ROBERT SANGSTER INHERITED VERNONS POOLS)

6. DAVID AND VICTORIA BECKHAM

7. MARK AND CAROL

8. THEY ARE MODELS

9. ALEC ROSE

10. BARBARA CASTLE

11. LORD LUCAN

12. CALEDONIAN CANAL

13. READING GAOL

14. ALL POETS LAUREATE

15. SOMERSET HOUSE

16. BRIGHTON

17. BEN ELTON

18. ROBERT ADAM

19. NORFOLK, NORTHUMBERLAND, NORTH YORKSHIRE, NORTHAMPTONSHIRE, NOTTINGHAMSHIRE

20. FAY WELDON

PEOPLE & PLACES 18/ANSWERS

1. WYSTAN HUGH

2. WILLIAM BUTLER

3. JOHN PETER RHYS

4. HENRY MORTON

5. ERNEST HOWARD

6. RONALD DAVID

7. LESLIE POLES

8. WILLIAM GILBERT

9. JAMES GRAHAM

10. EDWARD PALMER

11. WILLIAM HENRY

12. JOANNE KATHLEEN

13. THOMAS EDWARD

14. JOHN KENNETH

15. ANTONIA SUSAN

16. WILLIAM EWART

17. RONALD FREDERICK

18. RICHARD AUSTEN

19. WILLIAM SCHWENCK

20. JAMES MATTHEW

1. CHARLES DARWIN

2. MARGARET THATCHER

3. DAVID BAILEY

4. JOHN LOGIE BAIRD

5. STANLEY BALDWIN

6. MARY QUANT

7. FREDDIE MERCURY

8. HEATHER MILLS McCARTNEY

9. LEWIS CARROLL

10. MARGARET

11. ELIZABETH HURLEY

12. ST DAVID

13. WINSTON CHURCHILL

14. HAROLD WILSON

15. ANNIE LENNOX

16. BLACK PIG

17. CHARLES RENNIE MACKINTOSH

18. THOMAS BEWICK

19. SIR MARTIN REES

20. DURHAM

PEOPLE & PLACES 20/ANSWERS

1. ISLE OF MAN

2. DORSET

3. ORKNEY

4. BELFAST

5. LAND'S END

6. LERWICK, SHETLAND

7. CARDIFF

8. HEBRIDES

9. DUMFRIES

10. INVERNESS

11. PERTH

12. ABERDEEN

13. EDINBURGH

14. LIVERPOOL

15. ISLE OF WIGHT

16. NORTHAMPTON

17. BARROW, CUMBRIA

18. BRISTOL

19. KENT

20. ISLES OF SCILLY

PEOPLE & PLACES 21/ANSWERS

1. ROBERT AND JAMES ADAM

2. CHELTENHAM

3. KNIGHTSBRIDGE

4. BRUCE OLDFIELD

5. 1965

6. CAPTAIN HOOK

7. RUTH LAWRENCE

8. STAFFA

9. HAMPSTEAD AND HIGHGATE

10. CHARING CROSS

11. RICHMAL CROMPTON

12. DARCEY BUSSELL

13. ALL HAVE BEEN ARCHBISHOPS OF YORK

14. DAVID BAILEY

15. RUDYARD KIPLING

16. BILLY CONNOLLY

17. JOHN WESLEY

18. HAMMOND

19. THE CHURCH ARMY

20. BY STICKING A PIN IN A MAP OF THE USA - BAY CITY WAS THE RESULT

PEOPLE & PLACES 22/ANSWERS

1. DARLINGTON

2. BRADFORD

3. BIRMINGHAM

4. OLDHAM

5. HULL

6. BATH

7. LIVERPOOL

8. DUBLIN

9. GLASGOW

10. LEICESTER

11. DOVER

12. BRISTOL

13. WOLVERHAMPTON

14. WORCESTER

15. CARLISLE

16. EXETER

17. EDINBURGH

18. LONDON

19. MANCHESTER

20. NORWICH

PEOPLE & PLACES 23/ANSWERS

1. CAPTAIN OATES (MEMBER OF SCOTT'S EXPEDITION TO THE ANTARCTIC)

2. BENJAMIN DISRAELI

3. LORD BYRON

4. SIR CHRISTOPHER WREN (ST. PAUL'S CATHEDRAL)

5. EDWINA CURRIE

6. JOHN DONNE

7. KATHLEEN FERRIER

8. HAROLD WILSON

9. NANCY ASTOR

10. LORD TAYLOR

11. THE HOME GUARD

12. CHARLES II

13. THOMAS DE QUINCEY

14. IAIN DUNCAN-SMITH

15. JULIA LANG

16. SIR WALTER SCOTT

17. OSCAR WILDE 'THE BALLARD OF READING GAOL'

18. DR JOHNSON

19. FIELD MARSHAL MONTGOMERY

20. BILLY BUNTER

PEOPLE & PLACES 24/ANSWERS

1. LORD BEAVERBROOK

2. BASIL SPENCE

3. ROBERT FALCON SCOTT

4. MRS PATRICK CAMPBELL

5. SHIRLEY CONRAN

6. NEVILLE CHAMBERLAIN

7. NOEL COWARD

8. C. NORTHCOTE PARKINSON (PARKINSON'S LAW)

9. HAROLD WILSON

10. EMMELINE PANKHURST

11. A.J. COOK (BRITISH TRADE UNIONIST, IN THE 1920S)

12. EDITH CAVELL

13. ALFRED HITCHCOCK

14. ERIC IDLE (MONTHY PYTHON'S FLYING CIRCUS)

15. OSWALD MOSLEY

16. PAUL MCCARTNEY (DISCOUNTING RUMOURS OF A BEATLES REUNION)

17. MICK JAGGER

18. VIV NICHOLSON

19. DAVID HOCKNEY

20. DESMOND MORRIS

PEOPLE & PLACES 25/ANSWERS

1. GILBERT & GEORGE

2. CURSE OF THE BLACK PANTHER

3. GUCCI

4. BERTRAND RUSSELL

5. SIR ANTHONY HOPKINS

6. TORREY CANYON

7. 1995

8. YOKO ONO

9. HUMBER BRIDGE

10. NORMAN VAUGHAN

11. BRIAN ALDISS (IN 1971)

12. BILLY BUTLIN

13. D.W. WINNICOTT

14. SIDNEY & BEATRICE WEBB

15. ARTHUR ASKEY

16. DYLAN THOMAS

17. CHARLIE CHAPLIN

18. SHERLOCK HOLMES

19. ALAN COREN

20. EVELYN WAUGH

PEOPLE & PLACES 26/ANSWERS

1. KENNETH CLARK

2. TERENCE CONRAN

3. CECIL DAY-LEWIS (WRITING AS NICHOLAS BLAKE)

4. CECIL BEATON

5. 'STAR TREK' FANS

6. JACOB'S LADDER

7. CHEDWORTH ROMAN VILLA

8. CLEMENT ATTLEE

9. G.K. CHESTERTON

10. EDWARD DE BONO

11. THE ANGRY YOUNG MEN

12. LETCHWORTH

13. HOLKER HALL

14. LORD TENNYSON

15. QUENTIN CRISP

16. CARDIFF

17. WOOKEY HOLE

18. ANGELA RIPPON

19. ROYAL NATIONAL LIFEBOAT INSTITUTION

20. RAFFLES

PEOPLE & PLACES 27/ANSWERS

1. NORMAN LAMONT

2. T.E. LAWRENCE

3. KEVIN KEEGAN

4. CECIL BEATON

5. KATHERINE WHITEHORN

6. BOBBY ROBSON

7. DIDO

8. SIEGFRIED SASSOON

9. KENNY DALGLISH

10. IAN FLEMING

11. H.G. WELLS

12. ERIC CLAPTON

13. BERNIE ECCLESTONE

14. UMA THURMAN

15. RICHARD MEADE

POT LUCK 1/ANSWERS

1. SHOES

2. JOHN BUNYAN

3. CEEFAX

4. REAL ALE

5. DAVID OWEN

6. 1851

7. HAROLD WILSON

8. THE BRITISH STANDARDS INSTITUTION

9. A BREED OF TERRIER DOG

10. TAMOSHANTER

11. QUEEN'S ENGLISH

12. PUNT

13. OXFORD STREET

14. SUZY LAMPLUGH TRUST

15. TESCO

16. DANDY

17. MOUNTAIN RANGE IN GWYNEDD

18. LAURENCE STERNE

19. CHESTER

20. JOSEPH GRIMALDI

POT LUCK 2/ANSWERS

1. LEEK

2. GHILLIE

3. THE WORLD SERVICE

4. RUTH RENDELL

5. LOLLYPOP LADY (MAN)

6. REGENT'S PARK

7. BANKING

8. 2 SHILLINGS

9. DESDEMONA

10. LONGLEAT

11. 1971

12. 'THE ECONOMIST'

13. MARY SHELLEY

14. 'THE BEANO'

15. SPAGHETTI JUNCTION

16. STOCKTON AND DARLINGTON

17. ERIN

18. SCOTTISH NATIONAL PARTY

19. HYDE PARK, LONDON

20. STOKE MANDEVILLE

21. SOHO

22. EISTEDDFOD

23. 'LLOYD'S LIST'

24. REITH LECTURES

25. JOHN GODBER

POT LUCK 3/ANSWERS

1. JOHN CONSTABLE

2. TRACEY EMIN

3. SIR JOSHUA REYNOLDS

4. JOSEPH MALLORD WILLIAM TURNER

5. DAVID HOCKNEY

6. GEORGE STUBBS

7. SIR EDWARD COLEY BURNE-JONES

8. THOMAS GAINSBOROUGH

9. WILLIAM HOLMAN-HUNT

10. SIR EDWIN HENRY LANDSEER

11. NICHOLAS HILLIARD

12. SIR JOHN EVERETT MILLAIS

13. WILLIAM BLAKE

14. JOHN CROME

15. WILLIAM HOGARTH

POT LUCK 4/ANSWERS

1. b) 1616

2. b) A SMALL COTTAGE WITH TWO ROOMS

3. d) OVERLORD

4. c) HAMLET

5. b) 1960

6. c) A POLICE VAN

7. a) THE OUSE

8. b) ME AND MY GIRL

9. a) EDWARD LEAR

10. a) A TAX

11. a) 15TH FEBRUARY 1971

12. d) A WELSH BREAD

13. c) THE RED LION

14. c) EDINBURGH

15. b) TERRA NOVA

16. c) KENSINGTON GARDENS

17. b) REGINALD

18. d) 1956

19. b) BILLIARDS

20. a) HORSE RACING

POT LUCK 5/ANSWERS

1. LONDON'S BURNING

2. THOMAS CARLYLE

3. AMAZING GRACE

4. SIR STAMFORD RAFFLES

5. BLOOD CIRCULATION

6. THE RED ARROWS

7. THE ENGLISH CIVIL WAR

8. ERMINTRUDE

9. GEOFFREY CHAUCER

10. GEMMA CRAVEN

11. AKELA

12. WELSH FOR WALES

13. LORD PALMERSTON

14. RICHARD DIMBLEBY

15. MANCHESTER UNITED

16. NEW MUSICAL EXPRESS

17. CLIFF RICHARD

18. ORDER OF MERIT

19. THE WIND IN THE WILLOWS BY KENNETH GRAHAME

20. NEW MUSICAL EXPRESS

POT LUCK 6/ANSWERS

1. THE BAR

2. BAP

3. BILLY BUNTER

4. BROGUE

5. BUBBLE AND SQUEAK

6. BUCK'S FIZZ

7. BUCK HOUSE

8. BEN NEVIS

9. BURBERRY

10. BURSAR

11. BUTTY

12. BINGO

13. BROADS

14. BEEB

15. BRUMMIE

16. BROWNIES

17. BRIGHTON

18. BIRO

POT LUCK 6/ANSWERS CONT

19. BUSKER

20. BARD

POT LUCK 7/ANSWERS

1. ABERDEEN ANGUS

2. MI5 AND MI6

3. OXFORD

4. BRECON BEACONS

5. METHODIST

6. BSE

7. BLACK TIE

8. CHARTWELL

9. REGINA

10. BRITISH UNITED PROVIDENT ASSOCIATION

11. ANTHONY BURGESS

12. CLEOPATRA'S NEEDLE

13. DESERT RATS

14. THE ROYAL MINT

15. BLENHEIM PALACE

16. WINGS

17. 'WISDEN'

18. WOOLSACK

19. BAKEWELL TART

20. FATHER OF THE HOUSE

POT LUCK 8/ANSWERS

1. TREASURE ISLAND

2. THE CLEVELAND WAY

3. MARKS AND SPENCER

POT LUCK 8/ANSWERS CONT

4. THE SILENCE OF THE LAMBS

5. SUNFLOWERS

6. YELLOW

7. ST. GEORGE

8. MRS BEETON

9. DEE

10. STANSTED

11. TWO SHILLINGS AND SIX PENCE

12. MANCHESTER

13. JAMES DYSON

14. JOHN OPIE

15. ABERDEEN

16. DOUNE

17. GREAT PAUL

18. BACKBENCHER

19. BALMORAL

20. ANITA RODDICK

POT LUCK 9/ANSWERS

1. THE ROCKERS

2. NOTTING HILL CARNIVAL

3. BUCKINGHAM PALACE

4. FAUNTLEROY

5. DARBY AND JOAN

6. DARTMOOR

7. ROEDEAN

8. TABLOID

9. 1666

10. TERRITORIAL ARMY

11. CARDIFF

12. THE OLD BAILEY

13. LANCASTER

14. CRUFTS

15. GEORGE ORWELL

16. THE OVAL

17. TARTAN

18. CHAPEL OF REST

19. ORKNEYS

20. OXFAM

POT LUCK 10/ANSWERS

1. ALL BANK HOLIDAYS

2. TV CHEFS

3. SYMBOLS WITH A NATIONAL CONNECTION, WELSH DRAGON; IRISH HARP; BRITISH BULLDOG

4. ALL ROMAN ROADS

5. WORLD PROFESSIONAL DARTS CHAMPIONS

6. CHARACTERS FROM 'DAVID COPPERFIELD' BY CHARLES DICKENS

7. UNIVERSITY TERMS

8. CATS (FROM TS ELIOT'S POEMS)

9. ALL WON OLYMPIC GOLD MEDALS FOR SWIMMING

10. GOVERNORS OF THE BANK OF ENGLAND

11. NATIVE SPECIES OF DEER

12. WEATHERED PEAKS IN DOVEDALE, PEAK DISTRICT

13. BOOK SIZES

14. CREATURES FROM 'ALICE'S ADVENTURES IN WONDERLAND'

15. PRESENTERS OF 'BLUE PETER'

16. ALL PLAYS BY ALAN ACKBOURN

17. MEMBERS OF STATUS QUO ROCK GROUP

18. ALL SPEAKERS OF THE HOUSE OF COMMONS

19. ALL CHARACTERS FROM FRANK RICHARD'S 'BILLY BUNTER' STORIES

20. ORDERS OF CHIVALRY

POT LUCK 11/ANSWERS

1. SKEGNESS

2. THOMAS CHIPPENDALE

3. MATT JAMES

4. PEMBROKESHIRE COAST

5. CANCER RESEARCH UK

6. KEIRA KNIGHTLEY

7. BUXTON

8. DAN DARE

9. LEICESTER SQUARE

10. KNOT

11. THREE

12. THE LANDMARK TRUST

13. ALEXANDRA PALACE

14. JOHN LE MESURIER

15. OUTWARD BOUND

16. TROUSERS

17. WEDGEWOOD

18. BEEFEATERS

19. ARSENAL

20. WALTHAM FOREST; WANDSWORTH; WESTMINSTER

POT LUCK 12/ANSWERS

1. POPPY DAY

2. THE DAILY EXPRESS AS WELL AS THE SUNDAY EXPRESS

3. A HOBBY HORSE (WALES)

4. MARMITE

5. SIR ALEC DOUGLAS-HOME

6. DANIEL DAY-LEWIS

7. 1982 (21 JUNE)

8. MR LOCKWOOD

9. MICHAEL FOOT

10. STONEHENGE

11. NECKER

12. DAMIEN HIRST

13. WARWICKSHIRE; WEST SUSSEX; WILTSHIRE; WORCESTERSHIRE

14. DOVER

15. 0141

16. DREADNOUGHT

17. MRS HUDSON

18. THE BLACK PRINCE

19. 11 DOWNING STREET

20. BBC

POT LUCK 13/ANSWERS

1. 'NEWS OF THE WORLD'

2. THE MALL (NEAR ADMIRALTY ARCH)

3. ROMAN CATHOLIC

4. LADY LEVER ART GALLERY

5. INCH

6. A WINTER VIKING FESTIVAL IN LERWICK, ON MAINLAND

7. GLASGOW

8. CAMBRIDGE UNDERGRADUATE MAGAZINE

9. LAKE DISTRICT (SCAFELL PIKE)

10. ROBBIE BURNS

11. LADY EMMA HAMILTON

12. CIRCUS

13. 'BEING JORDAN'

14. YOUNG UPWARDLY MOBILE PEOPLE

15. 'THE GURU'

16. EDINBURGH

17. HUGH CASSON

18. T.S. ELIOT

19. MENAI STRAIT

20. GEORGE MELLY

POT LUCK 14/ANSWERS

1. TURNER PRIZE

2. EAST AYRESHIRE, EAST DUNBARTONSHIRE, EAST LOTHIAN, EAST RENFREWSHIRE

3. TAN HILL INN

4. R.C. CATHEDRAL, CHRIST THE KING

5. 0191

6. ERMINE STREET

7. EDINBURGH

8. MAXWELL FAMILY (ROBERT MAXWELL FELL OVERBOARD FROM THIS YACHT)

9. 'ENDURANCE'

10. 1935

11. THE BULL

12. JIMMY SAVILLE

13. 'TYNWALD'

14. SHIPPING AREAS

15. SIR JOHN BETJEMAN

16. A SLOW SCOTTISH DANCE

17. 'HERMES'

18. Z

19. SUFFOLK PUNCH

20. OXBRIDGE

POT LUCK 15/ANSWERS

1. ADVANCED PASSENGER TRAIN

2. BRITISH SUMMER TIME

3. CITIZENS ADVICE BUREAU

4. DIRECTOR OF PUBLIC PROSECUTIONS

5. EQUAL OPPORTUNITIES COMMISSION

6. 'FINANCIAL TIMES'

7. GENERAL CERTIFICATE OF SECONDARY EDUCATION

8. HEAVY GOODS VEHICLE

9. IRISH REPUBLICAN ARMY

10. JUSTICE OF THE PEACE

11. KNIGHT OF THE GARTER

12. LOCAL EDUCATION AUTHORITY

13. MARYLEBONE CRICKET CLUB

14. NATIONAL CAR PARKS

15. OLD AGE PENSIONER

16. PAY AS YOU EARN

17. QUEEN'S PARK RANGERS

18. ROYAL ACADEMY OF DRAMATIC ART

19. SPECIAL AIR SERVICE

20. TA TA FOR NOW

21. UNIVERSITIES CENTRAL COUNCIL ON ADMISSIONS

22. VALUE ADDED TAX

POT LUCK 15/ANSWERS CONT

23. WOMEN'S ROYAL VOLUNTARY SERVICE

24. YOUTH HOSTELING ASSOCIATION

25. ZERO POPULATION GROWTH

POT LUCK 16/ANSWERS

1. BRIAN KEENAN

2. FINE YOUNG CANNIBALS

3. 1981

4. JONATHAN EDWARDS, TRIPLE JUMP

5. JIM BROADBENT

6. OSCAR WILDE

7. TIM

8. BRIMLESS SCOTTISH HAT

9. EROS

10. HARPERS & QUEEN

11. B, C, P, M

12. ANNE WOOD

13. 'HARRY POTTER AND THE PRISONER OF AZKABAN'

14. MARCH 17TH

15. FISHERMAN

16. ENGLISH COUNTRY DANCE

17. HOLMFIRTH

18. OASIS

19. MALCOLM BRADBURY

20. ZANDRA RHODES

POT LUCK 17/ANSWERS

1. CHLOROFORM

2. THE MARY TYLER MOORE SHOW

3. 'THE FLORAL DANCE'

4. LIFE GUARDS; BLUES & ROYALS

5. MOIRA SHEARER

6. DURHAM

7. NICK HORNBY

8. 'OUTSIDE EDGE'

9. GARY HOLTON (WAYNE)

10. VITA SACKVILLE-WEST

11. TRACEY EMIN

12. STATE EARNINGS RELATED PENSION SCHEME

13. WILLIAM POWELL FRITH

14. HELEN SHARMAN

15. NORTHUMBERLAND

16. JIMMY YOUNG

17. PETER SELLERS

18. CLIFF MICHELMORE

19. GHANA

20. ALL DIED IN 2002

POT LUCK 18/ANSWERS

1. EDWARD WOODWARD

2. CANADA

3. BEN ELTON

4. ALL BLUE PETER PRESENTERS

5. 1947

6. VAUGHAN WILLIAMS

7. DENISE WELCH

8. £70,000

9. JASPER CARROTT

POT LUCK 18/ANSWERS CONT

10. ST. PAUL'S CATHEDRAL

11. NOEL COWARD

12. 1 JANUARY 1909

13. RICHARD ARKWRIGHT

14. 'THE LISTENER'

15. HAROLD MACMILLAN

16. CHRISTOPHER PATTEN

17. A HELMET (WORN BY THE BRITISH IN THE COLONIES TO PROTECT FROM THE SUN)

18. CUBS

19. THE SEVEN YEAR'S WAR

20. CUTHBERT

POT LUCK 19/ANSWERS

1. PATRICK MacNEE AND HONOR BLACKMAN

2. 1960

3. SEAMAN

4. COLIN COWDREY

5. TINKY WINKY, DIPSY, LAA-LAA, PO

6. MS DYNAMITE

7. WARS OF THE ROSES

8. SARAH BRIGHTMAN

9. SIR WILLIAM BEECHEY

10. JACK ROSENTHAL

11. 'GRACE AND FAVOUR'

12. ISLE OF WIGHT

13. JOANNE HARRIS

14. 'CARRY ON COLUMBUS'

15. PAKISTAN

16. 1988

17. SIR EDWIN LUTYENS

18. 'BALLYKISSANGEL'

19. NORWICH

20. TIFFANY CASE

POT LUCK 20/ANSWERS

1. PRISONS

2. SHOPPING CENTRES

3. ROMAN ROADS

4. ALL HAVE APPEARED ON BRITISH BANK NOTES

5. RAILWAY STATIONS

6. CONDUCTORS OF THE HALLE ORCHESTRA

7. ALL PSEUDONYMS OF THE WRITER ELEANOR HIBBERT

8. ALL HAVE BEEN HOME SECRETARIES

9. FOOTBALL TEAMS NICKNAMED 'THE U'S'

10. ALL MODELS OF FORD CARS

11. CARD GAMES

12. T.V. CHEFS

13. ALL PRESENTED TV'S 'ANTIQUES ROADSHOW'

14. ALL HAD HITS WITH THE SONG 'SHOUT'

15. MEMBERS OF THE ORDER OF MERIT

16. TV 'GLADIATORS'

17. ALL ARE THEME TUNES FOR 'TOP OF THE POPS'

18. T.V. DESIGNERS ON 'CHANGING ROOMS'

19. REAL ALE NAMES

20. CHARACTERS FROM TV's 'CROSSROADS'

POT LUCK 21/ANSWERS

1. ALSO KNOWN AS

2. BRING YOUR OWN

3. CASH ON DELIVERY

4. DOUBLE INCOME NO KIDS YET

5. ESTIMATED TIME OF ARRIVAL

6. FOR YOUR INFORMATION

7. GROSS DOMESTIC PRODUCT

8. HARD BLACK (PENCIL)

9. IN VITRO FERTILISATION

10. JUNIOR COMMON ROOM

11. KNIGHT COMMANDER OF THE ORDER OF THE BRITISH EMPIRE

12. LOCALLY UNACCEPTABLE LAND USE

13. MORTGAGE INCOME RELIEF AT SOURCE

14. NOT IN MY BACK YARD

15. OFFICE OF STANDARDS IN EDUCATION

16. PERSONAL IDENTIFICATION NUMBER

17. QUASI-AUTONOMOUS NON-GOVERNMENTAL ORGANISATION

18. REPETITIVE STRAIN INJURY

19. SEALED WITH A LOVING KISS

20. TEACHING ENGLISH AS A FOREIGN LANGUAGE

21. UNION OF SHOP, DISTRIBUTIVE & ALLIED WORKERS

22. VIDEO HOME SYSTEM

23. WHAT YOU SEE IS WHAT YOU GET

24. YEAR 2000

25. ZERO ECONOMIC GROWTH

POT LUCK 22/ANSWERS

1. TRINITY COLLEGE, DUBLIN

2. THE SALVATION ARMY

3. FEAST OF THE ANNUNCIATION

4. OSBERT LANCASTER

5. TWO SMALL ISLANDS OFF THE GOWER PENINSULAR, WALES

6. HANGMAN

7. MASTER OF THE ROLLS

8. BENJAMIN BRITTEN

9. SAUCHIEHALL STREET

10. BLACKBEARD

11. 'REACH FOR THE SKY'

12. HOLY LOCH

13. 28

14. 'ABSOLUTELY FABULOUS'

15. A PEKINESE DOG

16. OLD KENT ROAD

17. 'THE LEAGUE AGAINST CRUEL SPORTS'

18. 'THE SINGING DETECTIVE'

19. 1997

20. THE WINTER OF DISCONTENT

POT LUCK 23/ANSWERS

1. BELLY

2. RUM

3. TEA

4. HOUSE

5. CANDLE

6. SHIRT

7. DINNER

8. RAIN

9. BIRD

10. PHONE

11. KIPPER

12. FISH

13. UMBRELLA

14. SUPPER

15. STEAK & KIDNEY

16. BOOK

17. FIST

18. PICKLES

19. DRIPPING

20. POCKET

21. BOIL

22. SHIRT

23. MORMON

24. JUDGE

25. AUNT

<u>POT LUCK 24/ANSWERS</u>

1. THE 'WAR CRY'.

2. ROWAN WILLIAMS.

3. LHR.

4. ROBBIE WILLIAMS.

5. THE SPARROW.

6. 15 JUNE.

7. GOLDEN EAGLE.

8. THE 'DAILY RECORD'.

9. M11.

10. SIR DAVID WILKIE.

11. 'FREEDOM ORGANISATION FOR THE RIGHT TO ENJOY SMOKING'.

12. 'BILLY LIAR'.

13. JACK DEE.

14. ANT & DEC.

15. DAVID LLOYD GEORGE

16. GENERAL WILLIAM BOOTH

17. 'O COME, ALL YE FAITHFUL'

18. 1978

19. DOG-COLLAR

20. KENSINGTON GARDENS

POT LUCK 25/ANSWERS

1. B) PLAYSCHOOL

2. D) 1969

3. D) GRAHAM SUTHERLAND

4. C) BIRMINGHAM

5. B) JIM DAVIDSON

6. D) RICHARD HAMILTON

7. C) BAMBURGH

8. B) KENNETH WILLIAMS

9. C) IAIN DUNCAN-SMITH

10. D) SARACEN

11. B) STABBED HIMSELF WITH A PENKNIFE

12. D) 1964

13. A) SALISBURY

14. D) ALAN BLEASDALE

15. B) SISTER

16. A) BLUE ENSIGN

17. D) JEFF BANKS

18. B) ROBERT LOUIS STEVENSON

19. A) 'JUDE THE OBSCURE'

20. D) A DRINK OF BEER, EGGS & BRANDY

POT LUCK 26/ANSWERS

1. BAMBURGH

2. QUAKERS

3. DAVID PUTTNAM

4. JULIE PANKHURST

5. 1926

6. A TYPE OF CHEESE

7. EIGHT

8. BASS

9. BASIL BRUSH

10. CLAUDIUS

11. THE GUILDHALL, LONDON

12. WOODEN SHOE

13. THE 'DANDY'

14. REVD. W. AWDRY

15. FOSTER

16. GOLDFINGER (1964), DIAMONDS ARE FOREVER (1971)

17. WILLIAM SHAKESPEARE

18. BIRMINGHAM

19. NORRIS & ROSS McWHIRTER

20. 220 YDS

POT LUCK 27/ANSWERS

1. BLOODY MARY

2. ELGIN

3. DAME

4. CAERPHILLY

5. EARL GREY

6. CAPTAIN FLINT

7. VICTORIA

7. VICTORIA

8. DORCHESTER

9. LADYBIRD

10. OXO

11. HARROW

12. POSH

13. HEART OF MIDLOTHIAN

14. DOLLY VARDEN

15. ROCHESTER

16. VISCOUNT

17. MAIDEN (& MCANTLE)

18. CHICESTER & (SIR FRANCIS) CHICESTER

19. MAGPIES

20. CUTTY SARK

POT LUCK 28/ANSWERS

1. TEESSIDE

2. 102

3. LICHFIELD CATHEDRAL

4. LADY PENELOPE IN 'THUNDERBIRDS'

5. MUTE SWAN

6. GEORGE CAREY

7. M62

8. WILLIAM KENT

9. DEPARTMENT FOR ENVIRONMENT, FOOD & RURAL AFFAIRS

10. ALL SHARE THE SAME BIRTHDAY, 8th January

11. WILLIAM WORDSWORTH

12. SANDHURST

13. JOHN TAVERNER

14. THE POWERS THAT BE

15. PUFFIN

16. ST ALBAN

17. CLAPHAM JUNCTION

18. 'THE HUNTER'

19. 'CONSIGNIA PLC'

20. ALI G (AKA SACHA BARON COHEN)

POT LUCK 29/ANSWERS

1. MUTE SWAN

2. SIR THOMAS BEECHAM

3. REBECCA WEST

4. RINGO STARR

5. GARDENERS' QUESTION TIME

6. ROBERT HERRICK

7. HAROLD WILSON

8. MAX BEERBOHM

9. 'CHARGE OF THE LIGHT BRIGADE'

10. A SCOTTISH WHISKY-BASED LIQUEUR, FLAVOURED WITH HONEY & HERBS

11. 'THE EAGLE HAS LANDED'

12. MARY BELL

13. MRS GASKELL

14. RED

15. WOODROW WYATT

16. GEORGE DU MAURIER

17. UB40

18. MUSTIQUE

19. BIRMINGHAM

20. SEAN O'CASEY

POT LUCK 30/ANSWERS

1. YORK

2. NATIONAL INSURANCE

3. NEW FOREST

4. THE NATIONAL THEATRE

5. NATIONAL DEBT

6. BIRMINGHAM

7. DEPARTMENT OF NATIONAL HERITAGE

8. NATIONAL YOUTH THEATRE

9. NATIONAL TRUST

10. NATIONAL PORTRAIT GALLERY

11. BRADFORD

12. NATIONAL MARITIME MUSEUM

13. NATIONAL ECONOMIC DEVELOPMENT COUNCIL

14. NATIONAL ART COLLECTIONS FUND (ART FUND)

15. BEAULIEU

16. THE NATIONAL YOUTH ORCHESTRA

17. CHELSEA HOSPITAL

18. NATIONAL CURRICULUM

19. NEWMARKET

POT LUCK 31/ANSWERS

1. ARCHIE ANDREWS

2. MICHAEL YOUNG

3. VIVIEN VAN DAMM

4. PETE MURRAY

5. TERRY MALLOY

6. GROUP CAPTAIN PETER TOWNSEND

7. DR JACOB BRONOWSKI

8. WREN

9. EDGAR WALLACE

10. STAR TREK

11. RADCLYFFE HALL

12. BENNY HILL

13. JOHN PEEL

14. BASIL SPENCE

15. TOM STOPPARD

16. JOHN PARROTT

17. LALLANS

18. HIS MASTER'S VOICE

19. COURT OF ST. JAMES'S

20. JOHN LENNON

POT LUCK 32/ANSWERS

1. IF IT DON'T PAINT IT'

2. 'FORGIVE'N'FORGET (1985); 'JODAMI' (1993)

3. BILLY FURY

4. OLIVER SACKS

5. 'THE PRISONER'

6. CHILLINGHAM CATTLE

7. PETER SELLERS

8. HERBERT SAMUEL (LORD SAMUEL)

9. ALEX COMFORT

10. DAVID LODGE

11. JOHN LENNON

12. R.D. LAING

13. SAKI

14. JOHN ALDERTON & PAULEEN COLLINS

15. NAVY, ARMY & AIR FORCE INSTITUTES

16. LIVERPOOL

17. DAVID MELLOR

18. NEWPORT

19. GEORGE SQUARE

20. BRIGIT FORSYTH

POT LUCK 33/ANSWERS

1. SINGLE LOADED FEMALE

2. CHITTY CHITTY BANG BANG

3. GAMEPLAN

4. STAFFORDSHIRE

5. JACOBEAN

6. CHRISTOPHER NOLAN

7. STANLEY GIBBONS

8. 1948

9. THE PROFUMO AFFAIR

10. BLACKPOOL PLEASURE BEACH

11. EARL OF STOCKTON

12. THE TOMB OF TUTANKHAMEN

13. BRIAN KEENAN & JOHN McCARTHY

14. 1984 (OCTOBER)

15. MICHAEL FRAYN

16. HARROGATE

17. ASLEF & RMT

18. ALL HAVE WON THE BBC 'SPORTS PERSONALITY OF THE YEAR' AWARD

19. TILLER GIRL (THEN SECRETARY)

20. GAMEKEEPER

POT LUCK 34/ANSWERS

1. STELLA RIMINGTON

2. ST. ANDREWS UNIVERSITY

3. RICHARD ROGERS

4. ROWAN ATKINSON

5. MAN ON FIRE

6. BEATRICE

7. MAJOR RIDES IN BRITAIN'S THEME PARKS (THORPE PARK; CHESSINGTON WORLD OF ADVENTURE & ALTON TOWERS)

8. LEDBURY, MALVERN HILLS

9. TOBERMORY

10. MAMMA MIA!

11. CLAIRE RAYNER

12. PAPA WESTRAY, ORKNEY ISLES

13. NEWPORT PAGNELL

14. GORDON RAMSAY

15. SIR ANTHONY EDEN

16. BEN ELTON

17. ALL PRESENTED TV'S 'CRACKERJACK'

18. ANTON DOLIN

19. ANTHONY CROSLAND

20. THE EASTER RISING

POT LUCK 35/ANSWERS

1. BRITISH AIRWAYS

2. BRITISH SUMMER TIME

3. BRITISH MUSEUM

4. BRITISH GRAND PRIX

5. BRITISH LEYLAND

6. BRITISH EXPEDITIONARY FORCE

7. BRITISH CALEDONIAN

8. BRITISH ANTARCTIC TERRITORY

9. ROYAL BRITISH LEGION

10. BRITISH TELECOM TOWER

11. BRITISH EMPIRE MEDAL

12. BRITISH HONDURAS

13. BRITISH HOME STORES

14. BRITISH NATIONAL PARTY

15. BRITISH COUNCIL

ROYALTY & TRADITION 1/ANSWERS

1. CAERPHILLY

2. VISCOUNT TONYPANDY

3. GEORGE II

4. ANDREW MORTON

5. £8

6. ANGUS OGILVIE

7. PRINCE ANDREW OF GREECE

8. THE COUNTESS OF HAREWOOD

9. EDWARD II

10. 1964

11. MAJOR HUGH LINDSAY

12. OXFORD

13. EDWARD II

14. 1964

15. 32

16. DULWICH COLLEGE

17. 1979

18. THE DUCHESS OF KENT

19. ALBERT, CHRISTIAN, EDWARD

20. HEY JUDE

ROYALTY & TRADITION 2/ANSWERS

1. PRINCESS ANNE

2. JAMES I

3. PRINCESS ALICE OF GREECE

4. LANCASTER HOUSE

5. GORDONSTOUN

6. HENRY IV

7. GEORGE III

8. VISCOUNT LINLEY

9. 2 JUNE 1953

10. YORK, GLOUCESTER, EDINBURGH, CORNWALL, KENT

11. ELIZABETH BOWES-LYON

12. GATCOMBE PARK

13. HONOURABLE ARTILLARY COMPANY

14. DUKE OF GLOUCESTER

15. PRINCE ANDREW, THE DUKE OF YORK

16. WINDSOR CASTLE

17. LADY

18. SOPHIE HELEN RHYS-JONES

19. ROYAL LEAMINGTON SPA

20. DUKE OF GLOUCESTER

ROYALTY & TRADITION 3/ANSWERS

1. KISS THE BLARNEY STONE

2. QUEEN VICTORIA (REFERRING TO WILLIAM GLADSTONE)

3. WEDNESDAY

4. MALCOLM III

5. ELIZABETH II

6. EDWARD VII

7. 1986

8. THE LAMBETH CONFERENCE

9. PRINCE OF WALES (THE FUTURE EDWARD VII)

10. LEEDS

11. LORD HAREWOOD

12. HOUSEHOLD CAVALRY

13. EDWARD IV

14. PAUL BURRELL

15. OSBOURNE HOUSE ON THE ISLE OF WIGHT

16. COUSIN

17. ANNE ELIZABETH ALICE LOUISE

18. HONITON

19. THE HONOURABLE (HON.)

20. PALACE OF HOLYROODHOUSE

ROYALTY & TRADITION 4/ANSWERS

1. DURHAM

2. PRINCESS MARGARET

3. 42

4. EDWARD VIII

5. SUNNINGHILL PARK

6. BILL OF RIGHTS

7. PRINCE MICHAEL OF KENT

8. 1987

9. MARY II

10. ST. ANDREWS

11. KING ALFRED THE GREAT

12. HIGHGROVE

13. JAMES II

14. GLAMIS CASTLE

15. HENRY VIII

16. LOCH LEVEN CASTLE

17. HENRY CHARLES ALBERT DAVID

18. DUKE OF GLOUCESTER

19. DISTRIBUTION OF MAUNDY MONEY

20. DUKE OF ROTHESAY

ROYALTY & TRADITION 5/ANSWERS

1. PRINCE EDWARD

2. GARRARDS

3. ROWAN WILLIAMS

4. PRINCESS BEATRICE OF YORK

5. LADY ANTONIA FRASER

6. PRINCE WILLIAM OF GLOUCESTER

7. 1953

8. GEORGE II

9. 1972

10. GRAY'S INN, LINCOLN'S INN, INNER TEMPLE, MIDDLE TEMPLE

11. PRINCESS ANNE

12. ROLLS ROYCE

13. DUKE OF KENT

14. EDWARD V

15. 25 SEPTEMBER

16. 'THE TIMES'

17. ANNE BOLEYN

18. LORD LOUIS MOUNTBATTEN

19. ADMIRAL OF THE FLEET

20. MARGO ASQUITH

ROYALTY & TRADITION 6/ANSWERS

1. HENRY II

2. WILLIAM II

3. HENRY VI

4. EDWARD I

5. JAMES II

6. LADY JANE GREY

7. (ALSO WAS JAMES VI OF SCOTLAND) JAMES I

8. GEORGE III

9. MARY I

10. WILLIAM IV

11. EDWARD VIII

12. HENRY V

13. EDWARD II

14. KING JOHN

15. HENRY VII

16. ANNE (QUEEN ANNE'S BOUNTY)

17. QUEEN VICTORIA

18. GEORGE VI

19. EDWARD VII

20. GEORGE V

ROYALTY & TRADITION 7/ANSWERS

1. DEBRETT'S

2. THE CHANGING OF THE GUARD

3. PETER & ZARA PHILLIPS

4. THE CHIEF WHIP

5. KENSINGTON PALACE

6. 'THE OBSERVER'

7. OSBORNE HOUSE

8. THE KING'S (OR QUEEN'S) SHILLING

9. LAND'S END TO JOHN O'GROATS

10. ELIZABETH I

11. CRATHIE CHURCH (BALMORAL)

12. QUEEN MARY (1934), QUEEN ELIZABETH (1938)

13. JENNIE BOND

14. ELIZABETH BOWES-LYON (QUEEN MOTHER)

15. HENRY IV

16. MINISTRY OF DEFENCE

17. PATRICK, LORD LICHFIELD

18. THE PRINCESS ROYAL

19. KING GEORGE II

20. 21 APRIL 1926

ROYALTY & TRADITION 8/ANSWERS

1. ROYAL ARMOURIES

2. ROYAL ACADEMY

3. ROYAL LYTHAM & ST. ANNE'S

4. ROYAL VARIETY PERFORMANCE

5. ROYAL SHAKESPEARE COMPANY

6. ROYAL AND ANCIENT

7. ROYAL ASSENT

8. ROYAL FREE HOSPITAL

9. ROYAL EXCHANGE

10. ROYAL GEOGRAPHICAL SOCIETY

11. ROYAL MARINES

12. ROYAL INTERNATIONAL HORSE SHOW

13. ROYAL NAVAL RESERVE

14. ROYAL SOCIETY FOR THE PROTECTION OF BIRDS

15. ROYAL WARRANT

16. ROYAL TOURNAMENT

17. ROYAL SCOTTISH ORCHESTRA

18. ROYAL ARMOURED CORPS

19. ROYAL EXCHANGE

20. ROYAL OBSERVATORY

ROYALTY & TRADITION 9/ANSWERS

1. LADY DIANA SPENCER

2. JANE SEYMOUR

3. SEVEN

4. HM CUSTOMS & EXCISE

5. ETON COLLEGE

6. ANTONY ARMSTRONG-JONES (LORD SNOWDEN)

7. BERNARD WEATHERILL

8. JAMES V (OF SCOTLAND)

9. ARTHUR PHILIP

10. BLACK ROD

11. WOBURN ABBEY

12. THE DUKE OF NORTHUMBERLAND

13. THE QUEEN

14. NEW BOND STREET

15. EARL SPENCER

16. EDWARD IV

17. CAERNARFON

18. SARAH ARMSTRONG-JONES

19. CHARLES II

20. LUNG CANCER

ROYALTY & TRADITION 10/ANSWERS

1. ALDEBURGH

2. CHIEFTAIN

3. PRINCE MICHAEL OF KENT

4. CLARENCE HOUSE

5. SARAH FERGUSON

6. ARCHBISHOP OF CANTERBURY

7. ASCENSION DAY

8. ZARA PHILLIPS

9. QUEEN VICTORIA

10. GEORGE FREDERIC HANDEL

11. BELVOIR

12. ALNWICK

13. LORD LIEUTENANT

14. GEORGE V

15. FUNERAL OF DIANA, PRINCESS OF WALES

16. CANDLEMAS, WHITSUNTIDE, LAMMAS, MARTINMAS

17. DUKE, MARQUESS, EARL, VISCOUNT, BARON, BARONET

18. PRINCESS MICHAEL OF KENT

19. GEORGE IV

20. BEATRICE ELIZABETH MARY & EUGENIE VICTORIA HELENA

ROYALTY & TRADITION 11/ANSWERS

1. DAVID & ELIZABETH EMANUELLE

2. PRINCESS ANNE

3. PRINCE CHARLES

4. SUBFUSC

5. GEORGE III

6. LOUISE

7. THE VICTORIA CROSS

8. RIPON

9. 1992

10. STANLEY BALDWIN

11. 1968

12. BLIGHTY

13. HOW SHALL WE EXTOL THEE, WHO ARE BORN OF THEE

14. JANE SEYMOUR

15. DUCHESS OF WINDSOR (WALLIS SIMPSON)

16. 2002 (30 MARCH)

17. THEY ARE WORLD HERITAGE SITES

18. GEORGE V

19. EDINBURGH

20. ALISTAIR COOKE

ROYALTY & TRADITION 12/ANSWERS

1. DIANA, PRINCESS OF WALES

2. THE PRESS

3. 1978

4. THE CELLARS (AFTER THE GUNPOWDER PLOT OF 1605)

5. CHATSWORTH

6. WHITE HART

7. MARY QUEEN OF SCOTS

8. NORMAN, PLANTAGENET, LANCASTER, YORK, TUDOR, STUART, HANOVER, WINDSOR

9. 1985

10. QUEEN ELIZABETH II

11. LORD LINLEY

12. MARY ROSE

13. PRINCE EDWARD

14. THE NATIONAL GALLERY

15. 1992

16. LORD MITFORD

17. PRINCESS MARGARET

18. LIEUTENANT PHILIP MOUNTBATTEN

19. JAMES V, KING OF SCOTLAND

20. 1957

ROYALTY & TRADITION 13/ANSWERS

1. ELIZABETH I

2. 1960

3. GEORGE II

4. ANNE BOLEYN

5. EDWARD II

6. TIM LAURENCE

7. LORD LONGFORD

8. WILLIAM IV

9. ELIZABETH I

10. A SUMMER'S DAY

11. POPE JOHN PAUL II (1982)

12. CHARLES I

13. ST. GEORGE'S CHAPEL, WINDSOR

14. PRINCESS ALEXANDRA

15. 1958

16. CIVIL LIST

17. HENRY VIII & JAMES II (Mary and Anne)

18. GEOFFREY FISHER

19. DUKE OF WELLINGTON

20. PRINCE ANDREW, DUKE OF YORK

ROYALTY & TRADITION 14/ANSWERS

1. AULD LANG SYNE

2. BOATER

3. THE KNAVE

4. DIVORCED BEHEADED DIED, DIVORCED BEHEADED SURVIVED

5. BOW BELLS (OF ST. MARY-LE-BOW)

6. A DEED OF COVENANT

7. CAERNARFON

8. WHITE CLIFFS OF DOVER

9. ST. SWITHIN (IF IT IS WET OR DRY ON THIS DAY, IT IS SAID TO SET A PATTERN OF WEATHER FOR THE NEXT 40 DAYS)

10. THE TRANSPORT & GENERAL WORKERS' UNION

11. 1984

12. NELL GWYN

13. BURKE'S PEERAGE, BURKE'S LANDED GENTRY

14. DUKE OF KENT

15. 1901

16. 1996 (28 AUGUST)

17. LONGLEAT

18. CARLISLE

19. BURNS NIGHT (BIRTHDAY OF POET ROBERT BURNS)

20. MARY OF TECK

SPORTS & PASTIMES 1/ANSWERS

1. KELLY FISHER

2. COLONEL MUSTARD, PROFESSOR PLUM, REVEREND GREEN

3. PLAS Y BRENIN

4. SURREY

5. WIDNES

6. BIG BREAK

7. GAZZA IN 'FOG ON THE TYNE' (REVISITED)

8. SUE BARKER

9. MEADOWBANK STADIUM (EDINBURGH)

10. 'SIX NATIONS' TOURNAMENT

11. 1982

12. GARY LINEKER

13. BRITISH LIONS

14. HEART OF MIDLOTHIAN (HEARTS)

15. AMAZON

16. LIVERPOOL F.C.

17. GO TO JAIL, FREE PARKING, JUST VISITING, GO

18. RAY WOOD

19. AUSTRALIA

20. MURRAY WALKER

SPORTS & PASTIMES 2/ANSWERS

1. BLACKBURN ROVERS

2. DARLINGTON

3. DUNDEE

4. YORK

5. HIBERNIAN

6. SUNDERLAND

7. BURY

8. WATFORD

9. TRANMERE ROVERS

10. BRENTFORD

11. BOLTON WANDERERS

12. CHELTENHAM TOWN

13. WOLVERHAMPTON WANDERERS

14. CARLISLE UTD

15. RANGERS

16. STOKE CITY

17. PRESTON NORTH END

18. OXFORD UTD

19. MIDDLESBROUGH

20. PETERHEAD

21. SOUTHAMPTON

22. IPSWICH TOWN

23. ARBROATH

24. PETERBOROUGH UTD

25. ROCHDALE

SPORTS & PASTIMES 3/ANSWERS

1. THE DERBY

2. DOUGLAS, ISLE OF MAN

3. BROOKLANDS

4. JOHN CURRY

5. TYRRELL

6. SNOOKER

7. THE LONDON MARATHON

8. ROMAN ABRAMOVICH

9. WILLIAMS

10. BARRY McGUIGAN

11. ROYAL ATHLETE

12. SANDY LYLE

13. JENNY PITMAN/CORBIERE

14. IAN BOTHAM

15. LENNOX LEWIS

16. WILLIE CARSON

17. PAULA RADCLIFFE

18. NOTTS COUNTY

19. CURLING

20. JUDO

SPORTS & PASTIMES 4/ANSWERS

1. MOHAMED AL-FAYED

2. EDDIE IRVINE

3. WILLIE CARSON

4. FOOT & MOUTH CRISIS

5. JOHN LANDY

6. LINCOLN & GRAND NATIONAL

7. DISQUALIFICATION OF A DRIVER

8. 6

9. AUDLEY HARRISON

10. WORLD'S STRONGEST MAN

11. TONY ALLCOCK

12. EMBASSY

13. WIRES

14. MISS SCARLET, MRS WHITE, MRS PEACOCK

15. BOBBY CHARLTON

16. CURLING (WOMEN)

17. CHEPSTOW

18. STIRLING ALBION

19. PROFESSIONAL FOOTBALLER

20. GARY LINEKER

SPORTS & PASTIMES 5/ANSWERS

1. SWIMMING

2. POLO

3. CROWN GREEN BOWLS

4. RIFLE SHOOTING

5. YACHTING

6. GOLF (WOMEN)

7. RIFLE SHOOTING

8. DIVING

9. SHINTY

10. BOXING

11. ROWING

12. SHOWJUMPING

13. CRICKET

14. ROWING

15. RUGBY LEAGUE

16. JUDO

17. LACROSSE

18. SWIMMING & WATER POLO

19. SQUASH

20. RUGBY UNION

SPORTS & PASTIMES 6/ANSWERS

1. FRANK BRUNO

2. DARTS

3. TATTENHAM CORNER

4. KENT COUNTY CRICKET CLUB

5. 400 METRE HURDLES

6. THE OVAL & LORD'S

7. JAVELIN

8. STEVE DAVIS

9. AUSTRALIA

10. QUEEN'S PARK (HAMPDEN PARK, GLASGOW)

11. DERBY COUNTY

12. KARREN BRADY

13. DESERT ORCHID

14. JOE BUGNER

15. ROWING

16. HEPTATHLON

17. CESAREWITCH & CAMBRIDGESHIRE

18. FIRST FEMALE JOCKEY IN 'THE GRAND NATIONAL'

19. 28 INCHES (71.1 CM)

20. OXFORD

SPORTS & PASTIMES 7/ANSWERS

1. 16 LB

2. CHINAMAN

3. TEDDY SHERRINGHAM

4. GOLF (WOMEN)

5. M DWYER

6. HIBERNIAN

7. DERBY

8. OIL ON THE TRACK

9. MODERN PENTATHLON (INDIVIDUAL EVENT)

10. DAVID BRYANT

11. 12 AUGUST (GLORIOUS TWELFTH) - 10 DECEMBER

12. KARATE

13. QUEEN'S PARK RANGERS

14. FLOOR, ASYMMETRIC BARS, BEAM, VAULT

15. POLO

16. HARROW

17. REVOLVER, ROPE, CANDLESTICK, LEAD PIPE, SPANNER, KNIFE

18. FRANK SKINNER & DAVID BADDIEL

19. VIV ANDERSON (1978)

SPORTS & PASTIMES 8/ANSWERS

1. 100M HURDLES; HIGH JUMP; SHOT; 200M; LONG JUMP; JAVELIN; 800M

2. SURREY

3. BRITISH DARTS ORGANISATION

4. KENNY DALGLISH

5. 14

6. GORDON RICHARDS

7. 300

8. THE BRITTAS EMPIRE

9. SHEFFIELD UNITED

10. 58 FT

11. JOE JOHNSON

12. LILLESHALL

13. HORSE OF THE YEAR SHOW

14. TREVOR FRANCIS

15. KING'S CROSS; FENCHURCH STREET; LIVERPOOL STREET; MARYLEBONE

16. MARYLEBONE CRICKET CLUB

17. THE MILK RACE

18. JOHN SURTEES

19. 8

20. ABERDEEN

SPORTS & PASTIMES 9/ANSWERS

1. PRESTON NORTH END

2. ASTON VILLA

3. ASTON VILLA

4. WEST BROMWICH ALBION

5. SHEFFIELD WEDNESDAY

6. NOT HELD

7. PORTSMOUTH

8. BURNLEY

9. EVERTON

10. LIVERPOOL

11. LIVERPOOL

12. MANCHESTER UNITED

SPORTS & PASTIMES 10/ANSWERS

1. CANOE RACING

2. THE GRAND NATIONAL

3. GOLF (ST. ANDREWS, SCOTLAND)

4. JUNE

5. 60

6. THE OAKS

7. A GAME BETWEEN FOOTBALL RIVALS CELTIC AND RANGERS

8. ROWING (COXED PAIRS)

9. LINFORD CHRISTIE

10. BADMINTON

11. 1954

12. BOXING

13. ELLEN MacARTHUR

14. STEVE OVETT

15. ERIC BRISTOW

16. DIVING

17. WIGAN

18. TRIPLE JUMP

19. THE CURRAGH

20. RANGERS 2 (CELTIC 1)

SPORTS & PASTIMES 11/ANSWERS

1. THE WEE ROVERS

2. THE HONEST MEN

3. BLUES

4. SEASIDERS

5. BLUE BRAZIL

6. BLUEBIRDS

7. RAILWAYMEN

8. EAGLES

9. QUAKERS

10. THE TERRORS

11. GRECIANS

12. COTTAGERS

13. THE BAIRNS

14. MARINERS

15. TIGERS

16. THE JAM TARTS

17. HATTERS

18. LIVI LIONS

19. COBBLERS

20. OWLS

21. THE SAINTS

22. THE WARRIORS

23. SADDLERS

24. DONS

25. MINSTERMEN

SPORTS & PASTIMES 12/ANSWERS

1. DONINGTON PARK

2. HURLING

3. THREE

4. THE PENNINE WAY

5. ARGENTINA

6. DAMON HILL

7. ST HELENS

8. 1908, 1948 (1944 BUT NOT HELD DUE TO THE WAR)

9. HAMPDEN PARK

10. CHELSEA BEAT MIDDLESBROUGH 2-0

11. JANE TORVILL & CHRISTOPHER DEAN

12. HARROW SCHOOL

13. TONY JACKLIN

14. KILMARNOCK (BEAT FALKIRK 1-0)

15. HILLSBOROUGH STADIUM, SHEFFIELD

16. NAOMI JAMES

17. 'THE SPORTING LIFE'

18. SHROPSHIRE

19. MANCHESTER UNITED

20. CLIFF THORBURN (1983)

SPORTS & PASTIMES 13/ANSWERS

1. TORVILLE & DEAN

2. FRANK BRUNO

3. VIRGINIA WADE

4. GEORGE BEST

5. JOHN FRANCOME

6. GRAHAM GOOCH

7. ELLEN MacARTHUR

8. DAVID SEAMAN

9. JENNY PITMAN

10. PETER ALLIS

11. MIKE ATHERTON

12. AUSTIN HEALEY

13. BRIAN CLOUGH

14. EDDIE KIDD

15. GEORGE DUFFIELD

16. STEVE REDGRAVE

17. TRACY EDWARDS

18. REBECCA STEPHENS

19. RICHARD DUNWOODY

20. ALEX FERGUSON

SPORTS & PASTIMES 14/ANSWERS

1. 1951

2. 1984

3. 1993

4. 1955

5. 1979

6. 1994

7. 1977

8. 1964

9. 1981

10. 1960

SPORTS & PASTIMES 15/ANSWERS

1. FRANK BRUNO

2. DIANE MODAHL

3. PETER SCUDAMORE

4. DARTS

5. ELLEN MacARTHUR

6. ROUNDERS

7. MENS 2KG., WOMEN'S 1 KG.

8. AYR

9. CYCLING (KILOMETRE SPRINT)

10. ST. HELENS

11. DAVIS CUP (TENNIS)

12. IN RUGBY, ANOTHER NAME FOR AN UP AND UNDER

13. BAGATELLE

14. FLOOR, HORIZONTAL BAR, PARALLEL BARS, POMMEL HORSE, RINGS, VAULT

15. JUDO (MIDDLEWEIGHT)

16. WIDNES

17. EDDIE WARING

18. STANLEY MATTHEWS (1965)

19. VIRGINIA WADE

20. TED HANKEY

SPORTS & PASTIMES 16/ANSWERS

1. 35

2. 8

3. 77

4. 87

5. 6

6. 21

7. 50

8. 38

9. 9

10. 71

11. 80

12. 41

13. 90

14. 49

15. 42

16. 30

17. 56

18. 3

19. 89

20. 62

1. MANCHESTER CITY

2. TANNI GREY-THOMPSON

3. BROOKLANDS

4. SWIMMING

5. STIRLING MOSS

6. DWIGHT YORKE

7. LANCASHIRE COUNTRY CRICKET CLUB

8. IAN WOOSNAM

9. LEANDER

10. GRAHAM GOOCH

11. THE PHOENIX IN BRISTOL

12. BOB CHAMPION

13. BRIDGE

14. DOCTOR

15. HAMPDEN

16. DUNCAN GOODHEW

17. SUZUKI

18. THE KING'S & THE QUEEN'S

19. RIVERSIDE, CHESTER-LE-STREET

20. PROFESSIONAL DARTS COUNCIL

SPORTS & PASTIMES 18/ANSWERS

1. MOTOR RACING

2. IMAGINE

3. GRACE ROAD

4. DEVON LOCH

5. HARE & HOUND

6. STOKE CITY

7. BRIAN JOHNSTON & HENRY BLOFELD

8. HARLEQUINS

9. GINNY LENG

10. ROYAL BIRKDALE

11. TATTERSALLS

12. ANGLING (ALL FRESHWATER CHAMPIONS)

13. ROGER BLACK

14. 100M; LONG JUMP; SHOT; HIGH JUMP; 400M; 110M HURDLES; DISCUS; POLE VAULT; JAVELIN; 1500M

15. DURHAM

16. MICHAEL OWEN

17. DUNDEE

18. NICK FALDO

19. CLASSIC CLICHÉ (1995) & SHANTOU (1996)

20. MONTY'S PASS

SPORTS & PASTIMES 19/ANSWERS

1. SCORPIONS

2. DYNAMOS

3. EAGLES

4. DRAGONS

5. GLADIATORS

6. HAWKS

7. KENT SPITFIRE'S

8. LIGHTNING

9. FOXES

10. CRUSADERS

11. STEELBACKS

12. OUTLAWS

13. SABRES

14. LIONS

15. SHARKS

16. BEARS

17. ROYALS

18. PHOENIX

SPORTS & PASTIMES 20/ANSWERS

1. RIDING, FENCING, SHOOTING, SWIMMING, CROSS COUNTRY RUNNING

2. WARWICKSHIRE

3. PHIL TAYLOR

4. BEES (BRENTFORD), ROBINS (BRISTOL CITY), RAMS (DERBY)

5. 30

6. YELLOW

7. COXED EIGHT (ROWING)

8. ROBERT PIRES

9. MIKE RUSSELL

10. JUDO

11. K

12. ALAN SHEARER

13. TIM HENMAN

14. SHEFFIELD WEDNESDAY

15. JOHN PARROTT

16. MAYFAIR

17. VFB STUTTGART

18. RED

19. 10 POINTS EACH

20. 1985

SPORTS & PASTIMES 21/ANSWERS

1. PRESTON NORTH END

2. MANCHESTER UNITED

3. LIVERPOOL

4. STOCKPORT COUNTY

5. ARSENAL

6. ABERDEEN

7. EVERTON

8. HIBERNIAN

9. NOTTINGHAM FOREST

10. SUNDERLAND

11. KILMARNOCK

12. MIDDLESBROUGH

13. SHEFFIELD WEDNESDAY

14. CELTIC

15. CRYSTAL PALACE

SPORTS & PASTIMES 22/ANSWERS

1. CANOEING

2. STRAW (ALSO KNOWN AS MINI FLY)

3. EPÉE

4. BOB FITZSIMMONS

5. STEPHEN POTTER

6. GEORGE ORWELL

7. SIMON SHERWOOD

8. ALLAN WELLS

9. THE 'RACING POST'

10. DAVID BECKHAM

11. FRANK SKINNER & DAVID BADDIEL

12. MOTOR SPORT

13. LIVERPOOL F.C.

14. QUIZ BALL

15. CHRIS EUBANK

16. GARETH EDWARDS

17. ASHINGTON

18. JOE DAVIS

19. GRAHAM GOOCH

20. DAMON HILL

SPORTS & PASTIMES 23/ANSWERS

1. BOBBY ROBSON, GRAHAM TAYLOR & TERRY VENABLES.

2. DAVID COLEMAN

3. NOBBY STILES

4. REGENT STREET

5. JONNY WILKINSON

6. FOOTBALL

7. HELEN ROLLASON

8. DAVID BECKHAM

9. MARIA SHARAPOVA

10. LESTER PIGGOTT

11. RUGBY UNION (MJ), HURDLER (CJ), CRICKET (AS), FOOTBALL (DJ)

12. WILLIE CARSON

13. STEVE REDGRAVE

14. MIDDLESBROUGH F.C.

15. JENSON BUTTON

16. ROYAL TROON

17. MANCHESTER

18. DONINGTON

19. WAYNE ROONEY

20. BILL SHANKLY